IMPERFECT JUSTICE

IMPERFECT JUSTICE

An East–West German Diary

INGA MARKOVITS

CLARENDON PRESS · OXFORD
1995

Oxford University Press, Walton Street, Oxford OX2 6DP

Oxford New York
Athens Auckland Bangkok Bombay
Calcutta Cape Town Dar es Salaam Delhi
Florence Hong Kong Istanbul Karachi
Kuala Lumpur Madras Madrid Melbourne
Mexico City Nairobi Paris Singapore
Taipei Tokyo Toronto
and associated companies in
Berlin Ibadan

Oxford is a trade mark of Oxford University Press

Published in the United States
by Oxford University Press Inc., New York

British Library Cataloguing in Publication Data
Data available

Library of Congress Cataloging in Publication Data
Markovits, Inga.
[Abwicklung. English]
Imperfect justice: an East–West German diary / Inga Markovits.
p.   cm.
1. Law—Germany (East)—History.   2. Justice, Administration of—
Germany (East)—History.   3. Germany—History—Unification, 1990.
I. Title.
KKA190.M3713   1995
349.431—dc20
[344.31]   94-43453
ISBN 0-19-825814-3.
ISBN 0-19-825961-1 (pbk.)

1 3 5 7 9 10 8 6 4 2

Typeset by Best-set Typesetter Ltd., Hong Kong
Printed in Great Britain
on acid-free paper by
Bookcraft Ltd., Midsomer Norton, Avon

For Dick

Contents

Explanations, Apologies, Thanks

Some explanations, apologies, and thanks relating to this book.

First the explanations: my 'diary' is something of an artifact. Each conversation or event I describe took place on the day I list; each statement comes from the person to whom it is attributed; each sentence set in quotation marks is a literal quote. But I have also moved around descriptions and ideas better to suit my purpose, used other sources besides observations and interviews, and, in particular, relied on the information of many conversation partners whose names do not appear in the pages. Almost all names cited are the real names of the people who talked with me. A few names have been changed: usually less to protect a person's face than to leave him or her the anonymity that might make it easier to begin a new professional life.

The apologies: a report on the hopes and fears of people in the midst of momentous change treats these people—regardless of how much respect and sympathy the reporter might feel for them—at least to some extent as objects of observation. I can imagine that for this reason alone some of my conversation partners will be dissatisfied with my account: nobody likes to be an object. To make matters worse, they and I come from different worlds and, for that reason, will often see the same event with different eyes. This, too, is inevitable in a book about East–West encounters. And yet, despite our cognitive dissonances, I became convinced during this year of conversations that all of us, whether asking or answering questions, shared the same goal: to understand and describe what law and justice meant before and after the political turnabout as honestly and as precisely as possible. Without my East German colleagues this book could never have come about. They are its authors no less than they are its subjects.

It therefore seems almost inappropriate to thank my conversation partners for their time, their openness, their patience, and often also their hospitality—this is their book too. Other debts of gratitude must be acknowledged. Deans Mark Yudof and Michael Sharlot of the University of Texas Law School, with generous and unbureaucratic support, enabled me to spend a year in Berlin. The National Science Foundation helped with a travel grant. John Prater, David Gunn, and the staff of the University of Texas Law Library provided fast and professional support. Sue Arapian and John Ferrick ably typed the manuscript. My children generously acquiesced in their neglect. The greatest thanks go to him to whom this book is dedicated and without whose pushing, praise, scolding, cooking, and family management it would still not be completed.

Introduction

This is an account of the sudden death of socialist law in East Germany and of the reactions, hopes, and fears of some of its survivors.

It will be an ambivalent tale. Imagine: what happens when overnight a legal system is replaced by its ideological opposite? When people used to being coddled and disciplined by their law have to adjust to a state which expects them to look out for themselves? When men and women trained to serve and to legitimate their political system have to explain their complicity in its corruption? And when in this process of national soul-searching it is the Western victors alone who may ask all the questions?

I have written a book on East German law before, when, twenty-five years ago, I investigated East German struggles to transform an inherited system of bourgeois law into a socialist civil law system. Now—it is still hard to believe—I will look at the very opposite undertaking: the attempt to integrate the once socialist GDR into the capitalist *Rechtsstaat*. Twenty-five years ago I produced my first piece of legal scholarship—today I want to write a report on the experiences and beliefs of people whose everyday lives are thrown off course by the legal turnabout. Then, my data had to be gathered in the archives of West German libraries. Today it comes from the mouths of those living through the momentous changes: from the reports of East German judges and prosecutors, professors and students, lay assessors, and social workers. Then, all official East German doors were closed to me. Now almost all are open. And then, I came from inside: a doctoral candidate in West Berlin writing her thesis in the shadow of the Wall. Now, I come from outside: a law professor from the United States, revisiting familiar places with mixed feelings of old affection and new-won distance; for whom not only East Germans but also West Germans at times are 'the others' and who often finds herself searching with puzzled disappointment for some brotherly warmth in Germany's reunification.

I remember well when the thought first occurred to me to write a dissertation on East German law: one or two years after the construction of the Wall on a winter evening in East Berlin when I had stopped at the brightly lit window of a legal bookstore to contemplate its displays—the Marxist classics bound in navy or burgundy plastic leather; the Party pamphlets shining in bright cherry red; the academically grey and dull-looking monographs in which Party or union functionaries extolled the qualities of socialist law—and decided to investigate this symbiosis of power and law in its legal details. And I can pinpoint the moment at which my plan for the present book first took root: again in Berlin, in November 1989, two weeks after the opening of the Wall. I stood on the Potsdamer Platz in the heart of Berlin, listened to the hammering of tourists chiselling commemorative rocks from the Wall, looked through the first narrow slits into East Berlin, and thought: how will the GDR find its way into the *Rechtsstaat*?

In the intervening years, I had made repeated trips to the GDR to learn as much as possible about its legal system—always on a tourist visa, since scholarly requests for official assistance never yielded even so much as a reply. On these travels I had spoken with everyone willing to tell me something about East German law: with professors, attorneys, and legal counsel of state-owned enterprises; if I was lucky, with the occasional judge or prosecutor; with strangers sharing my table at restaurants in the socialist fashion, or with fellow travellers on the train. Many of my conversation partners were open and communicative. Some who had at first been willing to talk to me turned out to be unavailable at the appointed hour. A few rejected my request for a conversation with demonstrative outrage. On one occasion I noticed to my surprise that a conversation partner was well informed about the previous stops of my journey. Only once did I manage to attend an East German court hearing: in Erfurt, where the custodian of the local *Kreisgericht* (district court) passed on my request to a young family law judge who, without much ado, invited me into his courtroom. I should come back after lunch, he said at the end of the morning; he had a few more divorce cases left on his agenda that day. But by the time I returned in the afternoon, his superior must have gotten wind of my visit, and I was not even allowed to re-enter the courthouse.

While my travels taught me a great deal about socialist law, the knowledge had to be gathered in bits and pieces. Putting together the parts of the puzzle remained a hazardous enterprise. Far too many pieces were missing. Nor could I even be sure that the information received correctly described the workings of law under socialism. I never had reason to fear that my conversation partners might lie to me. But what important knowledge did they withhold? Our conversations were politically too sensitive to allow me ever to raise fundamental questions about the socialist legal system. I knew that at least those East German citizens holding positions of any importance would have to report all contacts with Westerners to the Party. Since most of our discussions took place in settings removed from state supervision—in restaurants, on a walk, at the coffee table of someone's apartment—these reports could be phrased with some narrative leeway. But just talking with me could prove embarrassing for an East German. I was all the more grateful to everyone willing to submit himself to my questions. I had to be careful not to provoke political indiscretions. As a result, almost all our conversations focused on practical, everyday legal issues. Questions of principle—about justice, about the relationship between law and power, about the self-perception of lawyers under socialism—in silent complicity between me and my conversation partners were almost always passed over.

Now, with the Wall collapsed, all questions could finally be asked. But I would have to hurry. Soon, the protagonists of the socialist legal process would have other things on their minds. But now memories were fresh and eyewitnesses, still reeling from the blows of political change, were eager to talk about the world they so suddenly lost. Now, not yet adjusted to the new life awaiting them, they could talk openly about their hopes and concerns under the new rule of law. East and West Germans had lived for so long in different worlds—how could each side do the other justice without understanding what 'justice' had meant on the opposite side of the Wall?

So in September 1990 I came for a ten-month stay to Berlin to sketch the last portrait of a legal system about to disappear into the belly of history. This book records my observations. I have chosen the form of a diary to preserve something of the spontaneity of my encounters, to enable readers to visualize people and places, and so to remind them that legal change entails not only the redrafting of constitutions and statutes but also the disruption and painful restructuring of human lives. If the reforms go well they will infuse these lives with new hope and energy. If they go badly they will leave behind new anger and disappointment.

Since my account is, in large part, based on the self-presentations of people deeply involved in the socialist legal process, it puts less emphasis on the oppressive features of socialist law than some readers might expect. Even people trying to give an honest account of their work are unlikely to dwell on its most negative aspects. Our conversations never avoided the issue of responsibility for perversions of justice under socialist rule; indeed, questions of political guilt or innocence cast their shadow over every one of our encounters. But I looked just as much for the non-scandalous, everyday aspects of socialist law; for that side which now, in the hullabaloo of one ideological system's victory over the other, is most easily lost: for its normalcy. Because it is not through its excesses but through its familiar, commonplace habits—on both sides of the former Wall!—that the past will longest exert its hold over the future.

When I arrived in Berlin in September 1990, four weeks before Reunification Day, I found an East German legal system very different from the one I had encountered on my previous travels. In the last months and weeks of its existence, East Germany's parliament, the People's Chamber, had worked with feverish energy to reform laws which for so long had been the product of Party fiat. Socialist legislators, it seemed, wanted at least to leave the scene of their former humiliations with their heads held high. But their last-minute efforts did not renounce all aspects of the GDR's socialist past. Some bills only abolished the politically objectionable terms of a statute, leaving its bulk intact. Others looked for new and original solutions which would neither repeat past socialist mistakes nor simply copy present capitalist approaches to a problem. Since much of the new legislation had been designed at a time when Germany's reunification still seemed to lie in the distant future, it was already outdated by the time it passed its first reading in the People's Chamber. As a result, East German legislation of those last few months had a somewhat surreal quality: a mixture of bad conscience and good intentions, of optimism, euphemism, and unacknowledged melancholy. But the GDR's legal system was, four weeks before its obliteration, still 'socialist' enough to warrant my observing the trials which had for so long been inaccessible to me.

So, I decided to spend the final days prior to reunification in East Berlin's central courthouse: the *Stadtgericht* in the Littenstrasse, only a few minutes' walk from the Alexanderplatz. It would be my last chance to see socialist judges in action. The Unification Treaty provided that on 3 October 1990 the GDR would become part and parcel of the Federal Republic of Germany. West German law would become the law of the land. East German courts would be reorganized to follow the West German model of court organization. And no East German judge would retain office without submitting to a judicial review procedure which would examine each candidate's political past and possible involvement in miscarriages of justice under the old regime.

The Unification Treaty softened the impact of this sudden turnabout with many transition rules. The lifespan of certain East German legislation would be expanded for a limited period of time. In the territory of the ex-GDR, socialist courts would continue to function until funds and personnel had been found to allow their reorganization along West German lines. Judges would remain in their posts for the time being, until the judicial review procedures could be completed. Special rules, however, applied to Berlin.

To overcome the city's division as quickly as possible, the Unification Treaty denied East Berlin's court system the grace period granted to socialist courts elsewhere in the ex-GDR. Instead, it provided that on 3 October 1990, the day of German reunification, the West German 'court structure' should 'be extended' into the eastern half of the city. The treaty contained no details of what that might mean.

West Berlin's city government, the Senate (which together with a few officials in the GDR Ministry of Justice had been instrumental in the drafting of the treaty's Berlin provisions), interpreted the clause not only to imply the immediate expansion of West Germany's model of court organization into East Berlin but also to authorize a total turnover of judicial personnel. In early September the Senate decided to close all East Berlin courts as of 3 October 1990. On that date all East Berlin judges and prosecutors would be suspended, at 70 per cent of their former pay, for a period of six months. All East Berlin court files were to be transferred to the authority of West Berlin courts, all ongoing cases to be reassigned to West Berlin judges, and future cases originating in East Berlin to be redirected to designated West Berlin court districts. Some court buildings would be refurbished for future use, others closed altogether. East Berlin judges would be offered courses on West German law to re-tool while awaiting review by the judicial selection committees. Those who failed the review process would be considered dismissed after the expiration of their six month suspension. Few were expected to pass.

Considerable internal debate preceded the decision. But at no point were representatives of East Berlin's judiciary consulted. On 6 September 1990, after weeks of rumors, speculation, and news reports, the West Berlin Senator of Justice, Professor Jutta Limbach, informed a meeting of East German judges and prosecutors of their imminent suspension.

This is where my story begins.

I

Last Days

6 September 1990

Caught by pure chance on television a segment of Jutta Limbach's meeting with East Berlin judges. A packed room in the *Stadtgericht*, East Berlin's highest court. I missed Frau Limbach's speech, but I can see its effects: the room sizzles with anger and resentment. The main reaction seems to be disbelief. Several people in the audience simultaneously call out objections: too much noise to hear what they say. A man in Professor Limbach's entourage shouts: 'You must understand: you come from a state of injustice to the rule of law! We can't just take everyone!' The words sound more emphatic in German: 'You come from an *Unrechtsstaat* into a *Rechtsstaat*!' At the word '*Unrechtsstaat*' a wave of indignation runs through the room. Raised voices everywhere. Frau Limbach, all agitated, tries to make herself heard above the clamor.

12 September 1990

At the court building in the Littenstrasse in East Berlin. It houses several legal institutions: two first-instance district courts (*Stadtbezirksgerichte*), the East Berlin Court of Appeals (*Stadtgericht*), the State Notary's office, and— in two separate wings—the Supreme Court of the GDR and the office of the Prosecutor General. In the past I had never managed to get beyond the little cubicle of the custodian: it was next to impossible to assemble the permissions necessary to attend a socialist court session. Today the guard does not even look up as I pass his window.

It is a beautiful building, almost art nouveau, which has been a court-house since its completion in 1904: under the Kaiser, the Weimar Republic, the Nazis, and now, though only for another three weeks, under the social-ists. At the center a large, light rotunda extending over four floors and surrounded at each level by balconies with ornamental white cast-iron railings. At each side a set of twin staircases, weaving back and forth from story to story, accompanied by the same white banisters on their swinging path to the top. Columns in pink and olive-green stone, beginning at differ-ent levels, all ending under the high-domed ceiling. White walls contrasting with the warm brick-red of floors and staircases. The tiles of the rotunda have been patched in many places, and one can tell which tiles survived two wars and two dictatorships: each is embossed with a small crown at its center.

Everything is light and cheerful; a festive space, perfect for a ball, and indeed the annual lawyers' ball has at times been held at this courthouse. But no one is likely to feel festive today. I look for Dr. Oehmke, acting director of the Court of Appeals, to inquire about some last East German court sessions I might observe. Dr. Oehmke, a slight, pale man, very smooth, very polite, is eager to help, but can't offer much choice. Many pending matters are no longer set for hearings, since it would be difficult to complete the case before 2 October, and even more difficult to get a decision typed: East German courts work fast, but they have few secretaries and next to no modern technical equipment. Most scheduled criminal trials cannot take place because the defendants no longer appear, obviously counting on a reprieve until the new system takes over or—better yet— hoping to get lost in the shuffle from East to West German law. My best bet, Dr. Oehmke says, will be family or labor law cases: family law because judges are reluctant to leave troubled family members in limbo, labor law because the East–West German monetary union (in effect since 1 July 1990) and the ensuing wave of privatizations of state-owned enterprises have led to many contested dismissals which both plaintiffs and judges rush to resolve under the protective rules of East German civil procedure.

While Dr. Oehmke arranges for a list of upcoming sessions, I chat with his secretary. Like many other people in this building, she learned about the upcoming court closures through the newspaper. She has no idea what will become of her after 2 October. She is so proud of her office, her position as *Chefsekretärin*: will she find another job, at her age, in times of rising unemployment? Many court employees, she tells me, have left the sinking ship to look for work elsewhere. Cleaning ladies, always rare under socialism, have vanished. The court's press secretary, who appears with my list of upcoming cases, plans to take his vacation next week to make sure he has used all his free days by the time the world comes to an end.

The same apocalyptic mood in the corridors. A group of angry and agitated people has gathered in front of one of the courtrooms. Why the excitement? A civil case: plaintiff and defendant had both appeared with their lawyers. But when everyone was ready to begin, the judge had shrugged his shoulders and walked out. 'Why bother?' he seems to have thought. A few doors further down, a young judge buttonholes a colleague. 'Can you lend me a lay assessor?' Under East German rules of procedure, laypersons elected every five years at their place of work participate in the resolution of most first-instance cases. But these days, few of them show up for court duty. In the past, they had been favorites of the socialist legal system: model workers, rewarded with bonuses and special citations and entitled to time off from work, at the employer's expense, if their presence was required in court. But now, with state-owned enterprises transformed into private companies struggling for survival, managers no longer like to see their workers take time off, and workers no longer dare to ask for the permission to do so. Only pensioners and the unemployed can afford to spend time in court, and judges must make the most of their presence.

On my way out, I pass a big blackboard announcing special notaries' hours for church leavers. Another sign of disintegration. In the old GDR, few people with political or professional ambitions dared to remain church members. But many ordinary people belonged; if only for the sake of the three big occasions of baptism, wedding, and burial. After reunification, these services will become expensive: West German law imposes sizeable church taxes on everyone who has not formally resigned from his church. Many people now rush to do so. And since they also fear the higher fees of private West German notaries after 3 October, they queue to testify to their lack of religion while the notaries' service still comes cheap. The Deutschmark completes what socialism did not quite manage to achieve.

13 September 1990

Back at the Littenstrasse courthouse at 7:45 a.m. East German judges cannot sleep in; working hours are from 7:45 a.m. to 4:15 p.m., and presence in the building is mandatory.

I search for Room A334, for a family law case on my list. Once you leave the light and cheerful internal courtyard, this building becomes gloomy and confusing. There are A-corridors, B-corridors, corridors without any letter, and unexpected cross-passages leading you further astray. An architecture at odds with the plain language and didactic character of socialist law. Instead, the building echoes the complexity of the bourgeois legal system for which it was built, whose intricate structure and logic were never accessible to laymen. You have to think like a lawyer to find your way around here.

But Room A334, finally discovered, is plain enough: an elongated table, a little raised, for the judges; two smaller tables in front, facing each other, for the parties and their attorneys; two rows of creaking wooden folding seats in the back, for the audience. I am the only observer. On the wall behind the judges' table a big circle in cleaner white shows where the GDR emblem with its compass and hammer within a wreath of corn has already been removed. Neon light.

The case involves an appeal from a first-instance custody decision. As would be the case under West German law, the court will review issues of fact and law. No lay assessors serve at this level; the Stadtgericht sits with three professional judges. All three are women; all are wearing dark suits with white blouses. Although GDR law does not provide for judicial robes, all judges I encounter in this court wear formal clothes and dignified colors. 'We just fell into the habit,' someone explained.

The presiding judge, Frau Fischer (in her mid-thirties, with short hair and an open face) introduces the court, then quickly summarizes the decision under appeal. At its center is a 9-year-old girl. When her parents divorced six months ago the district court gave custody to the mother. Now the father claims that the mother is spoiling the child; that his daughter has become nervous and irritable; that her school performance has dropped. The mother listens. Both parents sit stiff and intense at their opposite tables and avoid looking at each other.

Judge Fischer does what any American family court judge would do in her place. With careful and detailed questioning she tries to find out which parent is the child's primary caretaker. Her task is complicated by the fact that the family still lives together; neither parent has yet been able to find a separate apartment. The daughter shifts between sleeping on a cot in her mother's room and sharing the former marriage bed with her father. Since Sigmund Freud has no place in socialist cultural heritage, nobody seems to worry about these sleeping arrangements. Rather, the court sees the child's daily closeness with both parents as assuring her attachment to both, and I can soon see that Judge Fischer will not find cause to overrule the district court's award of custody to the mother. But the tricky issue—tricky in this twilight zone between socialist and capitalist law—is visitation.

Six months ago, when the district court decided this case, GDR family law treated custody after divorce as a win or lose issue: no joint custody, no visitation rights for the losing spouse unless the custodial parent consented, and no parental standing to sue for modification of custody decrees. Social peace seemed more important than the equities between the ex-spouses. Eight weeks ago, in a last-minute attempt to bring GDR family law into line with the new respect for individual entitlements, the legislature reintroduced visitation rights, though not as the right of the non-custodial spouse but as the right of the child to keep in touch with both his parents. And in three weeks West German law will apply, which treats parental visitation primarily as the right of one adult against another.

On the face of it, three radically different visitation models. The issue illustrates how much East German legal ideology has changed in just a few months, from the pursuit of social welfare to the protection of individual rights, by way of a short-lived and probably illusory attempt to find a new and distinctive East German legal voice which would retain some of its socialist accent. But Judge Fischer's problems are practical. She wants to find a solution that will outlast reunification. That means a settlement with an eye on soon-to-apply West German custody law. Most East Berlin

judges have used the last months to read up on West German law. Those
who could afford it have bought West German legal literature; in many
offices, I can spot the familiar red-bound copy of the *Schönfelder*, the
looseleaf collection of West German private law. The numerous recent East
German enactments, on the other hand, hurriedly passed before the first
and last democratically elected GDR government would cease to exist, are
much harder to come by; the new code of civil procedure, I am told, became
available to the court only two weeks after it took effect.

   But Judge Fischer is not very interested in procedural issues. This hearing, for instance, was scheduled with insufficient notice to allow for the
proper exchange of briefs through the mail: a letter has not arrived. The fact
is mentioned and by general agreement soon dropped. No reason to worry;
everyone knows what the case is about. Socialist law has never been very
finicky about procedural precision; what counted was substantive justice,
and the old inclination not to be side-tracked by formal rules is now reinforced by the knowledge that time is running out. That does not prevent
the judge from listening carefully to the parties. But the emphasis is on
human, not legal, communication. The tone is quiet, civil, unauthoritarian.
Polite addresses are used: Madame Judge, Herr Dr. Scholz (for one of the
lawyers). When the attorneys get too technical, the judge speaks above
their heads directly to the parties and lets them tell their side of the story.
From time to time, Frau Fischer summarizes the deliberations for the tape
recorder (there is no court stenographer; too expensive), asks whether the
parties agree with her synopsis, on one occasion lets herself without any
defensiveness be corrected, and proceeds. Almost no questions from the
assistant judges. The attorneys participate more, but the trial belongs to the
presiding judge and the parties. Although the court will not announce its
custody decision until the afternoon (previous judgment affirmed, I later
learn), the parties agree, whatever the outcome, on a visitation schedule in
line with the West German minimum number of contacts. At the judge's
suggestion they renounce their right to withdraw from the settlement within
the next two weeks. Both custody judgment and visitation settlement can
thus become final. Done.

   The whole proceeding takes about an hour and a half. East German
judges handle fewer cases than their West German colleagues but, on
average, spend more time on each individual case. While a West German
civil law judge is bound by the parties' motions, an East German judge must
raise unasked questions, request additional evidence, suggest useful motions, and generally ensure that the dispute is completely resolved. Civil
procedure serves not only to adjudicate disputes of the past but also to
prevent conflicts in the future. One more example of the socialist preoccupation with collective harmony at the expense of the individual's control
over his own procedural fortunes. It takes time.

After the trial I join Frau Fischer and her two colleagues for a cup of coffee in the judges' room. All three are still shaken by the meeting with Frau Limbach. They do not recognize themselves in the portrait drawn by their West German critics. The word *'Unrechtsstaat'* rankles. All women agree that the GDR was no *Rechtsstaat*: law did not control political power, but power controlled the law. But they do not believe that the law's corruption in other areas of public life infected their own work. All three insist that taking political orders would deeply offend their sense of self-worth. 'How else would I be able to look at myself in the mirror?' Judge Fischer says.

I admit that most civil, family, and labor law disputes in the GDR had no immediate political significance. Civil law did not cover transactions within the state-owned economy and thus dealt mostly with small sums and minor personal grievances. Labor law did not allow for collective bargaining or workers' codetermination and so again was limited to matters affecting the rights and obligations of individual employees. And family law, by definition, concerned itself with personal relationships. But does this mean that none of the legal disputes arising under these headings touched upon political issues? In family law, were there never political reasons to recommend a specific result? Have they never encountered what the Soviets call 'telephone justice': attempts by someone with political pull to sway a decision his way? What about custody disputes if one of the parents had applied for an exit visa to leave the GDR, or a divorce proceeding involving a high party official?

Yes, Frau Aschenbach, one of the assistant judges, has encountered such a case. A first-instance divorce suit involving some second-rank functionary at the Central Committee. Frau Aschenbach just happened to be in the room when the director of her district court received a call from the man. The judge listened; held the receiver far away from his ear to diminish the din of words; then, when the voice at the other end stopped, returned the phone to his ear, said shortly, 'I will inform the judge,' and hung up. She, Frau Aschenbach, had been the judge in the case. And? 'That was it.' Her director had thought it below his dignity to pass on the message.

The others agree. A good judge did not pass on such messages and certainly did not act upon them. And a bad judge? They do not claim to speak for the area of criminal law, although ordinary criminal judges, they assure me, were much more independent than their Western critics would have it. All politically touchy issues investigated by State Security (the Stasi) rather than the People's Police were adjudicated by special senates, the infamous 'Ia panels' (now dissolved), which were even physically separated from the rest of the court and so—my family law judges seem to imply—well out of people's way. But civil, family, and labor law judges were autonomous in their decisions. They insist on it.

Whatever the truth, I have to accept the fact that these judges believe that they have carried out their tasks without political interference. *Rechtsprechen*—the German word for 'to adjudicate'—means in literal translation 'to speak right.' These women do not feel that they have spoken wrong. Now, with the wisdom of hindsight, they admit that their courtrooms were luxurious shelters in an unpleasant political world. They always suspected, often knew, and now no longer can escape the fact that others were spied upon, manipulated, and repressed by the system in whose name they exercised their authority. 'That was our mistake,' Frau Fischer says, 'not to have looked around us.'

But even if I accept her self-characterization, I have difficulty matching it with the realities we now know: the corruption coming to light, the defamations, the fine-meshed web of state security surveillance. Justice cannot be quite as easily divisible as these judges make it appear. Even Frau Fischer admits that there is a difference between the reply 'I will inform the judge'—even if no action follows—and a number of other possible answers coming to mind: 'I will inform the prosecutor of your call,' for example. Whatever independence these judges enjoyed must have been more fragile than they can now admit to themselves.

Afternoon

One floor down at the first-instance district court, Berlin-Prenzlauer Berg. A small room, with dark wood panelling and a beautiful stucco ceiling. Jarring: the squat modern judges' table of light lacquered wood. Here the GDR emblem is still present, burned into the shiny table front.

A civil case: *Deutsche Reichsbahn* v. *Schulze*. The judge is Frau Dietz, an older woman with a mild, worried face, looking pale in her ill-fitting dark blue suit. She sits alone; under the new GDR rules of civil procedure first-instance cases other than divorces can be handled without lay assessors. The new rule represents a step away from the socialist preference for collectives and also, I assume, from the mutual supervision collective decisions implied.

The plaintiff is the East German state railroad company, which also runs the city trains in Berlin. Last year the defendant, a cheerful young man with a small golden ring in one earlobe, had been caught travelling without a ticket. He had been fined the usual DM 20, had not paid, had received a second notice, had objected, and now the *Reichsbahn* wants to collect the fine plus the cost of enforcement and 'handling fees': DM 31 in all. The *Reichsbahn* representative, a plump young woman with the resigned look of someone who has seen it all before, sits at the plaintiff's table chewing gum.

Earlier, in the hall, the young man had explained to me his views on the matter. Why should he be the only one fined if everybody else skips the fare just as often? Why pay good West German marks when he was caught in times of the worthless Ostmark? And hadn't it all happened too long ago anyway? A spirited young man with a well-developed capitalist rights consciousness, arguing equal protection, a fair rate of exchange, and the right to repose. But at least he came to the hearing; even brought his girlfriend, who sits next to me in the spectators' row.

The dispute turns on the appropriate rate for exchanging the old Ostmark debt into current West German marks. Both sides agree that the fine itself should be calculated at a rate of 2:1, since it had been issued before the monetary union of both German states on 1 July 1990 and since 2:1 had been set as the official rate of exchange for Ostmark debts incurred before that date. But how about the handling fee? Wasn't a letter mailed after the monetary union? And how about the court costs, also to be borne by the defendant? At least part of the debt, the plaintiff argues, should be calculated at the 1:1 rate.

Palaver back and forth. From time to time, the judge intervenes to clarify what item on the bill is being debated. Finally, both sides agree to exchange the whole thirty-one marks at the rate of 2:1, leaving a debt of DM 15.50 plus DM 5 court costs, the lowest possible fee. The judge suggests a settlement instead of a judgment, which lowers the court costs by half to DM 2.50. Do the parties renounce their right to withdraw from the settlement within the next two weeks so the decision can become final? They do. That means the defendant owes DM 18. How about paying it on the spot, the judge suggests? Herr Schulze grins and turns his pants pockets inside out: no money!

The whole affair lasted almost an hour, occupying one judge, one railroad employee, and one irreverent young man who would have been better off doing some useful labor. Only two months ago the trial would also have taken a large chunk out of the working day of two lay assessors. All this at a price which the state sets at DM 2.50. A regime contemptuous of individual dignity? In many respects, yes. But in this context, a regime with an almost touching faith in the pedagogic powers of the law. This trial was not initiated to compensate the *Reichsbahn* for its losses. It was meant to state a lesson in civic behavior. Many East German citizens do not take debts owed to the state very seriously. Herr Schulze is right: many passengers cheat on the train fare. Many tenants of state-owned housing do not pay their rent. Many utility customers 'forget' to settle their electricity bills. So, the state sues to discipline the delinquents and to set an example for others: the court as schoolhouse.

East German procedure reflected the law's pedagogic ambitions. Until this June's civil procedure reform, the court had several means at its disposal to emphasize its lessons. It could ask a 'selected public' to attend the proceedings: a trial form considered most useful in rent collection cases, when other defaulting tenants could be invited to watch as the judge ordered their fellow delinquent to pay up. The court could hold 'visiting sessions' at a defendant's place of work or residence if it believed that other members of the collective would benefit from the instruction. And the judge could draw upon the testimony of 'social representatives,' a defendant's neighbors or colleagues, whose knowledge of the setting in which a conflict arose might help the judge to find a response which would not only resolve the dispute at hand but also address its causes.

None of these procedural techniques is available in Herr Schulze's case. The East German legislature abolished the didactic features of GDR civil procedure before reunification could sweep them away. But the old hopes for collective socialization still show in the way this trial is handled. The patience of the judge, the relaxed squabbles between the parties, the unhurried pace of the deliberations all reflect a procedural system which cared more about social integration than about efficiency. Judge Dietz is very much a representative of this system. She treats the parties with the long–suffering resignation of a parent who is not optimistic about her offsprings' improvement but has not yet given up on them. The maternal tone is used for the plaintiff as well as for the defendant. 'Why don't you take that chewing gum out of your mouth,' Frau Dietz tells the *Reichsbahn* woman, who complies with a placid shrug of the shoulders.

But what has Herr Schulze learned from the proceedings? Probably not very much. The trivial back-and-forth of his arguments with the plaintiff show how ill suited civil procedure—even socialist civil procedure—is for teaching collective responsibility: structured as a dialogue between two conflicting viewpoints, the trial encourages each side to exaggerate the validity of its own position and to downgrade the other's. Egotism is rewarded. And it is unlikely that Herr Schulze will never again travel without a ticket: even for a young man with empty pockets, DM 18 is not much of a deterrent.

The case demonstrates how difficult it must have been for Frau Dietz and her Littenstrasse colleagues to turn civil law hearings into socialist learning experiences. All too often, the courts' pedagogic effort was undercut by the fact that East German civil or labor law did not provide steep enough sanctions to discourage antisocial behavior. How can a judge teach tenants that the punctual payment of rent is an important socialist obligation if rents are absurdly low and if the law makes evictions for failure to pay almost impossible? Or teach workers the importance of labor discipline if sanctions amount to no more than a fraction of the costs incurred by the employer and if the law, to all intents and purposes, rules out dismissals? East German law wanted to persuade its addressees to rank collective interests above private advantage. But all too often, it was to the private advantage of socialist citizens simply to disregard collective interests. Only the already converted could be expected to listen to the sermon.

The socialist state also overestimated the pedagogic enthusiasm of its judges. Most spent—by capitalist standards—a great deal of time on their cases. Forty-five to sixty minutes, Frau Dietz tells me, is the average length of her trials. But most judges did not make much use of the fancier procedural options that might have increased the educational impact of their hearings. Time and again, Frau Dietz says, the judges of her court pledged to hold at least five trials a year outside of the court-house. But whether because of overwork, skepticism, political lethargy, or plain laziness, they never lived up to their goals. And if a judge decided to invite a 'selected public' to the hearing, usually in housing cases, chances were that the state housing administration would fail to provide the necessary list of suitable invitees.

The young woman from the *Reichsbahn* packs her briefcase. She has to rush off to her next trial. Beside Herr Schulze's case, she tells me, she has 14,000 other cases of unpaid fines to deal with, assisted by only one colleague. But things are looking up. In anticipation of its capitalist reorganization, the *Reichsbahn* has recently increased its number of ticket controllers from sixteen to thirty. And on the date of reunification, fines for travelling without a ticket will rise from DM 20 to DM 60. That should make a difference.

After the trial I sit in the judges' office, and Frau Dietz tells me about herself. Born 1935. Her father, a bricklayer, was a Communist. On 11 October 1944 he was murdered in a concentration camp. Frau Dietz wants me to know the date; it seems burnt into her mind. She learned it after the war when her mother was no longer afraid to tell her the truth.

When Frau Dietz was 20 her mother died of cancer. By then, the young woman was at university. The bricklayer's daughter became a lawyer. The new workers' state supported her and showed pride in her, and she in turn trusted the state. Even today she feels guilty about not having taken up work right after completing her studies. Instead, she married and stayed at home until her two children had grown up. 'I probably should not have done that' she says, still worrying that she might have disappointed the hopes placed in her. But she talks with pride about her son and daughter.

In 1975 she joined the judiciary and has stayed at the district court level ever since. Not a steep career. Like everyone else, Frau Dietz learned about the imminent closure of her court through the newspaper speculations and the meeting with Professor Limbach. What had happened after that meeting: had people gathered, talked, made plans about how to react? No, she had just walked home, stunned, and the others, she thought, had done the same.

Now, she wants to apply for review by the judicial selection committee. But at age 55 she doubts that they will have her. She has sent in her résumé and filled out the first questionnaire provided by the West Berlin government. They want to know whether she was 'socially active.' Like any other judge, she was a member of the Communist Party; is now, unlike most of her colleagues, a member of the PDS (*Partei für demokratischen Sozialismus*), its much maligned successor. Like other judges, she supervised social courts or gave pep talks on socialist law to high school graduates. Once a month she attended the Party meeting at the courthouse. 'What did you talk about?' She is a little evasive: 'nothing much.' How to improve the work of the judiciary, mostly. In former years, that must have meant an emphasis on ideological conformity. More recently, it seems to have meant efforts to conduct speedier and pedagogically more effective trials.

Has she ever had doubts about the East German political system? Oh yes; especially during the last few years, when the Soviet journal *Sputnik* was forbidden because of its critical views and when the Party put down *perestroika* as a mere 'change of wallpaper.' But she did not want to admit that things had gone seriously wrong. She thought mistakes could be corrected. She forgave Honecker's repressiveness and rigidity because of his years in concentration camp. 'He wanted to do the right thing.' That is what Frau Dietz wanted to do, too: the right thing.

The radical political change has left her tired and confused. She seems burdened by the new joys of consumption. Her children might now leaf eagerly through the catalogues of the big West German mail order houses, but she couldn't. 'Maybe I should do something about my clothes,' she says doubtfully. There it is again, the old attempt to live up to someone's expectations. But in this new world, she does not know how to do the right thing anymore. She no longer fits in.

If, by some stroke of magic, she could undo last year's events: would she want to? Frau Dietz' voice is so low that I have difficulty catching her reply. 'I wanted socialism,' she says.

14 September 1990

Lunch, of sorts, in the court cafeteria on the third floor. A bleak room and a minimal menu, but the place is always busy. Now more than ever: people search each other out to exchange rumors, worries, addresses to keep in touch after 2 October. A judge at my table tells about running into a West Berlin colleague. The Westerner had mentioned the Littenstrasse courthouse: 'It is said to be such a beautiful building. . . .'

'Said to be . . .'—he had not seen it himself. There were next to no contacts between East and West Berlin judges before the '*Wende*,' the 'turning-point': East Berlin judges were not allowed any 'West contacts'; West Berlin judges were not interested in what happened beyond the Wall. Then, in the euphoria following 9 November 1989, people on both sides could not see enough of each other: there were visits, common seminars, workshops, invitations of all kinds going back and forth. But as time wore on and as reunification became a rapidly approaching reality, the mood changed. The Westerners began to realize that their East German colleagues were not quite so similar to themselves as they had first believed. Noticing some differences, they began to suspect others. Largely ignorant about the East German legal system, they did not know how to interpret their own perceptions. The eagerness and simplicity of socialist lawyers made Westerners feel intellectually superior. And as more and more details about the corruption and repression in the old GDR came to light they began to doubt the sincerity of their socialist colleagues' will to reform. Was not every one of them tainted by the association with a totalitarian state? Why struggle to differentiate between degrees of contamination by a system which should be rejected in its entirety?

As Western attitudes towards East Berlin lawyers changed, so did the Easterners' view of their West Berlin colleagues. Where they had first met with good-willed curiosity, they now sensed reservations and disbelief. Westerners seemed to expect excuses, then rejected them as disingenuous or as admissions of guilt. Communication, which at first seemed pleasant and easy, turned complicated and full of pitfalls. The greater technical complexity of Western law made East German lawyers feel slow-witted and boorish. They began to realize that they were being looked down upon. The initial excitement about the new intellectual freedom gave way to worries about one's ability to compete. Feeling rejected, East Berlin lawyers became defensive and angry.

And so the Cold War, forgotten in the happy moments of reunification, seems to have ended in a cold peace. For a few more days East Berlin judges can huddle in this cafeteria. But everyone knows that the winners are preparing to take over and that the losers must get ready to pack their bags. 'It is said to be such a beautiful building. . . .' I can imagine the exchange: the gleam in the eye of the West Berlin speaker; the sinking heart of the East Berlin listener.

17 September 1990

Room A322: a labor law case before the East Berlin Court of Appeals. One of the many dismissal cases which still keep judges in this courthouse busy. It involves employees of the 'Fashion Institute of the GDR,' once the headquarters of the East German fashion industry, such as it was, and now the 'Fashion Institute Ltd.,' a private company which, like many other

recently privatized companies, fights for its survival. In January 1990 the
Institute had 375 employees; at present it has 120. The lay-offs which are
the subject of this trial happened in March 1990. The employees successfully challenged their dismissals in the district court; the Fashion Institute
now appeals.

The eight respondents, all women, sit in the front row of the spectators'
benches. You cannot tell by their looks that all of them were involved in
fashion design and marketing. One stylish pants suit (bought in West Berlin, as I learn later); the other outfits drab and conventional. One can see
why the Fashion Institute had to let go two-thirds of its workforce.

The judge, Frau Schomburg—tall, blonde, energetic—sits with two lay
assessors. Unlike in civil law cases, laymen participate in labor law cases in
both first and second instance. The respondents' attorney, also a woman,
sits on the left at a small table below the judge's bench. Opposite her, three
representatives of the Fashion Institute: the head of personnel (a sullen-
faced middle-aged woman), a smart young lawyer (obviously from the
West), and the Institute's *Justitiar*, its own in-house counsel from socialist
days, whose pained look suggests that he wants to dissociate himself from
the entire affair and who does not utter a word throughout the proceedings.

As a business decision, the respondents' dismissal in March must have
seemed reasonable enough: with the opening of the border and the influx of
Western goods East German fashion was no longer competitive, and the
Institute could not survive without drastic cutbacks. But these firings were
plainly illegal. Since they took place in March, they had to conform to the
GDR Labor Code's rules on dismissals. Under these rules the employer had
to offer reasonable alternative employment within the same enterprise or a
'contract of transferral' with a different enterprise which the employer had
to locate. Even then, the dismissal would not be valid without the prior
consent of the enterprise's union organization.

The Fashion Institute had not even vaguely complied with these requirements. How could it, considering that its own desperate situation was
shared by thousands of other East German enterprises equally close to
collapse? So the management had not offered alternative employment
(since its goal was to cut labor costs), had not arranged for a transfer
contract (with whom?), and had not even asked for formal union consent
(although the union, also worried about the enterprise's future, had apparently not opposed the dismissals). Plain as can be, the district court ruled, a
violation of section 54, paragraph 2 of the Labor Code.

As she goes over these facts, Judge Schomburg tries to find out whether
the employer did anything to help the dismissed women locate new jobs.
The results of this enquiry are meager. One of the women had been offered
work outside of her own department, but the offer was a repetition of a
previous proposal rejected several years ago for reasons of ill health, and

the work bore no relationship to the woman's occupation and training. 'A sham offer,' says Judge Schomburg. What else? The head of personnel had passed on a tip from the state employment office: North Vietnamese enterprises were looking for textile experts. One of the women had been alerted to a television program on new employment opportunities. Another had been handed an architect's newspaper advertisement searching for office help. In no instance had the Fashion Institute itself contacted possible alternative employers. What it had done instead was to make sure that the dismissals would go through whatever the outcome of the present law suit. To that effect, the management had fired the eight women two more times: in early June, right after its defeat in the district court, and in July, when the East German legislature replaced section 54, paragraph 2 of the Labor Code with the less stringent West German Job Protection Act (*Kündigungsschutzgesetz*).

It is obvious that Judge Schomburg takes a dim view of the management's efforts. She does not seem to expect formal compliance with section 54, paragraph 2. But she searches for some sign of compassion, of regret at losing colleagues who for decades were part of a collective endeavor. She finds none. And it is this absence of caring, it seems to me, which also makes the women sitting in front of me so angry and resentful. At one point in the hearing, for instance, when one of them complains about some bonuses not having arrived at her savings account, the young lawyer from the West explains that the delay was due to the near-collapse of bank transfers in East Berlin: 'That is not something the Fashion Institute can be blamed for.' Sarcastic laughter from the audience. It is not directed at the pitiful condition of the GDR banking system but at the lawyer who believes that institutional failures can excuse the management's lack of interest in the welfare of its employees. The lawyer, who senses the rising hostility in the room, tries to soothe his opponents. 'I can understand your feelings . . . ,' he begins a sentence. 'You cannot understand anything' is the bitter response of one of the women.

It becomes clear to me that this is not a dispute about legal issues. Of course the Fashion Institute has violated the dismissal requirements of the Labor Code. So has another East Berlin enterprise whose appeal I observe on another occasion, again in Frau Schomburg's court. In that case, too, the employer had dismissed several workers without offering them alternative employment or a contract of transferral and without obtaining the formal consent of the enterprise union organization. But in that case the manager, a stocky, plain-spoken man, comes himself to the trial; the head of the enterprise union organization sits next to him at the plaintiff's table, manager and employees address each other with the familiar '*Du*,' and all, employer and employees alike, are upset at the dismissals. 'We loved our Labor Code, too, but there was no other way,' the manager says, and the judge believes him. So there is a settlement: two of the employees receive three months' wages as compensation; the dismissal of the third is deferred until a later date because a lengthier term of employment, in her case, will eventually result in higher unemployment insurance. After the trial, a chat between all participants in the hall and a general shaking of hands.

But in the present case I cannot detect any evidence which would suggest that the Fashion Institute's management still feels responsible for its employees. The only management representative at the trial, the woman from personnel, says nothing betraying regret or concern. The *Justitiar* stays wrapped in mournful silence. The attorney from the West defends his client's case with articulate detachment—and irritates his opponents by his very reasonableness. They seem angry at him because he can afford an impersonal judgment, because for him this trial has no existential dimensions, because he treats the case as a legal conflict to be decided by the quality of each side's legal arguments and as a job from which he can walk away after a good day's work to a secure and comfortable existence.

To the eight women, their firings result from human failure, not legal error. Three times in the course of the hearing the most articulate among them, the woman who supposedly was offered alternative employment, tries to explain how this very offer demonstrated the management's lack of interest in its employees. 'They did not even know what kind of work we were doing,' she says. And she means: they cared so little about us that they did not bother to find out. When the attorney from the West suggests that maybe she was a little too picky about available work, she gets even more agitated: 'You don't understand about these matters in West Germany!'

She is probably right. He does not understand a social system which swaddled its employees but also protected them; in which low pay was balanced by extensive social benefits; in which collectives confined their members but also shielded them against the outside; in which the absence of autonomy, of free play, of any room to maneuver was compensated for by the warmth of comradeship. With this world, the eight women had made their reluctant peace. After the trial they tell me how none of them—and these are fashion experts!—had ever been allowed to travel to Paris, London, or Rome. Every choice of color, cut, or material in their designs had been censored, dulled, and compromised. But the Institute also took care of them. Their jobs seemed forever safe. There were health care, child care, organized vacations, a collective subscription to the theater. One of the women had come to the Institute as a cleaner, had been sent to engineering school, and was now a fashion consultant. All had regularly been rewarded with bonuses, prizes, and special commendations for their commitment.

As recently as March they had received a letter of thanks from the management.

Now it turns out that all those professions of warmth and concern had been dishonest. The celebrated solidarity between management and workforce does not survive the political turnabout. Management and Party leadership concentrate on saving their own skins. The former cadre leader becomes head of personnel. The Party secretary turns technical manager and exempts her friends from the inevitable dismissals. The young daughter of a departmental director, who works in precisely the same field as one of the respondents, may keep her job, while the respondent, after twenty-five years with the enterprise, must lose hers. The deal which these women thought they had struck with the system and on which they had relied—security in exchange for autonomy—turns out to be void.

So, these women have not only lost jobs. They have lost the justification for the sacrifices, the limitations, and humiliations of all their working lives. For this they kept their mouths shut and patiently did their jobs? So that now—too provincial to compete with Western fashion, too old to begin again at the beginning—they will also lose their livelihoods? 'I feel lied to, robbed and cheated,' says one of the women, and she speaks for all of them.

The judge seems to understand. Her own situation is not all that different. But it can come as no surprise that the young attorney from the West cannot find words that do justice to the depth of his opponents' disappointment. When towards the end of the trial he summarizes the arguments supporting his client's position, I hear, for the first time in this case, a coherent legal discussion. No wonder that the statement so completely misses the issues of this trial.

Is there anything one can say to support the legality of the dismissals? The lawyer chooses the only possible path: he denies the applicability of section 54, paragraph 2 of the Labor Code under present conditions. Section 54, he says, was the product of a policy of full employment, which could only be realized under socialist conditions. With the abolition of planning, the monetary union, and the establishment of a market economy in the GDR, the provision lost its *raison d'être*. The Labor Code revision in June 1990, which adopted the West German rule permitting 'socially justified' dismissals, had only acknowledged existing changes. Even the GDR Labor Code, by the way, had not ruled out dismissals in the wake of structural changes. But the Code's very stringent prerequisites for such firings had to be redefined to fit the new economic conditions. And in any case: the management could never find alternative employment for the appellees. No law could obligate its addressees to do the impossible.

From the subsequent exchanges it is clear to me that I am the only person in the audience to appreciate my colleague's efforts. Nothing suggests that the others even listened. Neither the respondents' attorney nor the judge refers to what has just been said. Frau Schomburg also does not react to the attorney's request to outline what she would consider an acceptable settlement. He undertakes one more try: suggests to the respondents that a settlement now, still in the shadow of the protective GDR Labor Code, will probably be more advantageous to them than settlement at a later stage, after a renewed dismissal, when West German law will apply. The response is outraged commotion. Shuffling, hostile voices, and shouts of 'Blackmail! Blackmail!'

I have to think for a moment. Blackmail? It seems perfectly natural to me that a settlement should take the risks of later developments into account and perfectly legitimate to remind one's opponent of the likelihood of such events. But this is—still—a socialist courtroom. For the last forty years, law as practiced in this room served above all as a means to protect public order and only in second place—often very much in second place—as a technique for reconciling conflicting private interests. To the eight women in front of me, this hearing, too, should turn on issues not of private rights but of public morality: the enterprise's responsibility towards its long-time servants. It must seem profoundly immoral to them that this conflict should be decided by their opponent's strategic exploitation of their own time pressures; that the law's moral authority should be compromised by the parties' wheelings and dealings; that law, in protecting a right-holder's individual entitlement, should also protect his ability to manipulate others. They want the court to restore order, not to play the role of impartial umpire. To be reminded now that the days of this order are numbered, that soon their own employment or unemployment will no longer be a question of public responsibility but a matter of personal concern, seems particularly bitter.

Judge Schomburg calls the audience to order, defends the professional stance of her capitalist colleague, and restores quiet in the courtroom. But it is plain to see that the attorney from the West need not be very optimistic about the outcome of this case. And in the afternoon, when the court announces its decision, all eight dismissals are indeed ruled void.

Afterwards, Frau Schomburg and I stay on in the courtroom and talk. She seems quite shaken by the trial. 'That was just terrible!' she says. Terrible? Depressing, yes: if I think of the women's middle-aged faces under the neon light, of the banality of their clothes, the bitterness in their voices, the new dismissal notices waiting for them at the enterprise. But they won, didn't they? Then it occurs to me that Judge Schomburg might not only be talking about the respondents. It was the hearing itself that was so terrible: the open hostility in the room, the inability of the judge to restore social peace, the fact that nothing she could do would have lasting significance. And, on a deeper level, the collision between two profoundly different legal world-views, one of them already defeated and knowing it, which had added a special sharpness to the proceedings.

Socialist law never liked conflict. It smelled too much of self-assertion and the wish to absent oneself from collective felicity. Although all disputes adjudicated in East German courts involved essentially personal matters (conflicts between state-owned enterprises were handled by special economic tribunals, while institutional conflicts and public law disputes were not subject to judicial review), courts were nevertheless expected to downplay the private elements in a dispute and to concentrate instead on its social dimensions. The technique was called 'generalizing a conflict' (*einen Konflikt verallgemeinern*): interpreting a specific controversy as a symptom of underlying social tensions and finding a solution that would not only right individual wrongs but also address their causes, prevent their recurrence, and thus ensure collective peace in the future.

By definition this feat could be achieved only with the co-operation of all participants. Social harmony is not divisible. Hence the pedagogic leanings of socialist procedure and its dislike for zero-sum solutions. Socialist trials were not supposed to divide a collective into winners and losers but to unite it in common allegiance to socialist norms of behavior. That explains the East German preference for unanimity and for settlements. Rather than fighting it out, the parties were encouraged to work at what was called an 'autonomous solution' (*eigenverantwortliche Lösung*).

But the term is misleading. The purpose of compromises and settlements in GDR law was not to increase the parties' autonomy. Western experiments with alternative dispute resolution often pursue the goal of empowerment: when we replace adversary proceedings with processes which give more voice to the parties themselves, we do so in the belief that people know what is good for them and should generally control their own lives. East German attempts to promote settlements were not motivated by the wish to limit state authority over private affairs. Socialist law did not strive for autonomy but for harmony. If to us settlements are better than judgments, to socialists settlements are better than discord. Our law thrives on conflict. But East German law was meant to prevent conflict, to overcome, or at least to diffuse it. Children, please no fighting! As always, it is the metaphor of the family that best conveys the intentions of socialist law. What other paradigm could explain the socialist claim of basic congruence between individual and collective interests? Or the leading role of the Party which, as materfamilias, presides over the family and ensures everyone's welfare? Children, please no fighting!

I am reminded of an exchange with a young judge in this court-house whom I had asked why he had chosen his profession. 'Because I never liked arguments,' he had replied. My translation is a little unfair: '*weil ich nie Streit mochte*,' were his words, and *Streit* could also be rendered as 'discord'

or 'quarrelling.' But 'arguments'—one's hostile, reasoned dissociation from
somebody else's viewpoint—defines very well what the system found unacceptable. This young judge did not like arguments, the Party did not like
arguments, and Frau Schomburg did not like arguments. Hence her dismay
at this hearing: because the depth of discord it had revealed—between the
participants and between the ideological systems for which they stood—
could not be bridged, because social harmony would only be in demand for
another two weeks, and because after that conflict would rule the law. 'That
was just terrible.'

18 September 1990

Back in Judge Schomburg's office. I want to pursue the issue of 'telephone
justice.'
  'Oh, they always meddled.' 'They,' to Frau Schomburg, were mostly
Party bosses at the district level, maybe because most of her examples of
'telephone justice' stem from the time when she was a district court criminal
law judge. She recalls a dubious case against the chairman of an artisans'
co-operative. The district First Secretary had called and said: 'We expect a
conviction.' Judge Schomburg talks about the call as one would about
a predictable occupational hazard. 'It was possible to fend that kind of
thing off.'
  Then there were the more formal and less controllable pressures of the
superior court. Judge Schomburg remembers a prosecution for one of the
most frequently used provisions of the GDR Criminal Code: 'attempted
unlawful crossing of the state border.' Since the defendant had been totally
drunk at the time of the incident she had acquitted for lack of intent. The
prosecutor appealed (as prosecutors in all civil law countries can) and the
regional court remanded: insufficient evidence. Frau Schomburg sub-
poenaed a second border guard, who testified how he and his colleague had
to carry the inebriated defendant from the scene of the crime, and acquitted
again. Again overruled; this time the regional court itself pronounced the
conviction but granted probation. Frau Schomburg tells this story with the
level voice of someone recounting commonplace events. I detect no criticism of a state that punishes its citizens for attempting to leave it, no outrage
at the court of appeals for applying the punishment to people who pose no
real threat to the system, and no self-righteousness on her part for having
persisted in disagreeing with her superiors.
  And how about labor law? Frau Schomburg cannot remember a telephone call suggesting a particular outcome in a labor law case. I believe her.
The typical labor law dispute involved issues of pay, terms of employment,
dismissals, and—the largest case-group—compensation claims of the employer for damages caused through the negligence of the employee. These

issues were of concern to the individual worker but unlikely to attract the attention of Party bosses. And the one politically critical group of labor law cases—lawsuits challenging managerial sanctions based on the plaintiff's decision to emigrate to West Germany—was considered important enough to require a uniform, centrally articulated response which would only have been undercut by local attempts at 'telephone justice.'

I ask Frau Schomburg about these *Ausreiser* cases. *Ausreiser* was the innocent East German term for people applying for exit visas: 'outbound travellers.' But in practice 'outbound' movements met with extraordinary bureaucratic obstacles, and the 'travellers' were treated like traitors. Socialism never could tolerate those who rejected its blessings. By requesting an exit visa, a humdrum socialist citizen became a dangerous civic outcast. In the labor law context, this change entailed, above all, the loss of a citizen's usual job security. Visa applicants in ideologically sensitive jobs were no longer considered trustworthy enough to serve the socialist state. Teachers, who ordinarily could be dismissed only at the end of the school year, if at all, were fired as soon as their visa applications became known. So were academics, administrators, and people working in the media. Visa applicants in politically more neutral positions might be pressured into accepting 'contracts of transferral' to less desirable jobs.

Most *Ausreiser* did not contest their dismissals but thought it wiser to acquiesce, lie low, and hope that it would not take too long before the state permitted them to leave. But some—'the courageous and the naïve,' as Frau Schomburg says—sued their employer for violation of the Labor Code. To forestall any possibility of their success, God forbid, and to prevent dissenters from using the courts as a stage for voicing their dissatisfaction with life in the GDR, a technique was needed for suppressing *Ausreiser* suits before they could do any damage. The needed pretext was found in section 28, paragraph 3 of the Code of Civil Procedure, which allows a complaint to be dismissed 'by decree' if 'reasons exist which exclude a hearing and a decision on the merits.' Ostensibly based on this provision, *Ausreiser*-related suits could be rejected without oral argument. This is how Frau Schomburg, and any other labor law judge in this courthouse, handled these cases.

But who devised and authorized this treatment of *Ausreiser* complaints? And how was this policy disseminated to judges? Frau Schomburg goes to her closet and comes back with what looks very much like my own haphazard collection of cooking recipes. A cardboard box full of folded sheets of paper, some bundled in envelopes, some held together by rubber bands. A few are typed on the typical greyish and brittle East German office paper. Most are covered with Frau Schomburg's round and orderly handwriting. She searches a bit and shows me: a set of notes on a meeting of labor law judges at the Supreme Court on 10 November 1988 dealing with legal issues relating to *Ausreiser*. A summary, again handwritten, of a decree of the Chairman of the Council of Ministers dated 8 December 1988 (decree number 192/1988, she has taken it all down) ordering that, in principle, no oral arguments are to be held in labor law suits involving applicants for exit visas. A note on an 'orientation' (probably issued by the Supreme Court) of April 1989 repeating the same position. A summary of a Supreme Court conference of 10 May 1989, again affirming the 'no oral argument' policy.

Doubtless, many similar memos sit in many other desk drawers and filing cabinets in this courthouse. They were needed because policies like the one dealing with labor law suits of visa applicants were not promulgated in written form. On less touchy issues of statutory interpretation the Supreme Court would issue 'Guidelines,' 'Viewpoints,' or sometimes 'Common Viewpoints' produced together with the office of the Prosecutor General or some ministry. The 'Guidelines,' which had statutory authorization, were published in the official gazette; the 'Viewpoints' were included in an un-published collection of Supreme Court decisions (called 'Supreme Court Informations') which in 1977 replaced the official volumes of Supreme Court case law. The 'Informations' were 'for internal use only' but they were distributed not only to judges, prosecutors, and other government officials but also to attorneys (although each copy was numbered and could thus be easily traced), and they were, if not printed, at least multiplied in typescript. The last issue of the 'Supreme Court Informations' appeared in the fall of 1989 in an edition of roughly 4,200 copies.

But directives like those instructing judges how to get rid of *Ausreiser* suits were considered too sensitive to be even semi-published in relatively accessible documents. These directives would be formulated at the top level of the Supreme Court (undoubtedly with the involvement of highest government and Party officials), circulated among those judges who worked in the area of law concerned, and passed on either to the directors of regional or district courts, who would inform their judges, or orally at 'specialized judges' conferences' (*Fachrichtertagungen*), which would as-semble judges working in a particular field, say labor law, at the Supreme Court or the regional courts of appeal. This is where Frau Schomburg would hear about the policy in question, take notes, and later add them to her boxful of similar instructions.

I once was shown an internal Supreme Court document dealing with *Ausreiser* suits which might have been used for such oral briefing of judges. It told the same story Frau Schomburg tells me, only in greater detail. According to this document, all complaints by visa applicants against their dismissals were to be transferred from social courts (the usual first-instance courts in labor litigation) to district courts. In district court, complaints were to be dismissed by the chairmen of labor law panels without the involvement of lay assessors. Prior to dismissing a complaint the judge was to report on the case, by way of the hierarchical ladder, via the regional court to the Supreme Court. Each report was to include a summary of the facts and a statement describing the efforts undertaken to co-ordinate the handling of *Ausreiser* cases with other authorities in the district.

All this typed on plain paper. No Supreme Court insignia, no addressee, just 'Senate for Labor Law' (to indicate the source of the order) in the upper left corner, the name of this copy's recipient handwritten at the top, and 'personal' marked in black felt pen. No signature either: no one, it appears, wanted to admit responsibility for the contents. A document with a bad conscience trying to leave no traces. I detect the same fear of embarrassment in another directive contained in the same piece of writing: that *Ausreiser* whose suits have been dismissed by lower courts and who apply to the Supreme Court for cassation (a *certiorari*-type proceeding open to all losing parties), 'as previously practiced' are not to receive a receipt acknowledging their complaint. If need be, they shall be informed orally that no action will be taken. Again: injustice careful not to leave fingerprints.

It cannot have been very efficient to co-ordinate the East German judiciary's response to important political questions with directives which many judges never even laid eyes on. What if they took incomplete notes? And how were judges to know whether a policy was still in force? Hence the many reiterations of essentially similar orders contained in Frau Schomburg's recipe box: to keep everyone safely in line. But another worry that would have seemed plausible to me—that the orders' secrecy might undercut their legitimacy—does not seem well founded. Asked whether she always followed such oral directives, Frau Schomburg answers with a matter-of-fact 'yes.' What would have happened had she not dismissed an *Ausreiser* complaint in the prescribed manner? She would have been overruled at the first try and lost her job at the second.

But I do not think that the likelihood of reprisals alone made Frau Schomburg follow the *Ausreiser* policy of the Supreme Court. She did not see this policy as unjust. Substantively, she could understand that this state would not tolerate teachers who had rejected the socialist way of life. Formally, she was satisfied that the generality of the Supreme Court's directives also implied their legitimacy. Although Frau Schomburg's own political choices would have been different, she did not see it as her job to question the state's policy decisions. Injustice, to her, began where state officials tried to intervene in individual cases. Such telephone calls had to be resisted if Frau Schomburg, like Judge Fischer, wanted to be able to look at herself in the mirror. 'We had freedom of decision,' she says with conviction. And: 'the lay assessors would never have played along anyway.' What she means is: within the narrow parameters of the individual case, it was both necessary and possible occasionally to resist outside interference.

Does Frau Schomburg's story reflect a lack of judicial backbone or differ-ent professional conventions than judges would follow under the rule of law? Her report on another case makes me uncertain. An *Ausreiser* teacher sued not to contest his dismissal but to force the school administration to provide him with the evaluation to which each employee is entitled at the termination of his employment. The school—seeing no longer the colleague but only the outlaw—had refused the request. Frau Schomburg still is incensed as she talks about it. Did she hold a hearing? No, but she called the school administration and threatened to hold one, whereupon the evalu-ation materialized. The Supreme Court had only ruled out oral arguments in cases where the *Ausreiser* challenged disciplinary sanctions. Since the withholding of an evaluation was not a permissible sanction under the Labor Code, Frau Schomburg did not consider herself bound by general internal rules. A skirmish with state authority on legal no man's land. But she did get into trouble on this account, as it turns out; just barely missed a disciplinary proceeding.

19 September 1990

At the District Administration, Berlin-Prenzlauer Berg, to talk with a young social worker (whom I had met at Judge Fischer's custody case) about the importance of family rights in everyday life.

Prenzlauer Berg is one of the poorer boroughs of East Berlin. Once-splendid houses from the turn of the century, but now in pitiful shape: crumbling façades, perilous hallways, apartments without central heating, and often even without indoor toilets. Many houses are no longer habitable and stand empty. The population is mixed: working-class families, old people, squatters, intellectuals. A district with a lot of business for social workers, I should think.

Frau Kerstin has brought along two of her colleagues, also young women in their early thirties. We talk about custody disputes and the East German rejection of enforceable visitation rights for the non-custodial parent. All three women liked this approach: it favored women and produced a 'cleaner' solution for the children. And the fathers? Oh, they would grum-ble. But they always got used to the law. No hint that this policy might pose an issue of fathers' rights. I can see why one of the many new associations brought forth by the political turnabout was an interest group of fathers pushing for more contacts with their children.

I want to hear about the women's work. Well, it was easier before the *Wende*, the 'turn-about,' when the Wall fell in November 1989. Not just because there was no unemployment, a lower crime rate, and no real reason to worry about drugs. They also had fewer obstacles to overcome: there was easier access to information, more support within the community, less resistance from the people they tried to help. Take a case of parental neglect. Since almost every child above the age of 3, and 70 per cent of children under 3 attended state nursery schools and crèches, mistreated or neglected children came quickly to the attention of the authorities. Once a problem was spotted, it was simple to investigate a family in trouble: parents brought, on their own, the required character evaluation from their employer; teachers and neighbors readily told a social worker what they knew. If help was needed, social workers could rely on the assistance of volunteers: there were 'youth assistance committees,' where professional and lay people together decided whether to remove a child from his family, and lay 'family helpers,' who could lend a hand with housekeeping or child care, or provide guidance and advice.

And—although the social workers do not say this—the law was on their side. Or rather: it was not on their clients' side. The only act of interference with family rights which needed court approval was the termination of parental rights. It was rarely used because even without it endangered children could easily be removed from their homes. Frau Kerstin checks her files: in 1989 there were only eight termination cases in the district. And how much state involvement short of termination? On Frau Kerstin's beat, an area with roughly 980 families with children, fifty to sixty families were clients of the State Youth Services.

As of now, the three young women have no idea how reunification will affect their job security. But they can tell that their working climate has already changed. Now, it occasionally happens that a client shuts the door in their faces. Managers no longer provide information on their employees. Nor do Frau Kerstin and her colleagues dare to ask. Under the old system a social worker could call an enterprise not only to enquire how a client was doing but also to suggest that management and work collective watch out for him and help him to reform. But now the request for information would only alert the employer to his employee's general failings and make him a more likely candidate for dismissal.

It is obvious that as far as social work is concerned, in these women's view, the *Wende* has brought a change for the worse. Frau Kerstin mentions the new buzz word 'data protection,' which now complicates access to personal information, with the exasperated tone one would use to describe a particularly trying boss. The protection, she feels, will often be at the expense of the protected. It robs people of chances to be helped, closes their lives off from the concern of others. Especially the weak, she thinks, will be weaker without collectives to sustain them.

Maybe. But why would clients' behavior change so quickly after the *Wende* if they had not all along experienced social work as intrusion rather than help? Would collective co-operation collapse so fast if it had been founded on true comradely feelings rather than on political incentives? I have no doubt that these three women are idealists: none was a Party member, and at DM 1,000 net a month (about $570) they had to be motivated by human concern rather than ambition. But they have fewer doubts about their capacity to do good than I would find warranted under any social system.

One of the women tells me that during the first months after the *Wende*, when East and West Berlin social workers eagerly got together to exchange ideas, the West Berliners often expressed envy at their Eastern colleagues' working conditions. 'You have all those possibilities that we are still pushing for,' they would say. The comment highlights the fact that the socialist state in many respects defined its own tasks as social work. At its best the GDR was a do-gooder society, a brother's-keeper state, which would allow no one to be left behind. Our conversation demonstrates the obvious costs: in three hours none of the women even once used the word 'privacy' or any of its synonyms or derivations. I know, because I listened for it.

20 September 1990

A divorce case under Judge Tauchnitz, a stout, cheerful woman close to retirement age, who never rose beyond the district court level. A typical GDR career, if the word 'career' applies: in a world in which professional advancement brought few financial rewards and no real increase in decision-making powers, but imposed greater obligations to demonstrate political orthodoxy, many people were happy to remain in inconspicuous posts.

This is my third divorce case in this courthouse. The first involved a drawn-out dispute over a garden allotment, which in the West would probably have been settled between the lawyers. The second was the kind of quick, consensual divorce of a young childless couple which in an American court would have taken ten rather than thirty minutes but otherwise would not have looked out of place. But this third hearing seems different to me: it combines the authoritarian and optimistic features of socialist law in a mixture which—at least at this undiluted strength—one would be unlikely to encounter in an American family court.

A sixteen-year-old marriage; one teenage son. The wife sued not for any drastic, isolated reason but because she seems deeply dissatisfied with the quality and intensity of the relationship. The husband appears puzzled and hurt; he does not understand what his wife wants from him. This is the second hearing. Three weeks ago Judge Tauchnitz interrupted the first hearing to give the spouses a chance to talk things over, employing a technique to foster reconciliation which is authorized by the East German Code of Civil Procedure.

Now the spouses are back in court, after an unsuccessful attempt to settle their differences. The wife still seems determined to go through with the divorce. The husband would like to give the marriage another try. Judge Tauchnitz talks gently to the wife: 'You have not really separated yourself yet from this marriage, have you?' Yes, she has. It makes no sense to continue the relationship. Judge Tauchnitz persists: should they not wait a little longer? No, waiting would make no difference. 'I don't want to persuade you,' says the judge, although it is obvious that she does; she speaks with warm authority, her eyes fixed on the plaintiff, her white hair shining through the courtroom. Hushed voices. The judge does not let go; she continues to urge reconciliation. The wife, with gentle obstinacy, resists.

From where does Frau Tauchnitz take the faith in her own judgment and in the law's ability to preserve this marriage? The GDR Code of Civil Procedure allows the judge to adjourn divorce proceedings for up to one year if 'reasonable prospects' exist to 'overcome the conflict.' East German family law experts have often told me that the provision is not successful. West German and American law have had the same experience: spouses split and reconcile for their own reasons, not the law's, and by the time marital disagreements are articulated in a divorce court it is usually too late to heal the break unless both spouses want to.

But Frau Tauchnitz does not doubt the law's capacity, as she says, 'to put things right which have gone wrong.' She adjourns for six months. 'I can usually tell the condition of a marriage,' she later tells me in the hallway. Could she be right? The wife is not visibly upset when told of the adjournment: because Judge Tauchnitz has correctly gauged her readiness to give the relationship another try? No, I rather think the wife so meekly accepts the result because she, too, does not dispute the court's authority to second-guess decisions affecting her own welfare. Later, she may try her best to circumvent the verdict. But she does not question its legitimacy. At no point during the hour-long proceedings do I sense irritation at the judge's insistence that a marital rift, which the wife herself thinks irreversible, can be healed. Frau Tauchnitz' maternal role is taken for granted. You can trust the law to want the best for you. Only towards the end does one of the lay assessors, a woman, shatter this harmonious picture with some practical advice. 'You don't have to wait the full six months before you can reapply for a divorce,' she tells the wife.

Afternoon

I want to learn something about East German judicial statistics. Now is the time to do it. Before the *Wende* I did not know whether comprehensive data on the workings of socialist courts even existed. Surely there had to be more of a record than the six miserly pages in the official GDR *Statistical*

Yearbook. But all that was available to an outsider were occasional isolated figures, often relating only to local institutions, strewn sparingly and haphazardly across the pages of newspapers and law reviews. While ferreting out and patching together these bits of information could be pleasurable detective work, the resulting overall picture remained hopelessly speculative.

Now Herr Krüger, the head of the Berlin Stadtgericht's Department for 'Legal Information, Analysis, and Statistics,' tells me that detailed data on GDR courts do exist. But they were 'for internal use only,' and even East German researchers needed security clearance to get access. That meant an application which no doubt exposed the applicant to increased state attention. Moreover—as East Berlin colleagues tell me—any manuscript containing precise figures was regarded with great suspicion by the authorities deciding on its publication. Under these circumstances, it comes as no surprise that East German academics did not show much inclination to do work which required the use of statistics, and that I found so little hard data in the legal literature. The main customers of the Department of Legal Information were judges composing their mandatory annual report to the parliamentary body which appointed them.

So Herr Krüger and one of his colleagues, who joins us for the usual cup of coffee, are quite pleased that I want to know about their work. They show me the master sheets used for collecting information on each type of legal dispute decided in this courthouse: civil suits, labor law suits, family law suits, and—registered separately—divorce suits. Nothing on criminal law: those data are kept separately at the Prosecutor General's office.

As Herr Krüger points out with obvious satisfaction, East German judicial statistics are actually more detailed than their West German counterparts. West German courts work with a short computerized questionnaire, filled out by a court employee, which records the main data on a particular dispute: parties, issue in controversy, number of hearings, participation of lawyers, type of verdict, value in controversy, and allocation of court costs (which under the civil law rule of 'loser pays all' also allows inferences about the litigation success of both parties). East German statistics ask similar questions but in much greater detail. If, to give the most extreme case, the West German question on 'issue in controversy' contains as one possible answer 'rent law dispute,' the East German list contains nineteen such answers relating to landlord–tenant conflicts, distinguishing between different types of housing (state? private? privately owned but state-administered?), different types of tenant complaints (apartment needs repainting? structural defects?), or different reasons for eviction suits (rent arrears? owner needs?).

But East German statistics also reflect different motives for recording data. West German statisticians seem to want to capture the social dimensions of legal conflicts: their questions allow us to determine who uses the courts, in what matters, and with what results. East German statisticians also want to know why disputes arose in the first place, and how society should respond to them. Several of the entries reflect the pedagogic ambitions of socialist law: did the prosecutor participate? Did representatives of the collective? Was a 'selected public' invited? No question, incidentally, about the participation of lawyers except in labor law matters: in most first-instance disputes, retaining counsel was officially regarded as a private (and considering the active role of the judges, largely unnecessary) luxury. But in labor law disputes, an employee could choose between a private attorney and a union functionary to represent him, and I suppose it was necessary to ask about the involvement of lawyers to measure the popularity of union counsel.

One item on the questionnaire asks about 'the circumstances and conditions of the conflict': what lay at its bottom? Depending on the type of dispute, the possibilities vary. Civil law conflicts, if one believes the questionnaire, are caused by 'carelessness,' 'ignorance or misinterpretation of the law,' 'inadequately structured legal relationships,' 'disregard for socialist law,' and—the only bow to a materialistic world view—'inadequate state of repair of rental property.' All other suggested causes of civil law disputes, at least according to this questionnaire, are located in people's heads rather than in external circumstances.

In labor law the causes of disputes are sought in the employer's or employee's faulty attitudes towards the law and in management errors. In divorce law the listed causes of marital breakdown include, besides conventional sins such as alcoholism, marital misconduct, or family violence, more subtle failings like lack of domestic co-operation between the spouses, 'hasty marriage,' or 'problems arising from one spouse's participation in job qualification programs.' Again, I spot only one cause on the checklist which might possibly be blamed not only on the spouse's personal shortcomings but also on society: 'material difficulties.' For the item 'unfulfilled wish for children,' nobody can be faulted, even under socialism.

Looking through these lists I can see why East German statistical questionnaires, unlike the West German data sheet, could not be filled out by some secretary or administrator. But how can even the judge be sure that a particular dispute was caused by 'ignorance' rather than 'misinterpretation' of the law, or define exactly the causes of marital failure? By drawing on the briefs and the oral evidence, Herr Krüger says. He does not worry that five different judges, all present at the hearing, would very likely arrive at five different interpretations of the same apparent reality. East German legal data-gathering rests on the assumption that truth—'objective truth,' as socialists used to call it—is accessible, that the causes of social relationships can be observed and understood, and that what has gone wrong can be put right through social planning. The law is seen as 'tool,' as 'social lever,' as 'instrument,' or whatever other terms were used to describe the optimistic assertion that law is an implement of the state to propel society in the right direction.

During the final years of the GDR this optimism had sounded increasingly hollow. Political and social lethargy appeared to undermine the former faith in the law's miraculous powers. East German society had come to a standstill. As socialist academics discovered the gap between law in the books and law in real life, they began to discuss the 'effectiveness' of legal rules at learned conferences and symposia. But since access to empirical data was still restricted, and since East German law professors still shared the German penchant for lofty (and politically safer) theoretical speculation, the search for more legal 'effectiveness' did not lead to noticeably greater use of Herr Krüger's files. And although fewer people may have believed in the feasibility of legal engineering, the official claims were never dropped.

I ask Herr Krüger about the mechanics of judicial data-gathering. Each judge in this courthouse, after each trial, filled out a questionnaire about the case. Herr Krüger's department collected the sheets and each month sent them—'whole suitcases full'—to the Ministry of Justice. There, the Berlin statistics, together with data from the entire GDR, were fed into the computer. The printouts of the Berlin results were eventually returned to Herr Krüger's office. The GDR data were kept at the Ministry of Justice. A telephone call to Herr Krüger's colleague at the Ministry. Yes, I am welcome to have a look at their files.

At the Ministry, legal statistics are kept in a cavernous room on the ground floor. Herr Schulz, the custodian, puts stacks of folders for me on the table. In another two weeks his files will be packed up in preparation for the West German takeover. The boxes will be transferred to the authority of the Federal Office of Statistics in Wiesbaden, West Germany. Lord knows when the data will re-emerge for scholarly use. Herr Schulz, by then, will most likely be unemployed. This is an occasion to show off work that soon will be forgotten.

I look at the large sheets, each tabloid size, printed on thin and porous paper in type so faint that some of the numbers almost seem to lift off the page. Each year, depending on the subject matter adjudicated, has between six and twenty-four of these sheets. Can I xerox some? Not at the Ministry if I want more than a few pages. Can I take files home to xerox them elsewhere? Herr Schulz hesitates. A year ago the question would have been preposterous, quite apart from the fact that I would never have gotten close enough to Herr Schulz' office to ask it. But he seems grateful for my interest in something that everybody else wants to bury as quickly as possible. If I xerox files now, at least a small part of his work will not be stacked away in some storage room in Wiesbaden. What do I want? I don't dare to ask for more than three years, in five-year intervals, of the data on civil, labor, family, and divorce litigation. All right, Herr Schulz says. If I return the sheets in two days. It is quite a stack so he even gives me a large vinyl bag to transport my loot home. I feel a little queasy as I carry it past the window of the entry guard.

Back at my desk, I pore over the tables searching for clues. Can I tell from the statistics how many *Ausreiser* suits were dismissed without oral argument? Labor law cases are subdivided by 'branch of economy' (for instance, 'construction' or 'agriculture and forestry') and by subject matter (such as 'wages' or 'termination of employment'). In 1989 twenty-eight suits in the field of 'public education' were dismissed by decree under Section 28 paragraph 3 of the Code of Civil Procedure—those must be teachers' suits. Nineteen suits, similarly dismissed, were brought by government officials. Three suits by people in the field of 'public health'—doctors or nursery school teachers. All in all, fifty suits (always assuming that all dealt with firings). I check dismissal suits: fifty-two complaints challenging discharges for cause were dismissed by decree. The figures roughly square.

But can they be right? About fifty such cases in the entire GDR seem very few, considering the traumatic role the issue played in East German judicial politics. Admittedly, the figure includes only those *Ausreiser* reckless enough to contest their firing in court. There is reason to believe that some judges persuaded such plaintiffs to drop their case to save time and trouble. In some instances, I am told, *Ausreiser* were also talked out of bringing suit by paralegals at the court's business office. Moreover, 1989 was an extraordinary year. Towards its end many *Ausreiser* no longer sued; they just left. And throughout the second half of the 1980s many people wanting to emigrate did not even bother to apply for exit visas but brazenly pretended to cross the border, were arrested, sentenced for a year or two in prison, and after a number of months were bought free by the West German government. The method was known as the quickest way to leave the country and, for my present purposes, transferred an *Ausreiser* from the labor law to the crime statistics. My figure of about fifty suits dismissed under section 28, paragraph 3 of the Code of Civil Procedure must be right, after all. But even classified statistics, I realize, tell only part of the story.

Somewhat sobered, I check the odds on whether Judge Tauchnitz' adjournment of the divorce which I watched will lead to the couple's reconciliation. In 1989, out of 62,329 divorce suits in the GDR, 2,492 were adjourned; 1,140 of the cases adjourned were not reopened during the trial period, and 597 divorce suits were brought after the trial period had lapsed.

Assuming divorce suits to remain constant over the years, that means 543 long-term reconciliations in cases where judges like Frau Tauchnitz decided that an adjournment would serve the couple's best interests: 0.9 per cent of all divorces in 1989.

I cannot decide whether this figure is high or low. Were the successful adjournments those to which both spouses consented? Would those spouses have reconciled in any event? And how about the unsuccessful adjournments: is it legitimate to restrict the freedom of many in the hope of increasing the welfare of a few? Always assuming that the court can define someone's personal welfare over his own objections, which in contrast to socialists I am inclined to doubt. But even East German divorce judges must have had some misgivings: judicial adjournments of divorce suits dropped from 6.3 per cent of all divorces in 1978 to 4 per cent in 1989. Resignation, liberalization, or both?

I am most curious about the 'circumstances and conditions' of legal conflicts: what do these figures tell me about the capacity of East German legal statistics to identify the causes of social problems and to help define policies for their solution? I check the rent cases. Of the 18,874 landlord–tenant disputes in 1989, if we believe the categories, 26.9 per cent resulted from negligence (whose?); 17 per cent from ignorance or misinterpretation of legal rules; 26.1 per cent from disrespect for socialist law; and only 2.9 per cent from the apartment's inadequate state of repair. What?! Considering the truly dismal condition of much GDR housing, the last figure is hard to believe.

But there is an explanation. East German tenants who are dissatisfied with leaking roofs, faulty plumbing, or broken elevators will often withhold their rent payments pending repairs. Since the Civil Code does not authorize such self-help, they will be in arrears and the landlord (most likely the state housing administration) can sue. The judge, when filling out his statistical questionnaire after the trial, will see the tenant's refusal to pay the rent as the cause of litigation and, depending on his mood and the tenant's behavior, will check the box for ignorance, misinterpretation, or disregard of the law. In this fashion, the dispute will be blamed on individual short-sightedness or ill-will rather than on the state's failing housing policy. The social trouble-spot identified by the statistics is 'faulty consciousness' rather than 'unsatisfactory housing conditions.' The cure would be 'more indoctrination and education' rather than 'more money for repairs.'

An amazing result for a legal system which set out under the banner of dialectical materialism and in the belief that 'existence determines consciousness' rather than vice versa. Wishful thinking, or a clever sleight of hand allowing all criticism of the state to be redirected against its critics? It hardly matters. These statistics were not meant for public use. One wonders whether they were even meant for what is stated on the top of each page: 'internal use only.' Leaving aside *ad hoc* requests by Party and government officials, the distribution list for the Ministry of Justice's annual and semi-annual printouts (I got it from Herr Krüger) shows as recipients only the originators of the data themselves, namely: the Ministry of Justice and the courts. No automatic sharing of information with other ministries, the planning authorities, the unions, or the universities. If law was indeed an instrument of social transformation, one would have expected widespread utilization of its insights. But the instrument was considered too sacrosanct to be subjected to rigorous investigation, and its functioning too sensitive to be exposed to public view. A system choking on its own obsessive secrecy.

23 September 1990

Last evening, a report on television showing prison riots in the East German city of Frankfurt-on-Oder. A night scene lit by floodlight: the camera searches for the shadowy figures of the inmates gathering on a rooftop against the black sky. They threaten to jump from the prison building unless their convictions by GDR courts are reviewed and measured against *Rechtsstaat* principles.

The report reminds me of a serious omission in my present inquiry: I am not dealing with criminal law. In part, because I never have been very interested in socialist criminal law and procedure: criminal punishment is such a convenient and simple tool of political repression that a totalitarian government will use it regardless of ideological justifications. While East German civil or labor law doctrine and case law could leave room for intellectual refinement and the human aspects of socialism, criminal law seemed either unashamedly apologetic or crude.

It would also be quite difficult at this time to obtain reliable reports on the workings of East German criminal justice. The 'Ia' departments of courts and prosecutors' offices—that is, those departments dealing with political crimes, investigated by State Security rather than ordinary police—have been dissolved (although some of their members are rumored to have found refuge in other judicial departments). Criminal judges are largely gone, criminal trials no longer held. Even if I were to get hold of them, criminal lawyers are less likely to tell me the truth than their less compromised civil law colleagues.

But I must keep the darker sides of socialist legality in mind if I want to find out how much and what kind of justice existed under socialism. In a way, criminal law provides a good example of the system's ambivalence and bifurcation. Political crimes—the 'Ia' offenses—were strictly separated from the rest of criminal law enforcement. They were investigated by special police, prosecuted by special state attorneys, and adjudicated by

special judges. The 'Ia' judges and prosecutors were more reliable support-
ers of the system, were ranked higher, and were unlikely to mingle with
colleagues of other departments. Often they were physically separated from
other court personnel.

The differentiation between political and non-political offenses was
reflected in conviction patterns. At the moment East Germany's prison
population is extremely low: about 5,000 inmates all told, 32:100,000
inhabitants. Soon after the *Wende* more than 18,000 prisoners were
released, many of them political prisoners, at least in the sense that their
offenses, while perhaps not motivated by political objectives, would nevertheless not have been penalized under a different ideological regime. By
comparison, the men who yesterday night huddled together on the prison
rooftop remained in detention even during the euphoric autumn of 1989
when most other prison inmates were set free. Although they may have
suffered injustice, they are unlikely to have been imprisoned for their
political beliefs.

But before the *Wende* East German prisons held very different inmates.
In 1988 the GDR had a prison population of 24,305, a ratio of 160 per
100,000 inhabitants: almost twice as high as the West German ratio of
85:100,000 but still considerably lower than the United States ratio of
351:100,000. But who was imprisoned in the GDR? Almost a quarter of the
inmates were convicted of 'asocial behavior' defined as 'infringing upon
public order and security by avoiding regular work' ('parasitism' in the
terminology of other socialist states). Another 10 per cent were people
caught while trying to flee the GDR or—in the words of the code—attempting to 'illegally cross state borders.' Six per cent of the inmates had 'interfered with the activities of state organs' (for instance, gotten into a fight with
a policeman) or had 'violated court-ordered restrictions' of movement or
association (mostly imposed for the ostensible purpose of reintegrating
previous offenders and social misfits).

In 1988 people who in one way or the other had run afoul of the state's
claim to absolute authority added up to 27.5 per cent of all offenders. But
they made up over 47 per cent of the East German prison population.
Obviously, the socialist state came down much harder on those who—
through their lifestyles or their attempts to escape—disputed its legitimacy
than on those who violated the law within the state's own political parameters. 'Parasites' were three times more likely to go to prison than were
thieves of personal property. Only 22 per cent of all thieves or embezzlers
of state property were sent to prison, compared to 54 per cent of those who
'interfered with the activities of state organs.'

The pattern confirms my previous impression of East German law: that of
a legal system distinguishing between insiders and outsiders. In labor law, it
had been the *Ausreiser*, those wanting to turn their backs on the socialist

state, who were deprived of the protection and concern that East German labor law judges usually displayed towards working people. In criminal law, the offenders punished out of all proportion to their 'crime' were again those trying to leave the GDR (clandestine *Ausreiser*, as it were) and those who, while physically remaining in the country, mentally dissociated themselves from the official socialist work ethic by preferring street life or vagrancy to regular employment. But ordinary criminals who sinned within the collective and whose offense was motivated by greed or aggression rather than a longing to escape could expect more conventional punishments. Even the convictions of the inmates protesting on that rooftop in Frankfurt-on-Oder, as I would eventually learn from one of the people involved in their review, showed 'no sensational deviations' from convictions for comparable offenses in West Germany.

While arbitrary and repressive towards some, East German courts could thus be benevolent towards others. As in a family, the system's favorite children were often those with special needs, provided the needs met with ideological approval. Privacy, for instance, was not an accepted need; housing and steady employment were. Accordingly, courts—as a rule—would favor tenants over landlords and employees over employers. Socialist law liked dependent people. It also liked people to remain dependent. Like a possessive parent, socialism could tolerate misbehavior but not rejection. What made the *Ausreiser* so unacceptable to the state was the fact that they were also *Ausreißer*, runaways, claiming adulthood and control over their own lives. East German law reacted to the rebellion with the harshness and bitterness of disappointed affection.

24 September 1990

Back at the Littenstrasse courthouse. Today I have appointments with two lay assessors. They were part of the army of lay people on which the East German legal system relied: as judges of social courts (already abolished) which adjudicated minor civil and criminal law conflicts and most first-instance labor law disputes, and as lay assessors who still sit, together with a professional judge, in civil, family, and labor law cases. Almost more important than these lay people's judicial role was their responsibility to explain and popularize the law among the collectives which elected them.

Herr Habermann, my first interviewee, looks so little like a foot soldier of socialist law that I at first mistake him for a plaintiff or defendant awaiting his case. Long, wavy, dark hair parted in the middle, mingling at shoulder level with a long, dark beard. In the midst of all this hair an earnest and friendly face. To my surprise, Herr Habermann is not only a lay assessor but a Party member since 1978. I would have thought that the Party required a more conventional appearance. What made him join? He read the Party Program and found it convincing.

We talk about the disappointment of socialist hopes. Herr Habermann was originally a math and physics teacher. He left teaching for an engineering job when he could no longer take the political indoctrination at school. 'The things they made us do!' 'They' are the Party functionaries with whom Herr Habermann shares the same political affiliation. To him, the Party seems divided into a top and a bottom, with the top—'those aged gentlemen'—largely divorced from reality, and the bottom a place where he and people like him 'tried to get things moving.' Engagement in local politics also led to his work as lay assessor: Herr Habermann himself had some problem with his apartment, became involved with the local housing administration, eventually joined the borough committee of the National Front, and was nominated as lay assessor.

The picture he conveys of the Party is one of local activism and central ossification. I look with some skepticism at this gentle Rasputin. From what I know, much mindless and docile rigidity also exists at local Party levels. But maybe Herr Habermann is one of those innocent and energetic people who forever spot jobs that need to be done and do them. His present work supports this hypothesis. He became unemployed when his engineering firm was privatized, Herr Habermann tells me, but now is an entrepreneur. Entrepreneur? Yes, he discovered a niche in the brand-new market. After the *Wende*, GDR stores no longer want to stock the modest, grey, East German school notebooks, which used to sell for ten pfennig, but only the colorful and glossy West German kind, which sell for up to one mark each. Herr Habermann has gotten hold of a large lot of the old notebooks and sells them, at a few pfennig apiece, to East German schools which can use the savings. He reckons his stock will last another month or two. By then he hopes to have found a job. He will in any case no longer be needed as lay assessor.

Herr Daschke, Herr Habermann's colleague, conforms better to my image of a lay assessor: a small, serious, official-looking man in a beige Sunday suit. I meet him in Judge Schomburg's office. He was, and still is, assigned to Frau Schomburg's court, and as I come into the room, he and his judge say a tearful goodbye. Today is Herr Daschke's last day in the courthouse, after thirty-seven years as lay assessor.

Herr Daschke, 62, was originally a carpenter. He started his community career as representative of his brigade, then became job-safety inspector, and now is a full-time union functionary. He obviously loves the law; besides his work as lay assessor, he represents employees in labor law cases and twice a week participates in the union's legal consultation service. In the early 1950s, when the East German government replaced all inherited bourgeois judges with so-called 'people's judges'—working-class men and women with some crash course training in law—Herr Daschke almost joined the judiciary. But his carpentry job paid too well.

What does he like about the law? It is useful for workers, and the workers use it; many employees consult him during the union's legal service hours. Herr Daschke thinks he does a good job when representing a fellow worker in court; better than a lawyer could do because he understands the setting and knows the enterprise's collective agreements. Would he take the case of a worker of whose claim he disapproved? Yes: 'law is law.' A worker has the right to representation. He sees nothing wrong with winning cases that his client should have lost; with respect to the individual worker, the law is clearly perceived as an instrument of protection.

And overall, does he think that socialist law did a good job? Law, for Herr Daschke, is labor law. Yes, for a long time the law kept everyone content. But it could not stem the collapse of labor discipline beginning in the early 1980s. The rules on 'material responsibility,' above all, did not work: East Germany's system of penalizing workers for damage caused to their employers through negligence, shoddy work, absenteeism, and the like. Interested more in education than restitution, the law on 'material responsibility' did not define liability in terms of damage done but operated with penalties measured by reference to the offender's wages. Since most sanctions amounted to no more than a fraction of the culprit's monthly pay and could be paid in barely noticeable instalments, employers were not interested in receiving the money and employees were not burdened by its loss.

Herr Daschke criticizes East German managers for not having taken advantage of the law on material responsibility to stage 'confrontations' in the enterprise which could have raised awareness about the need for better discipline. Instead, managers would either forgo sanctions (why bother about a few marks in an economy in which money counted less than labor, then in short supply?) or fire an employee (which was against the law). Who could be surprised? But Herr Daschke does not like an approach to law based on cost–benefit calculations. 'If you do not correct a worker's attitudes in his own enterprise, who else would do it?' 'The market,' I am tempted to reply. But Herr Daschke's labor law was meant to operate in a more personal way than anonymous market forces. It focused on each worker's needs and capabilities (hence the orientation, in material-responsibility cases, on an offender's individual wage) instead of abandoning him to the smacks of some invisible hand. I am reminded of what a judge in this courthouse said to me: 'The Labor Code was too good to us.'

I ask Herr Daschke why he spent so much time and effort on his community work. 'We were all people who did not want to stand aside,' he says. He talks about the Party in a fashion similar to Herr Habermann's: describes the distance between the top and the bottom; how criticism from below would get lost on its way up the hierarchical ladder; how reports would 'get more beautiful' each step closer to those in power. 'The Party has always had members and comrades,' he says. The comrades, he implies, were people like he: laboring in the vineyard.

A picture too idealistic not to instil suspicion. But I remind myself: Herr Habermann and Herr Daschke cannot be typical lay assessors. In this final week most laypersons no longer show up for court duty: they have more important things to do, have written off the system or never felt strongly about it in the first place. Herr Habermann and Herr Daschke must be more committed to socialist law than most of their colleagues. I find indirect support for this presumption when I ask Herr Daschke for his telephone number. It turns out that he has none: he has been on the waiting list for a telephone since 1975. 'Now I probably could get one but it will be too expensive,' he says a little apologetically. Surely as a full-time union functionary he could have pulled a few strings? The fact that Herr Daschke, after all these years, is not on the telephone confirms my image of him as the selfless servant of a legal system which expected selflessness to be human nature but rarely found this expectation fulfilled. It is not just that the East German Labor Code was 'too good' to the people to whom it applied: socialist law could have worked only if people also were 'too good' to be true: non-materialistic, diligent, eager to place the interests of the collective ahead of their own comfort. But how many Habermanns and Daschkes could there be?

Afternoon

An interview with Klaus Petzoldt, a civil law judge at the Court of Appeals, 31 years old. Unlike most other judges I have met, he does not come from a working-class background. Both his parents are lawyers: the mother a prosecutor, the father a retired military judge. Herr Petzoldt has the relaxed grace of someone to whom things have come easily.

How did one become a judge in the GDR? It took good grades and a politically acceptable background; fulfilling only one of these prerequisites was usually not sufficient. Students had to apply for admission to university a year or two before their high school graduation. At that age very few youngsters had any realistic image of the law; several people in this court-house told me that they chose law out of fascination with American court-room dramas on West German television. Herr Petzoldt, through his parents, knew a bit better what his choice entailed.

Students who wanted to become judges or attorneys—the so-called 'justice students'—were trained at the Humboldt University in Berlin (future prosecutors and economic lawyers were educated elsewhere). But the Ministry of Justice controlled the admissions process. High school students applied to the local district court and were eventually interviewed by an official at the Ministry whose apparent task it was to determine the applicants' political reliability. Nobody I talked to seems to have viewed this part of the application process as anything but a test of one's ability to recognize and plausibly articulate the desired answers. Nobody seems to have been offended by it either.

Before taking up his studies Herr Petzoldt completed three years of military service. Female students would do production or office work. One had to take part in working-class exertions before being allowed to set off on a more intellectual trail. The four-year study of law was highly structured; students of the same year attended most lectures together. Classes focused on general and abstract issues, with few practical exercises and case discussions. One-third of a law student's time was spent on the study of Marxism-Leninism and similar pursuits. Teachers tended to avoid embarrassing topics. The ruthlessly repressive use of law during the Stalinist 1950s and 1960s was never mentioned in class. Political criminal law—with the exception of issues relating to so-called border violations—was barely touched upon.

Most law students were Party members by the time they entered law school. With very few exceptions, those who were not joined the Party at some point during their university years. In either case the decision seemed so natural, so inevitable for future judges that neither Herr Petzoldt nor anyone else remembers noticeable external pressures or internal turmoil accompanying the event. During the third year of their studies students were 'directed' towards their future jobs: judge or attorney. Many students at the Humboldt University would have preferred the latter: attorneys made more money and enjoyed greater professional independence. But in a country with 592 private lawyers, and no significant increase in their numbers projected by the government, the Colleges of Advocates, who recruited their new members, could be picky. They tended to choose few women and only those men with good connections or the very best grades. Klaus Petzoldt did not care: he had wanted to be a judge in any case.

Why a judge? Because he had been brought up to believe in justice. And what does he mean by justice? 'A state in which everything is in legal order' ('*in dem alles seine gesetzliche Ordnung hat*'). Herr Petzoldt pauses for a second. 'And in which each individual gets his due. But not at the expense of others,' he adds. A mixture of old and new: legal discipline and the balancing and protection of rights. But the sequencing of the answers reveals something about Judge Petzoldt's image of himself: a keeper of order, a guardian of social peace rather than a defender of personal autonomy.

Did he, as a judge, feel burdened by the absence of free speech? No, not really. External political constraints, to Herr Petzoldt, mattered less than one might have thought because he could always speak freely among his colleagues. He admits that criticism would rarely produce results (how could it, I think, since it was kept within safe boundaries). Instead, the function of critical speech seems to have been therapeutic: it made it easier to respect oneself and others. In fact, conversations among Herr Petzoldt's colleagues were so open that he was shocked to learn, after the *Wende*, that a fellow judge at another court had lost his job for saying things that were routinely said within Herr Petzoldt's own collective. From his perspective, this courthouse—or rather, the dozen or so judges assigned to his court of appeals—formed a civilized and rational enclave within an oppressive society, allowing withdrawal from the unpleasant political realities on the outside. A simple, narrow, and contented professional life.

Later, thinking back on our conversation, I am struck most by Klaus Petzoldt's tone: neither defensive nor aggressive but artless, unguarded, human. I am probably so surprised because Herr Petzoldt is the first male judge whom I have interviewed at length. I must have expected a more 'male' style of expression. But in fact talking to him evoked the same impression I gained from talking to other legal professionals in the GDR: they do not sound like lawyers, certainly not like lawyers in the United States. I hear no cutting remarks or quick repartees; encounter no attempts to score points against an opponent; see no restructuring of every conversation into a win-or-lose debating competition. And there is another striking difference: male and female lawyers in the GDR speak in the same voice.

In the United States men and women seem to argue about the law in different ways. In the faculty lounge of my law school back home the talk is fast, sharp, and largely negative when the men dominate the conversation. Women among themselves are more relaxed, chattier, warmer, less rigorous, more willing to compromise. When men and women discuss an issue together, men are likely to raise 'men's' points and women 'women's' points. In the legal literature, you often can tell from the mere title of an article whether the author is a man or a woman: men write about legal principles and concepts, women (especially feminists) about human interactions: empathy, sharing, sexual domination.

Here at the Littenstrasse courthouse, men and women speak the same legal language. At its best it is simple, concrete, pragmatic, focusing on results. At its worst it is unintellectual and imprecise. But I can never tell from the words alone whether they are spoken by a man or woman. The flavor of a conversation in a group of men or women does not change if someone from the opposite sex joins in the debate. Much more than in Western discussions, speakers disappear behind their arguments; they seem less self-possessed than capitalist lawyers. Here, I notice little vanity among the men and no self-pity among the women. Both seem to find it easier to forget about the impression they make and instead to listen to what the other says.

It is surprising to find such effective human communication in a country in which speech had, for forty years, to take place under such precarious circumstances. Maybe the constraints and distortions of language in the world around them taught people in the GDR to listen closely to what was said. It is also likely that the presence of so many women in the East German judiciary (50 per cent overall, but more at the first-instance level) has softened the tone of communication between male and female judges. But I believe that the main factor in Klaus Petzoldt's intellectual socialization was not his female colleagues but socialist law itself.

American law has often been criticized by feminist writers for being 'male': abstract, hierarchical, competitive, coldly rational. Socialist law, one might be tempted to argue, is 'female': concrete, co-operative, caring, searching for collective warmth. Hence the 'different voice' of East German lawyers: contributive and conciliatory, echoing the voice of women.

But on second thought, an analysis of socialist law in gender terms loses much of its persuasiveness. The male/female dichotomy seems questionable enough if applied to capitalist law. Perhaps in the classic fields of private law—contracts, torts, and property—the metaphor 'male' might capture those features of the legal process which feminists and socialists both abhor: the emphasis on individual autonomy, on the exclusivity of rights, on conflict, the division of the world into winners and losers. But in other, more modern branches of our law the metaphor no longer fits. In many family or administrative law disputes, for instance, capitalist judges no longer operate as principled but heartless arbiters of individual entitlements. They function as managers: address issues in social context rather than in isolation, focus on the future rather than the past, and adjust ongoing relationships to fit people's needs rather than vindicate their rights. All these attitudes might be called 'socialist.' But it does not make much sense to call them 'female' if the feminist analysis of law as patriarchy is to hold up. The gender analogy in these cases no longer advances our understanding.

I find it more helpful to distinguish instead between adversarial and managerial styles of adjudication. Socialist law (and by now much American law) sees the judge as a social crisis manager rather than as an arbiter of private disputes. The law, in these instances, seeks to solve tasks, rather than to protect individual rights. While rights are best enjoyed alone, tasks are more effectively carried out with the help of others: hence socialist law's emphasis on collectives and the involvement of laymen. Lasting solutions to particular judicial assignments (a divorce, a dismissal case) will often require responses which take into account social connections and which focus on people's needs rather than on their entitlements: hence, the co-operative and often nurturing character of socialist adjudication. The analysis explains why East German judges so often sound like social workers rather than jurists.

In the terms of the American feminist, Carol Gilligan, one might characterize their approach as 'female' rather than 'male'—an 'ethic of care' rather than the law's usual cold and divisive 'ethic of justice'—were it not for those other East German decisions motivated by the very opposite 'non-ethic of rejection' applied to outsiders like the *Ausreiser*. But in any case the 'different voice' in which East German judges speak is not the different voice which Carol Gilligan attributes to the moral deliberation of women. Rather, it is the voice of subordinates, assistants, administrators. American critics of Gilligan have suggested that her analysis captures not so much the distinctions between women and men as between the dependent and the powerful. Viewed in this fashion, the 'different voice' analogy applied to East German judges works much better: they speak like people who are not masters of their own decisions but who carry out tasks set by another, the state.

Despite our law's increasing preoccupation with administrative functions, Western lawyers are still raised in the classic adversarial spirit. It is a fighting spirit, a spirit of self-importance, spelling the 'I' with upper case and the 'we' with lower case lettering; a spirit always wanting to be right. And our lawyers, accordingly, are often people who are full of themselves. But Klaus Petzoldt and his colleagues have been taught to serve a cause supposedly greater than themselves. They considered it their job to follow rules, to keep people housed, employed, and committed to their work, to preserve social peace, and to report to their superiors. They were serving, not self-serving. No wonder that their style is more modest, uncritical, charitable, and co-operative. No wonder also that they are looked down upon by their more self-assertive and quick-witted West German colleagues. But if I had to carry out some unglamorous, burdensome social project, I would love to have Klaus Petzoldt on my team.

26 September 1990

I pay a call on Judge Tauchnitz in her office and find her in the process of packing. She shows me the notice which finally came from the Senator of Justice, explaining details of the upcoming suspension of all East Berlin judges and prosecutors. It is only a circular. 'I ask for your understanding if the investigation of all personnel in higher positions (does that include first-instance judges like Frau Tauchnitz?) will be thorough,' the Senator writes. And: 'voluntary enrollment in retooling classes will be interpreted as a sign of your initiative and willingness to learn but will not be considered a factor that favors future continued employment.' Frau Tauchnitz plans to attend the classes in any case: they are free, they allow three more months of contact with former colleagues, and she wants to learn something about the new legal order. But she has no illusions about her 'future continued employment.'

Disregarding the jumble around her, Frau Tauchnitz digs into one of her boxes, finds cups and tea bags, plugs in the immersion heater, and is ready to answer questions about her life as a judge. Why is everyone so willing to talk to me? I need only to introduce myself, to explain why I am here, and people will ask me in, offer me coffee, and allow me to interview them about their work. And they are generous with their time: never look at the watch, never close conversations on their own account, never remind me of this or that task still awaiting them. 'Now I have taken so much of your time,' one judge apologized to me after a long conversation, when it was I who had imposed on her. Why?

It is true that judges in this courthouse now have a lot of free time on their hands: with only one more week to go before their world collapses there is little else to do but straighten out their offices and wait. But the main reason, I think, why my East Berlin colleagues are so eager to talk to me is that I am neither one of them, entangled in their present problems and anxieties, nor one of those West Germans whom they suspect of wanting to take their place. For people who up to a year ago were never allowed to travel to the West, I come from an almost exotic distance. I am neutral and safe. So I can be a useful listener: who understands but does not judge; prods with a question if an issue needs clarification; can steer the conversation back on course if the narrator should lose direction. My listening seems to spur on the questions which my conversation partners have asked themselves throughout this last year and longer: how could it all have happened, how could the law stray so far from their ideals, what was their own role in the events, what is left of their beliefs, what could they have done differently, what will become of them?

Conversations are poignant and intense, with a strong existentialist flavor. 'It is as if I woke up one morning to find myself a quadriplegic,' one judge said to me. Coming from a country in which most people's private lives were more important to them than their public position, my conversation partners are much better trained than I am in soul-searching talk: they are less guarded, less prepared to rush, also less conditioned than I am to look for a bottom line, draw a conclusion, and move on. At times I feel as if caught in a Chekhov play where talking gives the only weight and reality to lives adrift in a rapidly changing world. After two or three hours, when the person opposite me is still in fine fettle, I begin to tire: I wear out without the protection of formalities and small talk. And, to tell the truth, I am not used to all this East German chain-smoking. But then I am not among those whose life is suddenly thrown off course. My professional conscience is clean, my job secure, my rent paid.

27 September 1990

Today, a quite unsatisfactory interview with a prosecutor. The Prosecutor General's department is located in the same building as the Court of Appeals and the two first-instance courts in the Littenstrasse; in fact, it shares a corridor with them in the courthouse. But one cannot walk from one end of it to the other: a big iron grille rises in the middle and I have to leave the courthouse, walk down the road, enter another door, pass an entry guard, and obtain a permission slip stating the hour and purpose of my visit before I can meet with Prosecutor Karl Rewoldt, Director of Department III (General Criminality), who has agreed to talk to me.

Herr Rewoldt is an amiable man with a round face, thick curly hair, and a little paunch. If our conversation does not seem to get anywhere it is not because of his ill will, but because he and I are trying to pursue different topics. I want to know about the technicalities of his job: from whom did his orders come, what was their purpose, in what form were they transmitted. Herr Rewoldt wants to push aside the details of his work and present himself as a human being.

I had the same experience yesterday afternoon when I talked to another prosecutor: a round, motherly woman in her fifties whose face lit up when she told me about her grandchildren. She also was not interested in the command structure at her office. She seemed a little irritated at my insistence; it did not seem to matter very much to her through what channels and in what shape her orders arrived. She told me about the Prosecutor General's *Ausreiser* policy. One of a socialist prosecutor's main functions was 'general supervision': the task of monitoring the legality of all administrative decision-making. In this capacity, the prosecutor was one of the main recipients of citizen complaints in the GDR. But if people who had applied for exit visas complained about subsequent ill-treatment by the authorities, the prosecutor's office was instructed to tell them to petition the court instead. Never mind that a court, in most instances, was not competent to deal with the complaint (East German courts, with a few recent and limited exceptions, were not allowed to review administrative decisions), and that even in those cases subject to judicial review (such as labor law disputes) the courts, as I now know, would not examine *Ausreiser* grievances. Obviously the Prosecutor General's office knew that too. Its technique of getting rid of *Ausreiser* complaints by pretending incompetence strikes me as typical of the East German government's misuse of law: usually low-key; if possible denying justice by bureaucratic rather than physical interference; in most instances not violent but evasive and dishonest. I asked the prosecutor how she was informed of this policy. 'We always did it this way.' Yes, but how did you learn about it? 'I was told.' And by whom? 'By my predecessor, when I took over this office.'

Herr Rewoldt, today, is even more reluctant to talk about his political dependencies at work. The judges I interviewed in this building all seemed to perceive the relationship between law and power as problematic: they saw it as their role not to keep politics out of law—all law, in their eyes, is political—but to resist attempts to bend the law in individual cases. Even political law, to an East German judge, should be couched in generally applicable rules. But these two prosecutors do not talk as if the terms 'law' and 'power' might be dichotomies located at opposite ends of a continuum. To them the two are largely identical.

Of course, Herr Rewoldt would follow orders from the Prosecutor General: for instance, demand a harsher penalty if so told. Policy instructions usually came printed or typed and were 'for internal use only.' Herr Rewoldt would get a copy 'if there were enough.' If prosecuting on his own, he would ask for 'medium penalties': safely between the upper and lower reaches of the Code. In the case of 'illegal border crossings' that could mean one year in prison in simple cases and four years in 'aggravated' cases such as escapes attempted 'together with others' or involving 'the use of hiding places.' According to a 'Common Viewpoint' of the Supreme Court and the Prosecutor General, semi-published as late as 1988 in the Supreme Court Informations, such an aggravated attempt might have involved a defendant's planning to escape by hiding in a friend's car, even if the fugitive was arrested before he reached the vehicle. Herr Rewoldt would not be head of his department if he had seen anything wrong with such instructions.

I ask about Party interference with his work. Herr Rewoldt admits that 'there were such incidents.' Usually, the telephone call would contain not direct instructions but suggestions: 'I would bear in mind that X is the son-in-law of Y.' Callers would normally request to favor rather than disfavor someone: benign rather than malignant corruption. Herr Rewoldt tells a story of his resisting such a call, but as I listen I cannot help speculating about other, different stories which he is unlikely to tell me. How about his relations with the 'Ia' prosecutors, the ones who dealt with political offenses? 'Oh, there were never any problems,' he says. He explains: 'They kept to themselves.' There is a consensus among East German jurists that no excuses can be found for the activities of the 'Ia' departments, now dissolved and their prisoners released. But they still serve a useful function as foil for other legal officials: not to have been an 'Ia' prosecutor, Herr Rewoldt implies, and not even to have socialized with them in the cafeteria automatically absolves him from the guilt which in their case is undeniable. Innocence by dissociation.

We talk about the upcoming review of all judges and prosecutors by the judicial selection committees. Does he believe it makes sense to investigate each person's implication in miscarriages of justice under the old regime? Politically speaking, Herr Rewoldt can understand that the Westerners will not take on East German officials without close scrutiny (I think of the defiant remark of a young judge, shrugging off the anticipated rejection: 'if events had gone the opposite way, we wouldn't even have dreamt of retaining you.' After forty years of thinking in friend–enemy stereotypes, suspicion on both sides is plausible enough). But when I press for some criteria Herr Rewoldt would use to separate black sheep from white, he cannot come up with any. Does he believe that GDR lawyers are different from their West German colleagues? The only thing Herr Rewoldt can think of is that East Germans are used to working in collectives while West Germans, in his view, are 'solitary fighters.' Different ways of legal arguing? Not really: 'the lawyer's skills are applicable everywhere.' Does he know people at the Prosecutor General's office who in his opinion are so discredited by their past behavior that they should not pass the review ? No, aside from the 'Ia' people, no one comes to mind. 'Basically we are just jurists,' Herr Rewoldt says.

But he knows that the Westerners will not believe him. He plans to attend the retooling classes but has little hope of being allowed to remain a prosecutor. Could he not work as an attorney? The Unification Treaty allows GDR attorneys to continue the practice of law in the future united Germany, and many of Herr Rewoldt's colleagues (including the Prosecutor General) have applied for licenses. At present, only about seventy of the 130 East Berlin prosecutors are still in office, and their number is shrinking daily. But after fifteen years in a largely administrative and dependent job Herr Rewoldt does not feel up to the practice of law. I can see that he is afraid of having to compete with younger and more flexible colleagues and with those 'solitary fighters' from the West. To make things worse, his wife is also a prosecutor. How will they support their family? For six more months they will receive 70 per cent of their pay. But then? Herr Rewoldt confides that his wife has difficulty sleeping at night and that they have not yet dared to tell their children.

Looking at his bewildered and anxious face, I understand why Herr Rewoldt finds it so much easier to talk about his person than about his job. I cannot tell whether the prosecutor has reason to be displeased with his own performance or not. It would be surprising if there were nothing in his past to be ashamed of. But in any case his work is over, done with, discarded by events, and soon to be forgotten. The person remains very real. The prosecutor may never face up to the fact that he was involved in the administration of a largely repressive system of criminal law. The man will have to face the anxieties of unemployment and social descent. I discover that I find it much easier to believe the man than the prosecutor.

What has he done to find new employment? Herr Rewoldt has tried the Social Security Administration and written to a lot of insurance companies. No results so far. In any case he does not know how to work with computers and is not sure that he can learn. What else could he do? There seems to be a small chance of a job as manager of a chain store. He appears reluctant to talk about it, for fear, I think, that even this tiny hope might evaporate. I wish him luck.

28 September 1990

I can tell that the end is at hand. People in this courthouse are throwing out their books. This morning as I walk through the corridors I see stacks of discarded Codes, handbooks, commentaries, and official-looking materials of all sorts piling up near overflowing waste baskets, together with office junk and pots of wilting flowers. A little embarrassed, I check through the rubble for titles I might want to keep: a two-volume textbook on civil law, a couple of statutes, a copy of Karl Polak's *Zur Dialektik in der Staatslehre* (Dialectics and the Theory of the State), third edition, 1963.

I am particularly pleased about the Polak copy; I would not have suspected it still to be around. Karl Polak was Walter Ulbricht's legal mentor and speech writer—had returned, together with Ulbricht, soon after the war from Soviet exile to help build the legal foundations of the first socialist state on German soil. A brilliant man; quite crazy, as someone who knew him personally once told me; a Stalinist if ever there was one; and a vicious influence on East German legal thought for many years. There is something fitting in my having found his book, if not literally on the 'rubbish heap of history,' then at least on the rubbish heap of this courthouse.

Later, as I walk over to the Supreme Court of the GDR in an adjoining wing of this building to make an appointment with one of the justices, it is the same picture all over. I ask Justice Rudi Beckert (one of the few members of the court not yet to have gone home) about obtaining a collection of Supreme Court cases. Herr Beckert plans to keep his own set but says that I should have no difficulty finding another in the corridors. Together we search the waste baskets of the highest court in the land for discarded volumes of its own decisions.

1 October 1990

To fill the time until an afternoon meeting at the courthouse, I walk over to the State Contract Court in the Behrenstrasse in search of an economic judge. 'Contract courts' (called 'arbitrage' in other socialist states) used to resolve the legal disputes within East Germany's planned economy. With the monetary union of both Germanys implemented on 1 July 1990, and with the introduction of a market economy in the GDR, the contract courts were dissolved and their judges transferred to 'commercial chambers' attached to the civil courts. But the judges' offices in East Berlin remained in the old building, and I should be able to find someone to talk to me about his or her work.

As in other socialist planned economies, exchange relationships between state-owned enterprises in the GDR were not simply created by administrative fiat. Instead, they were based on a system of 'planned contracts': agreements between state-owned enterprises or their associations which translated Plan targets set by the state into contractual rights and obligations among the enterprises themselves. The 'contract system' was originally introduced in the Soviet Union in the 1920s, when it became obvious that the direct distribution of goods and services throughout the economy, based on central allocations and bookkeeping entries, simply would not work. By recasting Plan obligations in contractual terms, the contract system took advantage of each party's own interest in his partner's performance and thus, indirectly, in the other's timely fulfilment of Plan targets. Minor economic decisions which would have burdened the planning authorities with unnecessary details could be delegated to the parties themselves. And by monitoring each other's performance the parties contributed a useful element of decentralization to the cumbersome centralized state control over the economy.

GDR contract courts adjudicated disputes arising out of such contractual relationships between state firms. But since socialist economic contracts were so closely linked to the Plan, contract courts not only resolved contractual disagreements between two parties but also had to see to it that economic contracts were concluded in the first place and that their terms and conditions assured maximum Plan performance. Accordingly, the courts could operate in two different procedural modes: 'pre-contract' hearings would focus on the conclusion (and, if economically desirable, modification of contracts) and on the conditions necessary for their fulfilment; 'contract hearings' would serve to enforce the contractual claims of parties or to determine responsibility for contract violations. To handle these partly judicial, partly managerial tasks contract courts had far-reaching procedural tools at their disposal: they could initiate proceedings themselves, were not bound by the parties' pleadings, could thoroughly investigate the circumstances of each case, and could enlist the help of planners and administrators to sort out logistical problems beyond the reach of the parties. No wonder that the contract courts, despite their name, were considered administrative rather than judicial bodies.

When I arrive at the Contract Court in the Behrenstrasse, I find the building almost deserted. Empty corridors, locked doors, a secretary packing boxes, another whose boss is away on business in West Berlin. I am about to give up as I spot the young man at the end of the hall. Yes, he is a contract judge. Yes, he is willing to talk to me.

From what I know about the GDR's contract system, I expect a story of failure and frustration. Obviously, the economy has collapsed and the law has not been able to prevent its disintegration. How could it? From an East German manager's perspective, contract law can never have held much promise: since economic contracts had to incorporate an enterprise's Plan targets, real contract autonomy tended to be limited to decisions of secondary importance, like the packing or shipping arrangements for goods over whose production itself the enterprise had little control. If one's partner defaulted, damages or contract penalties could not possibly make up for the loss of actual goods or services. In an economy subject both to planning and scarcity, alternative resources would already be planned and monetary awards—at least awards in soft, socialist currency—could not buy replacements. I know that socialist managers felt ambivalent about the use of contracts: often neglected their timely conclusion (since the Plan targets— that is, the goals that really counted—could be followed in any case) or for a variety of reasons did not enforce contractual claims against their partners.

The most important aspect of socialist contract law, so it had seemed to me, was its function of assigning responsibility for economic failure: an enterprise that enforced contract claims against another could lay the blame for unsatisfactory Plan performance at the door of its defaulting partner, and so exculpate itself. But the spirit which animates our Western contract law and gives it such a central place in our legal thinking—our belief in individual autonomy and in the legitimacy of pursuing one's own interests—had to be absent under socialist conditions. Socialist contracts were planning instruments in civil law disguise, I thought, and basically a contradiction in terms. How could law ever gain real significance in an economy which believed neither in markets nor in money? And how could judges operating within this system not feel irritated at the law's subservience to the Plan?

But Rainer Hannemann, the young contract judge in whose tiny and overheated office we sit and talk (as in many East Berlin buildings, the radiator cannot be turned off), does not appear at all irritated or dissatisfied with his work. On the contrary, he seems to have thrived on it. Much more than other East Berlin judges I interviewed, he exudes energy, authority, and self-confidence. As he describes his work, I begin to see why.

It is true that during the seven years Herr Hannemann has spent at the Contract Court, East German economic law gradually grew powerless and

insignificant. As the planned economy (postulating total control over economic developments) continued on its collision course with the economy of
scarcity (in which projected resources and performances became increasingly unreliable), economic law could no longer plaster over the cracks and
fissures in the system. Neither planning nor contracting worked. Contract
judges, faced with disputes between enterprises who neither could trust the
Plan nor control their own performances, could not simply search the law
for the right answers. Instead, they had to fashion their own unorthodox, *ad
hoc*, and often extralegal solutions.

But as Herr Hannemann and his colleagues at the Contract Court more
or less muddled through the legal problems before them, their work, while
losing in judicial tidiness, gained in managerial authority. Contract judges
needed creativity to cut through economic tangles: they would coordinate
the goals of planners and managers if the Plan needed revision; would lower
statutory penalties if the law demanded the impossible; or find compromise
between two enterprises if fulfilment of a contract was beyond anyone's
control.

Because delay was costly in a troubled economy, judges had to work fast:
85 per cent of all disputes were targeted to be resolved within less than a
month, and Herr Hannemann's court stayed within this limit. Contract
courts could not issue temporary injunctions: too time-consuming, since
injunctions only deferred a dispute's definite settlement to a later date. Nor
could judges ask parties to submit expert opinions—again, too time-consuming—and so had to acquire much of the needed technical knowledge
themselves. Many hearings were held at the site of a particular conflict, to
gain a better grasp of its practical implications. Often, especially in pre-
contract disputes involving a chain of deliverers, each depending on the
other, or in damage suits where one party defaulted because of previous
snags in the production process, the judge would include other enterprises
beyond the immediate contestants in the hearing and rearrange a whole
web of economic relationships, rather than resolve only the most immediate
bipolar dispute.

Not surprisingly, black-letter law played only a secondary role in Herr
Hannemann's work. Sometimes it was simply ignored. For instance, since
contractual remedies were meant to signal economic malfunctionings to the
planners, East German enterprises were obligated to pursue contract penalties to which they were entitled even if, left to their own devices, they
would have preferred to forgo their claims. Contract courts, in these instances, could enforce the penalties at their own initiative and in the interest
of the public purse. But Herr Hannemann and his colleagues 'preferred not
to know about' such cases. Nor did they exercise their authority to initiate
pre-contract proceedings to secure the co-operation of enterprises in danger of defaulting on their obligations. Contract courts also no longer issued

specific instructions, as the law expected them to do, aimed at improving the contract and Plan performance of unco-operative enterprises. I get the impression that in the never-ending tug-of-war between East Germany's planning apparatus and its industry, Herr Hannemann and his colleagues did not align themselves as resolutely with the planners as the law had intended. If anything, they sided with the enterprises in viewing economic bureaucratization and red tape as their common foe. 'Our self-definition had changed,' Herr Hannemann says.

The picture he draws is that of men and women who are neither judges nor administrators but go-betweens: trouble-shooters in a steadily weakening economy. To do a good job they had to rely on their wits and on good relationships with all concerned. They toned down the 'gross discrepancies' between the expectations of the law and economic reality. They mediated between enterprises before a specific dispute could even arise. Instead of simply applying rules to cases they brought people together who between them might work out a compromise acceptable to all. They made telephone calls, wrote letters, arranged meetings. In an economy suffocating under the growing tendency to solve economic problems through administrative intervention, contract judges derived their authority from their capacity to remain flexible and pragmatic.

Listening to Herr Hannemann's description of his work, it occurs to me that his professional style is extraordinarily well suited to the specific characteristics of socialist law. Its preference for policy over principle, for instance, might be at odds with the protection of individual rights but works well if the primary purpose of legal intervention is to improve economic performance. Socialist law's, and the contract judge's, disregard for precise rules and predictable procedures might have made it difficult for an individual enterprise to manipulate the law to its own advantage but was likely to facilitate solutions acceptable to several parties trapped in the same economic deadlock. Herr Hannemann's close and constant co-operation with the planning bureaucracy might have blurred the line between judiciary and executive (which socialist law, rejecting the separation of powers, had not believed in either) but allowed him to find escape routes out of economic imbroglios. If the administration represented to other East Berlin judges a potential threat to their autonomy, it was to Herr Hannemann a natural and necessary partner.

All those features of socialist law which diminished its usefulness to individual citizens—the law's flexibility, its inexactness, its preoccupation with substantive rather than formal justice, its symbiotic relationship to power—contributed to Herr Hannemann's professional authority. His carefree way of handling the law could work only in a system which ranked social efficiency over individual entitlements. When I ask Herr Hannemann for his definition of 'justice,' he gives me a whole list of desirable attitudes and goals: 'avoidance of damages and hardships,' 'realization of legitimate claims within their social context,' 'awareness of other people's problems and constraints,' 'prevention of future conflicts,' 'compromise.' A mediator's answer. And an answer which echoes the parental concerns of socialist law.

How will he fit into the new legal system—if it will have him? Herr Hannemann believes that his past experiences have not prepared him well for work in the West German judiciary. His legal education 'only hinted' at what it means to think like a bourgeois lawyer. GDR law was too 'populist': 'the tricky bits were lacking.' He thinks that, as a civil judge, he would miss his former contract judge's broad procedural powers. But if anything Herr Hannemann looks forward to the challenge. His commercial law work, begun in July and now about to end with reunification, has been 'a lot of fun.' Conceptually harder than GDR contract work, but he likes it.

Maybe Herr Hannemann's rather free and roaming seven years of economic trouble-shooting have given him the self-confidence to tackle whatever lies ahead of him. He also seems to have a better political conscience than most other judges I have talked to. 'If they'll take anyone, they will take me,' he says of the judicial review committees. The words are spoken in a critical rather than a self-congratulatory tone, because Herr Hannemann disapproves of the Westerners' selection criteria for separating 'good' from 'bad' East German judges. But by their standards, he thinks he should pass.

He tells me the story which he believes will persuade the Westerners of his acceptability. Five years ago an officer from the infamous Ministry for State Security (the '*Stasi*') wanted to enlist Rainer Hannemann to spy and report on his colleagues. He said no. A week later a higher-ranking *Stasi* officer repeated the request. Herr Hannemann insisted that his wife be present during the conversation and said 'no' again. He was scared—for his career, he says, not his physical safety—and, when nothing happened, 'a little proud of myself.' He knew of others who, to their own disgust, cooperated with the *Stasi*. The knowledge cooled his relationships with some people at the court. But he never worried about being spied upon himself. 'I did not want to turn schizophrenic,' he says. I tell him about a friend in New York City who to my never-ending amazement finds it quite tolerable to live behind a door with four locks to it. Was life under the *Stasi* comparable to life under the constant and constantly repressed fear of burglars and muggers? Rainer Hannemann, who comes from a safe and orderly world, finds my example shocking. 'More like life behind a door with one lock,' he says.

But the *Stasi* experience seems to have awakened and alerted him sooner than others to the political fraudulence of really existing socialism. In September 1989 Herr Hannemann had 'trouble with the Party' about a letter to Honecker in which he complained about irregularities during the May elections. He initiated working groups at the Contract Court to prepare suggestions for a new Party statute. In November 1989 he resigned from the Party, to which he had belonged since he was 18. He says of himself: 'I reached essential decisions too late.' But he mourns the loss of utopian hopes in which he shared.

How should one go about selecting those judges who can be trusted to contribute to East Germany's transformation into a *Rechtsstaat*? Herr Hannemann agrees with the Western view that some review process is necessary. There is a real danger, he thinks, that those East German judges who tried to please the authorities in the past would simply continue to do so in the future. But if anything, the present selection process prolongs the old socialist habit of 'anticipatory obedience.' By intentionally humiliating their Eastern colleagues the West German authorities are undermining whatever self-respect GDR judges have left. Without some confidence in their own real strengths they will never achieve true independence. 'This is the wrong way to establish a democratic judiciary.' But Herr Hannemann does not know what the right way might be. I am reminded of the pessimistic prediction of another judge: 'Whatever they do, it will be the wrong people who pass.' Not in Rainer Hannemann's case, I hope.

Afternoon

2 p.m. A final meeting of judges and technical personnel in the Littenstrasse courthouse. It is held in the big 'culture room' next to the cafeteria. Dr. Oehmke, as acting director of the *Stadtgericht*, explains tomorrow's procedure for handing over the courthouse and its contents to the West Berlin authorities. About fifty to sixty people are present: shifting a little nervously on their chairs, chatting, distancing themselves with studied inattentiveness from the event.

Dr. Oehmke outlines everybody's duties. 'Ten colleagues from West Berlin's Court of Appeals will come to handle the transfer,' he says. The word 'colleagues' sounds strained; like cheerfulness at a sickbed. But Dr. Oehmke is still head of this court, still an equal to the future occupants, and he appears determined to act like it. All files should be deposited at the Registrar's office, he continues. 'Valuable office machines should be handed over against receipts, if possible.' ('Good grief!' says a woman next to me. 'Most aren't even working!') Presiding judges should remain in their rooms and report to Dr. Oehmke when the transfer has been completed. At 4 p.m. the big enamelled signs at the entrance door, listing the different courts housed in this building, will be removed. Everyone should retain his ID card, since employment relationships will continue during the six-month suspension. All offices should look clean and orderly. 'And please, no empty bottles!'

Then Dr. Oehmke hands out a few last bonuses to deserving employees ('Why let the Westerners take the cash, too?' the Personnel Council, who now approves of these decisions, must have thought) and makes a little speech. He praises the socialist judiciary's closeness to the people. He apologizes for 'inadvertent' injustices, quickly touches upon the issue of guilt. But 'we did not know any better,' Dr. Oehmke says. And: 'The good aspects of our work have formed us.' And: 'Justice and legality always were the primary concerns of our judicial process.'

No, Dr. Oehmke, things were not quite as pretty as that, I think. The others around me may have thought the same; people are leaving while the meeting still winds to its end. If I half expected this final gathering to turn into a moving occasion I was clearly wrong. The group was too large, too impersonal to allow an honest reflection about common successes and failures. It lacked cohesion.

One of the questions I usually ask in my conversations with East Berlin jurists is: 'What features or institutions of socialist law would you like to carry over into the new age?,' and one of the most common answers I receive is: 'The relationship with my collective.' Officially, a person belonged to several collectives: the immediate group of colleagues in one specific work unit (all family law judges at the Court of Appeals, for instance); the larger group of colleagues within a specific institution (for the judges and employees at the Littenstrasse courthouse, for example, everyone present at today's meeting); and the largest and ultimate collective: society. Unofficially, a person's collective consisted of one's immediate and trusted colleagues. Officially, collectives cut across hierarchies and included judges together with secretaries and technical personnel. Unofficially, collectives tended to be horizontal groupings of people with similar interests and backgrounds. Officially, primary collectives were expected to link their members, by way of the larger collectives surrounding them, with their highest aggregate, the state, and thus to encourage the fusion of individual and societal interests. Unofficially, collectives sheltered their members against pressures and demands from the outside. If today's meeting seems fragmented and unresponsive to the common crisis, it is because those present form at best an official collective.

Like so many other institutions under socialism—like the official and the 'second' economy; like socialist and 'real,' hard, Western currency; like wooden Party Mandarin and the everyday, straightforward, human language spoken by ordinary people—collectives in the GDR thus came in two forms: as the official collectives, marching under the same banner in May Day parades or walking together to the polls on election day, and as the real, human, close and often close-knit groupings of people sharing the same work. Sometimes the two would overlap, when the real collectives displayed that solidarity and concern for each other which the Party valued as socialist comradeship. Collectives in the GDR, real or official, would not just share such mundane pleasures as picnics, theater outings or the obligatory office birthday party. Good collectives also supported their members in times of need: filled in for a sick colleague or helped in a family crisis. The women I talked to especially praised the reliability and helpfulness of their collective. Men might get by without it. But how could a young woman judge with two small children—in an impoverished and consumer-hostile economy—juggle family and profession if she could not count on her colleagues to step in when needed? 'The times we sat around this table working out babysitting arrangements!' Judge Fischer said when describing the relationships among her female colleagues. This was an aspect of collectivity the Party approved of: shouldering together the tasks that would advance the cause of socialism.

But often the very same collective solidarity would turn into a threat to Party goals. Members of a collective also helped each other in ways considered impermissible by those in power: covered up for colleagues who came late to work or did their shopping during office hours; found excuses for the hundred little ways in which socialist citizens cheated on the state; kept to themselves the kind of political talk that in the outside world counted as subversive. By sheltering their members against the appeals of official morality they compromised and subverted the socialist state's claim to the total man or woman. In their unofficial version, collectives were part of that 'society of niches' into which socialism had developed: an aggregation of unconnected enclaves facilitating withdrawal from the totalitarian state. In this version socialist collectives did not reflect a common public philosophy but rather its absence: what counted for each individual were not the official articulations of correct or incorrect behavior but his or her own collective's definition of right and wrong. Hence the paradox which always struck me on my pre-*Wende* travels through the GDR: that this society, which put such extraordinary emphasis on ideology, should not have been able to produce any real ideological cohesion within its citizenry. Socialism, which set out to abolish man's division into the *citoyen* and the *bourgeois*, ended up with a society split more deeply into public and private spheres than any other I know of. Nowhere else have I encountered such discrepancies between a fake and hollow public morality and the private beliefs of ordinary men and women. East German collectives—the real collectives that is, which provided bits and pieces of that civic culture absent in public life—were part of the moral fragmentation of socialist society without which its rapid physical disintegration would not have been possible.

Today's meeting in the 'culture room' reminds me again of the absence of a public dialogue in the GDR. Dr. Oehmke's talk does not succeed in striking a common chord. The few questions from the audience concern only matters of pay and other personal claims. The same people who within their real collectives can sometimes talk with painful honesty about the collapse of socialism find no public voice on this occasion. But I am worried that even the private cohesion within their small groupings may not survive for long. Most of my conversation partners fear the same. They are afraid that the competitiveness and self-assertiveness of capitalism will undermine their limited but very real and reassuring solidarity. East German collectives remind me of invertebrates whose skeletons do not support them from within but hold them together from without. Under the pressures of a totalitarian state the outer shell of collectives grew hard and resistant. But with the disappearance of political coercion it may soon soften. For a while, common anxieties may keep people together. But unemployment and financial worries, I should think, pose threats too diffuse and corrosive to motivate people, as under socialism, to close ranks against a common opponent. Already, people seem preoccupied only with saving their own skins. The men and women I observe at today's meeting do not look like comrades held together by feelings of solidarity, but like individuals trying to keep a stiff upper lip.

2 October 1990

The last day of socialist law in this courthouse; of socialism, or what is left of it, in this country. The last day of this country. Tonight at midnight, when the reunification will be celebrated with music and dances and fireworks, the GDR will cease to exist.

Most people I have talked to do not plan to attend the festivities. All of them welcomed the *Wende*. Almost all, despite their anger and confusion, would not exchange their present for their former lives. But they are too disappointed about the ways in which they feel manipulated, again, into the position of objects rather than subjects of political change to want to engage in much revelry. 'One should not celebrate a bad occasion,' Klaus Petzoldt said sternly when I asked about his plans for tonight. People also fear the aggression that may accompany gatherings of large masses in a society in which public demonstrations are not as thoroughly staged as they used to be under socialism. So most of my East Berlin colleagues plan to spend the historic night at home, or at their garden allotments on the outskirts of the city, 'away from it all.'

As if silenced by the common mood of dejection, the courthouse this morning seems quiet, almost mute. Near the entrance, four or five grey-suited men consult with the custodian; they must be members of the delegation from West Berlin. No other person in the corridors. The East Berliners seem to prefer to stay in their rooms. Dr. Oehmke, who yesterday had anticipated a day of forced leisure and suggested that I come by his office for a little chat, has to confer with the visitors and disappears. While

I wait for his return I am joined by a stylish woman in her early forties, also looking for Dr. Oehmke. She turns out to be Dr. Heidrun Quilitzsch, Vice Director of the Court of Appeals and Presiding Judge of the Senate of Administrative Law. Just the right company.

Dr. Quilitzsch's Senate is a recent institution. The GDR was the last East European state to accept judicial controls over its executive, trailing behind not only more liberal countries like Poland or Hungary, but also more repressive ones like Romania or Bulgaria. The statute on the Competence of Courts to Review Administrative Decisions was passed on 14 December 1988 and took effect in July 1989, only four months before the political turnabout.

Prior to the new law, East German citizens who felt aggrieved by some official act could only complain: first to the agency which had rendered the offensive decision, then if still dissatisfied to the next highest office. For want of other remedies, the complaint system was widely used; by East German estimates, each year at least one citizen in ten lodged a complaint against the authorities. The system held some advantages over litigation: complaints were informal, costless, and unconstrained by any requirements of standing. Occasionally they produced results. But as an internal review depending entirely on the goodwill and insight of the administration itself, the procedure gave the citizen no control over the vindication of his rights. It was useless in cases in which a complainant either questioned crucial state policies (such as the denial of free speech) or in which his request, though supported by law, was not feasible economically (such as an application for a larger apartment). But even in other cases, the absence of any procedural bite meant that officials could pretty much deal with complaints as they pleased. Here, as elsewhere, the socialist citizen depended on the benevolence of the state.

Over the years it became obvious that East Germany's complaint system served neither the interests of its government nor of its citizens. It was too arbitrary to instil civic trust in the authorities and too easily dodged by the bureaucracy to ensure the state's control over its own administration. Everyone in the GDR, Frau Quilitzsch says, knew from personal experience of its 'miserable public service.' A 1987 high-level study of the legal knowledge and practices of local state functionaries, known to Dr. Quilitzsch only by way of rumors, apparently revealed 'shocking' conditions. When reform finally came in 1988 it was supported not only by academics (some of whom had for decades pushed for judicial review) but also by the Foreign Ministry and the Ministry of Justice. Ninety-three new judges and over 8,000 new lay assessors were elected to staff the new panels for administrative law at the district courts. Frau Quilitzsch was appointed to supervise eleven of these new administrative law judges at this courthouse. Litigation, it was hoped, would domesticate the bureaucratic excesses of socialism.

But the short history of the new statute on judicial review shows how unwilling, and in the end how unable, socialist law was to reform itself. From the beginning, the courts' authority to investigate the legality of administrative decisions was narrowly circumscribed. To counteract the implication that conflict between citizen and state might be a legitimate state of affairs, the statute went to great lengths to avoid any adversarial confrontation of citizen and administration in the courtroom. The plaintiff citizen was the only 'party' to the proceedings; both the prosecutor and the administration were only 'participants.' More restrictive than most of its East European counterparts, the East German statute allowed a citizen to sue the administration only in limited and specifically enumerated instances. And the court could examine only whether the disputed decision conformed to the letter of the law, not whether the administration had misused or exceeded its discretion.

The last restriction was fatal to the effectiveness of the reform. Experts in the Ministry of Justice, academics, and judges had wanted a limited review of discretionary decisions. But one of the items on the statute's list of reviewable matters, placed there, says Dr. Quilitzsch, to impress the international community, was the 1988 Decree on Travels of Citizens of the GDR to Foreign Countries. This decree gave the authorities great leeway in deciding whether or not a citizen should be allowed, temporarily or permanently, to leave the country. In administrative practice, many denials of visas were not even accompanied by reasons. If courts had been enabled to review such decisions for the misuse or excess of discretionary powers, one of the most sensitive areas of Party policy would have been laid open to outside scrutiny and criticism.

There they were again, the *Ausreiser*. To allow them to successfully contest the denial of an exit visa in a court of law would have implied the admission that a socialist citizen might actually have the right to disassociate himself from the best of all possible worlds. It was more than the Party could accept. The Supreme Court produced one of its 'guiding resolutions' ordering judges not to review the administration's use of discretion under the 'travel decree.' In a meeting in East Berlin's City Hall, officials of the Department for Internal Affairs instructed judges and administrators accordingly. Dr. Quilitzsch, who was present at the meeting, tells of 'the sigh of relief' which ran through the audience when the executive was told that it would, after all, not have to worry about the judiciary.

And the result? Judicial review of administrative decisions in the GDR turned into 'a farce.' Few people made use of the new right to sue the state: about 750 in all of East Germany in the first three months of the statute. Since 'the vast majority' of these suits attacked the denial of exit visas, the vast majority had to be dismissed for failing to establish the illegality of the contested decision. Judges, Frau Quilitzsch says, were 'helpless.' At best, they might try to dissuade a citizen from bringing suit in cases turning on the use of discretion. In non-discretionary matters plaintiffs could and did win some cases against the state. But these small triumphs were too rare seriously to worry the administration; too rare, also, to redeem the system in the eyes of its potential users.

What would have happened had the *Wende* not intervened? People would have become increasingly impatient. Frau Quilitzsch is not the first judge to tell me about the disappointment and frustration of East German judges when it turned out that the new statute would not enable them to check abuses of power. Internally, the issue was hotly debated. According to Frau Quilitzsch's description, those meetings at which all presiding judges of administrative law panels were convened at the Supreme Court and told how to handle the review of discretionary visa denials, were not passive occasions. People could raise objections and did. 'My eleven were not just patient recipients of commands!' she says of her judges. And: 'Nothing happened in Berlin to people who spoke their minds at such meetings.' At least, nothing serious. Frau Quilitzsch herself, five weeks before the opening of the Wall, was called in for a 'conversation' with the Vice-President of the Supreme Court after she advocated the review of administrative discretion in professional lectures. But such remonstrations, it appears, were annoying rather than threatening.

So, disagreement was possible. But did it matter? Could criticism contained within the four walls of a lecture room ever affect policies decided in the Central Committee or the Politburo? Or did speaking one's mind merely enable the speaker—and Frau Quilitzsch uses the same words as several other judges before her—'to look at herself in the mirror?'

She does not seem to think so. Even purely internal opposition may eventually effect changes on the outside. The official policy of non-reviewability of discretionary decisions had critics in high places; Frau Quilitzsch mentions several justices at the Supreme Court. Those in power were afraid of judges, she says: 'Because, after all, we were judges.' Klaus Petzoldt had phrased it differently: 'They were afraid of us, although there really was no reason.' I don't know who is right. Dr. Quilitzsch reports that in November 1989, when the Wall fell, a new draft of the statute on judicial review, greatly extending the powers of the courts, was already in existence. Whether because of the fact that most judges, in her words, 'were really in complete agreement on this issue,' or because of the thousands of citizens who gave up on courts and laws and fled the country by way of Hungary or the West German Embassy in Prague, I cannot tell. When the new statute went into force on 1 July 1990 nobody cared any longer.

But whatever the impact of their opposition, such as it was, I am no longer so certain that East German judges were necessarily less 'independent' than their Western colleagues. As I write it down, the statement looks ludicrous. But if we measure independence not by the extent to which a country's courts are actually insulated against interference from the outside but by the energy spent in warding off impositions—measure it in units of resistance, as it were, a sort of judicial 'ohm'—then many of the judges I talked to must have manifested more rather than less resistance than their West German counterparts. They operated under incomparably larger pressures. They responded, or many of them did, by trying to fend off extraordinary interventions, and by criticizing, more or less surreptitiously, the ordinary interference of a state used to providing authoritative interpretations of the law. Many times their resistance did not prevent abuses of power. Yet, if measured on our scale of judicial ohms, it might still register higher than the resistance expended during a Western judge's ordinary working day. Not good enough, most Western critics will say. Good enough, I should think, to discredit Western feelings of moral superiority. There is a passage in the final scenes of Brecht's *Galileo* which often came into my mind during these last four weeks. 'Unhappy the land that has no heroes!' Andrea says. 'No,' Galileo replies. 'Unhappy the land that needs heroes.'

It is past lunchtime. Dr. Quilitzsch and I, between us, have polished off the last bag of pretzel sticks on Dr. Oehmke's coffee table. He finally comes, if only for a minute. With an embarrassed little grin he presents each of us with a flat, black box with silver trim. I open mine and find a large gold medal. 'Forty years of legal work in the service of the people,' it says. And in a circle around it a legend still innocent, at the time of mintage, of the events which would transform the award from an honor into a joke: '8 December 1949–8 December 1989.'

On my way out I pass by Judge Fischer's office. She had promised to show me the questionnaire which had recently arrived in preparation for her investigation by the judicial selection committee. It begins with the usual biographical enquiries. Then come the nasty questions: the ones that mirror both West German suspicions and the East German political quagmire which gave rise to them. Were you a member of the Party? An unnecessary question, since every judge was. Were you exposed to Party disciplinary proceedings? Was your work ever the subject of citizens' complaints? Were you a member of a 'Ia' senate? Were you a collaborator of the Ministry for State Security? Were you ever asked to collaborate? With what results?

Frau Fischer shakes her head as we go through these questions: at the ugly image they draw of her professional life; at the fact that all these distasteful connections existed and that the image, in some instances, must be correct; at the hopelessness of explaining to Western examiners what it meant to be a judge in a socialist state. At the bottom of the page she is asked to sign a release making the information available to the Senate Administration of Justice, the Judicial Selection Committee, the Presiding

Council of Judges, 'and other offices participating in the investigation.'
'Who could that be?' Frau Fischer asks me. I have no idea. She is first
puzzled, then upset. Who else could want to know about the details of her
biography? Isn't the passage rather vague? Don't they have to tell her to
whom they pass on information? She will not sign it, Frau Fischer says. She
will add a passage explaining her refusal but not sign it. Anyone could be
meant by that passage, and she will not have it. Judge Fischer looks at me
with angry eyes. 'I can't start ducking again right away, can I?' she says.

II

First Steps

10 October 1990

Back at the *Stadtgericht* (now I should say: the former *Stadtgericht*) in the Littenstrasse. I want to listen to some of those classes on West German law which the Berlin city government is offering to (now former) East Berlin judges and prosecutors. Before the renovation crews arrive, East Berlin courthouses—once again—are to be used as places of education. I am also curious to see whether, one week after Reunification Day, I can already spot traces of the new *Rechtsstaat*.

The internal courtyard with its pair of swinging staircases looks unchanged. And the building's smell, that mixture of floor wax and pungent socialist disinfectant, is the same as always. But the big iron grille that used to separate the procuracy's wing from the rest of the courthouse is now gone, and I find a new Registrar's office at the end of the corridor. 'Enter only when called,' says a sign on the door. Nobody is around, and I enter anyway. I want to know who uses the new office and what kind of legal complaints the new citizens bring to court. But the West Berlin official who listens to my usual introductory explanations does not want to talk to me. I should speak with his superior. 'You must understand,' he says, not unfriendly. 'I'll only get into trouble.'

I understand and search for the main destination of my visit: a lecture for prosecutors on the subject of basic rights. It meets in a small second floor room in the east wing of the building. About thirty people attend, two-thirds of them women. Almost everyone has brought a copy of the constitution. Through the open window I can see the rails of the city train leading to the Alexanderplatz.

The retooling classes for East Berlin judges and prosecutors are taught by a variety of instructors. Most responded to newspaper advertisements by the Senate Administration of Justice searching for teachers. There are West Berlin judges and prosecutors, attorneys, retired lawyers from all branches of the profession. Even young graduates fresh out of law school applied, who are presently doing their two-and-a-half-year apprenticeship, which is required prior to the final bar examination. At 150 marks for a two-hour class, their motives must have been patriotic rather than financial. Today's lecturer, I would guess, is an attorney: a short, agile man with a gigantic black briefcase with a combination lock. He begins his lecture with some practical advice.

It may well be necessary. 'Look for the publication date when you buy your book!' he says. 'One or two years, in the law, is a long time! Don't get stuck with old textbooks!' I think back to the legal literature in GDR times, when only one treatise existed in each area of law and when a new edition of this text had to be authorized and prepared years ahead and was an event of almost national proportion. Socialist jurists were not to be led astray by a profusion of opinions. Even so, in 1983 an official in the GDR Ministry of Justice complained to an American visitor about the excessive bulk of East German legal teaching texts. The books currently in use together weighed seventy pounds, he said, when about forty-five pounds, in his opinion, would be ample to do the job. He was not joking.

I shudder at the thought of the combined weight of American and West German law books in print. But I must pay attention: the lecturer has turned to substantive matters. He begins with article 70 paragraph 3 of the 'Basic Law,' the German constitution, and its 'immutable' guarantee that certain central principles of the constitution shall not be altered even by absolute majority vote. A city train rumbles past the open window. The faces around me look inscrutable. The notion that law should be able to bind those in power even in situations in which an entire nation is willing to snub its commands must seem doubtful not only to socialists. Only yesterday, these men and women were taught that law is class law and an instrument of those in power to cement their rule. Are they now to believe that law can nonchalantly abstract itself from its power base and control its own makers? Does the Basic Law suffer from wishful thinking? From delusions of grandeur? But nobody lifts a hand to raise objections. Only a few take notes. Again, the rattling of a passing train fills the room.

Someone closes the window. The speaker moves on to issues of constitutional litigation. Most writing utensils still lie unused on their owners' noteblocks. But this is important, I think. Are the men and women in this room aware of the political power of capitalist courts? Do they realize that much of our political discourse uses the adversarial language of litigation? Or do they not believe what they are told? It is only when the lecturer addresses doctrinal issues, outlining categories and sub-categories of constitutional rights, that his students begin to take notes: record distinctions between human and civic rights, between general and specific constitutional guarantees, between liberty rights and those providing procedural protections. Why this sudden attention? Because conceptual definitions seem safer and more manageable than complex discussions about the relationship between citizen and state? Because scholastic classification games are pleasantly abstract and innocuous enough already to have been popular in the days of socialism?

These students like the mechanics of the law better than its principles, I think. They do not want to be converted. They are not interested in policy debates. They want clear-cut instructions that can be written down, studied, and applied when the need arises. The lecture nears its end. The teacher accelerates his pace, now just summarizing important points as he approaches his conclusion. His audience is restless. Only once do I sense rekindled interest: when the lecturer discusses the impact of constitutional law on private law relationships. He offers an illustration: a sign in a restaurant, warning 'foreigners not admitted.' Is that legal? A number of people in the audience suddenly look alert. But I can see that they are not satisfied with the lecturer's response. He talks about the tensions between different constitutional values, about the illegitimacy of discrimination, the constitutional belief in contractual autonomy, about balancing. What? What did he say? Is the exclusion of foreign customers legal or is it not? Again, no clear-cut answer—nothing that the students can store in their briefcases and carry home.

On the way out, I puzzle over the audience's inattentiveness. Why hadn't people taken more notes? Was the subject-matter too complex? The teacher's bent too academic? But in the afternoon I discover another possible explanation. I attend another lecture on constitutional rights, this one taught by a young administrative judge from West Berlin in the Plenary Chamber of the former GDR Supreme Court in the west wing of the building; a large, light room furnished with green-yellow curtains of dubious taste, in which the long judges' bench has disrespectfully been pushed aside to make room for more chairs. Again, only a few students take notes. Neighbors whisper with each other. But the lecturer, irritated by the general lack of attention, enquires about its reason. Maybe people are already familiar with the subject? Yes. And do they know the pertinent case-law? The *Lüth* decision? Yes. The *Blinkfuer* case? Yes. It appears that the students have been more diligent in their studies of the new law than their Western teachers anticipated.

15 October 1990

A visit with Rudi Beckert, the former East German Supreme Court justice who a few weeks ago helped me to rescue that collection of Supreme Court cases from the waste-baskets in the Littenstrasse court-house. Now he is not only unemployed but, to all intents and purposes, unemployable. No need for him to apply for readmission in the judiciary, since the Berlin Senate Administration does not accept applications from former Supreme Court justices. And, unlike many of his colleagues from the bench, Herr Beckert has not sought to join the Bar. He dislikes the idea of serving prospective clients necessarily worse, he believes, than more experienced attorneys would do. And who else would hire him these days, at his age: a judge coming from the highest court of a state now ignominiously collapsed, a specialist on the doctrinal intricacies of a criminal law system now scorned and despised? Instead of a job, Herr Beckert has found refuge in an undertaking for which unemployment provides time and freedom: the investigation of his own professional past. '*Aufarbeitung der Vergangenheit*' the Germans call it these days: 'giving the past a workover' and the term evokes mountains of files to be read and sorted amidst clouds of dust. Will the labor produce a clean desk? In simpler days, the German word *Aufarbeitung* used to describe the alteration of ill-fitting or outdated clothes: turning an old suit or dress into a serviceable garment. Can it now produce a past as good as new? And then there is *Vergangenheitsbewältigung*, another expression much in use to describe soul-searching investigation into Germany's recent history: 'coming to terms with the past,' or, in literal translation, 'mastering the past.' Can it be mastered?

Herr Beckert has no illusions that it can. He will be content just to understand what happened. Like I, he is interested in the relationship between law and political power under socialism. Rudi Beckert always knew more about this subject than most other people in the GDR. But now, for the first time, he asks questions about events and practices which once seemed to need no explanation. He digs into his memory for details, reconstructs events with almost self-destructive disregard for his own role in them. I want to learn something about the mechanisms that insured the conformity of socialist case law with Party policy. Over a glass of orange juice, Herr Beckert explains to me how the Supreme Court guided the East German judiciary.

Imagine a difficult case, he says; a situation in which a judge is unsure about how to decide a particular issue. For political or legal reasons? I ask. For one or the other reason, says Herr Beckert. He admits that obviously there were instances in which a judge wanted to protect himself against political criticism from above. This could be done with a telephone call to the District Party Office—couched in terms of a request for legal advice, to be sure, since an outright solicitation of political guidance would be considered in bad taste. But this kind of assurance could also be found closer to home: 'after all, there was a Party secretary in every institution.' Would a judge regularly check his decisions with the Party? No, no: 'don't assume complete servility.' A judge would not submit a draft of his decision to the Party secretary, either. But if he was worried about making a mistake in a politically touchy criminal case, for example, he might be tempted to test Party reactions prior to his judgment. 'Yes, I think that is a good solution,' the Party secretary might say if informed of the judge's intended approach. Such a conversation would greatly reduce the risk of later Party remonstrations.

But, at least in principle, requests for advice which only served to protect the questioner were frowned upon by the system. Anyway, these are not the types of cases Herr Beckert has in mind. Rather, he thinks of a situation in which a judge has honest doubts about how to decide an issue. For political or legal reasons? I ask again. 'Let's say for both,' Herr Beckert replies. But I can see that my question misses the point. To distinguish between political and legal considerations may seem natural to me. But it must seem spurious to Herr Beckert. All law, to a socialist, is political. An East German decision was legally correct only if it also displayed 'Party spirit': indebtedness not to one or the other party before the court but to the Party and to its policies and goals. A good socialist judge should neither allow himself to be influenced by a telephone call from the Party secretary ('telephone justice' served the interests of local bosses rather than those of the system) nor give in to the temptation to view a dispute 'unpolitically,' that is, without consideration for its political and social implications.

So let's assume a truly complicated case in which the decision might go either way, Herr Beckert says. Maybe a criminal prosecution involving an uncertain line-drawing between murder and manslaughter. 'In this situation, the court will look for help.' The presiding judge might telephone a criminal law colleague at the Supreme Court: 'Have you already read about the matter in the *Wochenmeldung*?' The *Wochenmeldung* (weekly report), also irreverently called *Wochenkrimi* (the week's whodunit), was part of a reporting system under which each week every court in the GDR had to inform its superior court of any noteworthy event. The report had to include all cases of possible political significance: cases involving foreign and particularly Western parties; cases affecting Party personnel (like the upcoming divorce of the council chairman); information on important local problems or trends, on citizen's complaints, and on matters of practical significance affecting the court's administration or its staff. A district court's weekly report would go to the regional court; a regional court's report to the Supreme Court. Copies were sent to the Central Committee, the Prosecutor General's office, the Ministry of the Interior, and of course to the Ministry for State Security. The reporting system was intended to increase the law's usefulness as an instrument of state planning and control.

In our murder hypothesis, chances are thus that news of the impending case has already reached the Supreme Court by way of the *Wochenmeldung*. If the trial judge now telephones for advice, the Court's Criminal Law Panel will get together and talk the matter over. Maybe some reference to recent literature or case law would be helpful. Maybe a Panel member could use the Supreme Court's greater resources or better connections to obtain additional information: for example, consult a psychiatrist 'in contact' with the Court on issues of imputability. The justice then calls back the trial court to discuss the case. The lower judge outlines his intended approach. 'Yes, this is definitely a solution I could support,' the Supreme Court justice might say. But the lower court judge need not follow the advice. Disagreement—within politically acceptable limits—is per-missible. 'Well, then do it your way,' the Supreme Court man might say if his colleague at the trial court prefers his own solution to that of his superiors.

Of course, justices at the Supreme Court, too, might feel uncertain about how to handle a particular matter. Then it is their turn to look for advice. A member of the Court will call the Administration of Justice section at the Central Committee's Department for State and Law. He will be asked about his panel's own view: 'Well, how do you propose to handle the case?' The justice will outline suggestions. His contact at the Central Committee will be careful not to give obvious orders. 'Yes, that seems a reasonable approach,' he might say. Or: 'you may want to consider the possibility . . .' 'The tone of these conversations was civil enough,' Herr Beckert says. I detect a hint of pleasure in the way in which he spreads the organizational innards of the Court before my eyes; like someone lifting a flagstone in his garden and observing with reluctant fascination the creeping, crawling life he has set free. Herr Beckert explains. Even between the Supreme Court and the Central Committee differences of opinion were not unheard-of. The Court could, if it so chose, follow its own approach. But if in doubt, it was a better idea first to ask and then to do things one's own way than not to ask at all. One had to 'recognize a problem,' had to show that one did not want 'to shirk political confrontations.'

Whatever judicial independence existed in this scheme of things was thus restricted to the decision of the case at hand. But as a rule, there would be no unprompted instructions from above; a judge did not have to ask for advice; or, if he asked, did not have to follow the advice received. There was no direct political pressure—'to claim there was would imply that the actors were victims'—or if, against the rules, someone with clout tried to influence the outcome of a particular case, such pressures could be resisted. Which is not to say that they always were. But all in all, 'the system worked far more efficiently,' Herr Beckert says. The telephone conversations back and forth, 'the week's whodunit,' the constant flow of information between different court levels all contributed to persuade each member of the judiciary that he or she took part in an important collective enterprise that had to be carried out according to a common plan. In this network of permanent communication, it was not difficult 'to know what they wanted.'

And if a judge had somehow missed his cue, he certainly would be told so—after the verdict, when the decision was evaluated at one of the Party meetings at the courthouse. There would be a 'political discussion' with the culprit. It was possible to make up for individual deviations from the Party line. But too many instances spelled trouble. The result? Judges learned to operate within the limits of the system. If someone strayed too far, even family members might be enlisted in the task of returning the

errant member to the fold. 'Why don't you talk some sense into your
husband (or wife)?' spouses might be told. Or it could happen that a judge
was sent to the Party Academy (a useful career move, too, for someone
interested in promotion). Substantively 'a total waste of time,' Herr Beckert
says. Nevertheless, most judges did their stint at the Academy. And so
the system worked: fast and without noticeable friction. Even consultations
by mail would, as a rule, take no longer than a week. 'Speed, too, was a
matter of socialist legality,' Herr Becker says, in a tone that mixes irony and
pride.

Consultations thus served to eliminate uncertainty or doubt about the
proper application of the law to individual cases. Other mechanisms steered
GDR judicial policy in a more general fashion: regular court 'inspections,'
for example. They complemented the weekly reporting system: while the
'whodunit' alerted higher-ups to budding problems at the bottom, 'inspections' were to ferret out shortcomings at lower levels at the initiative of
those above. Three or four court 'inspectors' from each regional court thus
investigated matters at each of the region's district courts; regional courts in
turn were investigated by inspectors coming from the Supreme Court. In
the 1970s, Herr Beckert had served as an inspector for a while himself.
What did one look for: political deviations? No, not really. At least, not
during his time. Politically touchy cases would be handled by the 'Ia' departments, anyway, who were not subject to inspections and whose problems, incidentally, were not included in the regular 'whodunit'—they had
their own reporting system. No, Herr Beckert and his collegues were simply
searching for judicial trouble spots: trying to discover defects in the system
before they could cause serious damage, and initiating timely repairs.

And who decided what should be investigated? The Supreme Court,
together with the Ministry of Justice, drew up 'inspection plans,' which
guided the regional courts in designing their own inspection projects. Sometimes, the Court would send its inspectors to check up on specific areas of
the law: review, for instance, all trial court decisions dealing with property
infractions. Sometimes, it would order a lower court to report on its own
work—its efforts to improve the collection of rent arrears in the district, for
example—and have inspectors double-check and evaluate the local account. Inspectors were never allowed to give orders to the judges they
investigated. They could observe trials, ask questions, and they had access
to the records and files—that was it. Still, an inspector's disparaging report
might, at a later stage, cause trouble for the judges concerned. To pre-empt
it, the inspected would occasionally make use of the visitors' presence in the
courthouse and consult them on the spot about some upcoming matter.

What type of judges were appointed inspectors: party hacks? eager
beavers? Rather those with a reputation of being thorough and circum-
spect, Herr Beckert says. Of course, inspectors had to be politically reliable.

But not 'super-reliable.' Above all, they had to be 'good writers': inspectors needed that essential socialist talent of composing beautiful and persuasive reports. If it was the official task of the Inspectorate to uncover weaknesses within the socialist administration of justice, its unofficial task was to represent the system to the Party in its rosiest light. Reports always described how well things worked. Occasional deficiencies were exceptions that proved the rule. The optimistic and reassuring narrative style of the accounts may also explain why none of the judges whom I interviewed about their experiences with the Inspectorate admitted to ever having found its visits the least bit disquieting.

And finally, Herr Beckert goes on to explain, there were the Supreme Court's Plenary Sessions to guide the judiciary, the 'reports' based on these sessions, published in law reviews, the 'Guidelines,' often in the making for years (and, on their face, increasingly unpolitical and technically more sophisticated than in the past), and the many 'Orientations,' 'Viewpoints,' 'Resolutions' and what have you, which the Supreme Court used to impress upon lower courts the proper attitude towards the various legal problems of the day. One problem in particular comes to mind: the treatment of *Ausreiser*-suits contesting firings based on the plaintiff's wish to leave the country. How did the orders to dismiss such suits without oral argument—of which I learned from Frau Schomburg—make their way into her files? Who instigated this policy? What role did the Supreme Court play in the process?

Herr Beckert's field is criminal law; he was not involved in the articulation of labor law policies. But he can imagine how things must have happened. Maybe the Ministry for State Security, worried by the increasing number of citizens leaving the GDR, had taken the initiative: could not the Ministry of Justice suggest some way to discourage applications for exit visas? The idea might first have been aired at one of the 'heads of departments' meetings which, three to six times a year, brought together the Ministers of Justice and of the Interior, the Procurator General, the President of the Supreme Court, and of course high-level representatives of the Central Committee and of State Security to discuss important matters of legal policy. From there, the issue would have been passed on to the 'Deputies' Round': a periodic gathering of officials from the same institutions, one notch down, which also regularly included a member of State Security (participating in the group's debates but never signing its resolutions). 'We need some suggestions from you people to help us tackle the *Ausreiser* problem,' the representative from the Supreme Court might have been told at one of these meetings.

He, in turn, would have approached the head of the Court's labor law panel about the matter. And like as not it was one of this panel's members who first came up with the idea of using Section 28 paragraph 3 of the Code

of Civil Procedure as a pretext for dismissing *Ausreiser* labor law suits
without oral argument. I know the rest of the story: a final draft, which only
few people would ever set eyes on; a meeting at the Supreme Court, at
which the presiding labor law judges of regional courts would be informed
of the new policy; a series of 'judges' conferences,' at which the lower
ranking labor law judiciary would be told how to handle *Ausreiser* complaints. The usual method.

But I would do the Supreme Court injustice simply to think of it as a
handmaiden of politics. It was also what it claimed to be: the most sophisticated and authoritative tribunal in the land. The Court's ambitions
seemed to vacillate between political loyalty and professional perfection-
ism. The same judges who together with Party and *Stasi* functionaries could
cook up flimsy pretexts for denying justice to prospective emigrants could
also complain about the procedural sloppiness or political over-eagerness
of lower-court decisions. At the Court's Plenary Session in the summer of
1986, speakers thus criticized the lack of spirit and self-assertiveness common among GDR judges. One of the discussants, director of the Court of
Appeals in Karl-Marx-Stadt, called a spade a spade and asked for more
judicial independence. He knew whereof he spoke: 'In my experience, the
judicial autonomy of courts in our region depends on the steadfastness and
personal integrity of each court's director.'

The claim confirms what a judge in East Berlin once told me about her
independence: 'Oh, my director's broad back was a pretty effective shield.'
If a court's director guarded his judges against interference from the outside, they did not have to worry about 'telephone justice.' But it was the
director's pluck (or, if need be, their own backbone) that protected judges,
not the dignity of their office. How could the system itself be made more
resistant? Maybe—thus the resolution at the 1986 Sixth Plenary Session—
with a nineteen-point program whose first provision demanded 'to enhance
the individual responsibility of courts for the management and resolution of
their cases.' 'We know that in this important political endeavor we can
count on the support of our leading Party organs,' said, almost imploringly,
the discussant from Karl-Marx-Stadt, obviously himself a man with a broad
back. But he also knew: 'This is a very complicated process. . . .'

Indeed. Was not the court's political subservience an integral component
of the system? Had not the very same 1986 Plenary Session resolved to
require all courts 'to ensure the complete transmission of all information
relevant to central decision making'? Did not the Supreme Court justices,
who in one breath called for 'increased judicial autonomy' and for prompt
notification of 'all politically significant trials liable to cause public unrest,'
want to eat their cake and keep it, too? Under the rule of law, the independence of the third branch can fairly easily be reconciled with the political

powers of the other two. Our hopes for justice are modest. We are agnostics at heart, don't claim to know what is good for other people; let everyone follow his own path to salvation and are content if we can agree on and keep to some basic rules of the game. Hence the crucial importance of procedure in our legal system. Whether this procedure, however scrupuously observed, will actually further the individual welfare of each player of the game is not our concern. It is people's own business.

But socialists hoped for more: not only formal but substantive justice. Unlike ourselves, they knew how to advance the welfare of each citizen. At least, they claimed to know it: from the Marxist classics; from the teachings of history; from the Party, which alone was able correctly to interpret and apply these teachings. And since 'there was a correct answer to each and every question, it was—from the socialist viewpoint—quite reasonable to ensure that judges would find it.

Assume for a moment that courts did not have the task of resolving legal disputes, but, say, of building bridges or roads. Then, all the troubling practices of East Germany's judicial process—the Supreme Court guidelines and directives, the weekly reports, the inspection system—would suddenly make sense. Building bridges does not require impartiality and fairness but expertise, quality controls, a plan. Roads must not be just, but properly designed and executed. GDR law, too, was less concerned with doing justice to the individual than with finding correct solutions to social problems. Hence, its complex and costly apparatus of control. If difficult construction jobs are to be carried out according to plan, it is important to keep a close eye on the crew.

Within this scheme of things, it was unrealistic to complain about the courts' political adaptability and compliance. They were part of a legal system which believed in a central authority's capacity to determine right answers. The calls for more judicial autonomy growing increasingly audible during the 1980s thus suggest not the strengthening of socialist law during its final years but rather its disintegration: socialist judges began to doubt the omniscience of the Party. With no address to turn to for the perfect answer, judges indeed had no other choice than to search for reassurance in formality and procedure. Their diminished faith understandably increased the Party's fear of losing control. Did the political climate at the Court improve or deteriorate in recent years? I asked Herr Beckert. 'Deteriorate!' he says. And: 'You can't imagine the flak I would have gotten had I dared to appear for work without my Party pin!'

Now, it is not just Herr Beckert's Party pin which is no longer in demand. But he has found new and rewarding compensation for his losses: honesty with himself. Why ever did you decide to become a lawyer, I want to know from him on my way out. Because, when he entered university, places were available only in law and teaching. At the time, law seemed the better choice. But had it been up to him, Rudi Beckert would have studied music.

25 October 1990

In the Plenary Chamber of the Administrative Court in West Berlin to attend a discussion about the integration of former GDR judges into the Berlin judiciary. The Association of Administrative Law Judges (Western, of course) has organized the event. One of the instructors at the Littenstrasse courthouse had told me about it. Despite his willingness to help with the retooling of his Eastern colleagues, he felt skeptical about the advisability of employing formerly socialist judges in the service of the *Rechtsstaat*. It is a hotly debated issue these days, and on both sides of the argument passions are running high. Strangely enough, I cannot predict even in the case of acquaintances or friends whether they will preach a spirit of generosity and acceptance towards the *Ossis* [the Easterners] or whether they will advocate reservation and distrust. The usual criteria for divining someone's stand on a contentious issue—is he a liberal or a conservative? a practitioner or an academic?—are of no use in this case. If anything, it is a person's age that may help to predict his attitude towards the Easterners. Young people, full of moral outrage, are unwilling to forgive a socialist judge's past; they reject all compromises; insist that this time, the forbearance Germans showed old Nazi judges after the Second World War shall not be repeated. Older people tend to be less certain of their moral superiority. Would they, if fate had let them grow up as East Germans rather than West Germans, have acted any differently? Maybe the memory of their own past mistakes, too, stands in the way of outright condemnation. Still, even among older West Berliners most colleagues I talked to seem more than reluctant to welcome ex-socialist judges or prosecutors with open arms. I am curious about tonight's debate.

The speakers are Dr. Karl-Heinz Beyer, until three weeks ago presiding judge of a civil law panel at the Stadtgericht in East Berlin, and Professor Horst Sendler, President of the Federal Administrative Court. Both men, at least through hearsay, are no strangers to me. Dr. Beyer's name was mentioned many times during my interviews in the Littenstrasse. 'You must talk to Dr. Beyer!' people would say, or 'Dr. Beyer would never have stood for that!' or 'Dr. Beyer was a role model for each of us.' I cannot recall ever having heard such consistent praise for any member of a big bureaucracy. And of Professor Sendler, too, I have the affectionate description by a former associate: a smart, warm, open, energetic man, thus the report; both combative and tolerant. With a good man on each side, East and West should be able to reach some sort of understanding tonight.

The topic has attracted a full house. I count an audience of about 120 people; most of them lawyers, I am sure; most men; most, by the cut of their suits, easily recognizable as *Wessis* (Westerners). Here and there, a cluster of East Berliners, the objects of tonight's debate, are huddling in nervous little groups. They look younger and more colorful than their West Berlin colleagues, like students in a gathering of corporate lawyers, and many of them are women. Dr. Beyer is the first to speak. Personally, the issue of today's debate does not affect him: he has taken early retirement. It is for his young colleagues' sake that he has come. They are 'good-willed, reasonable and knowledgeable young people,' he says, and 'this generation is worth something!' How can he convince the *Wessis* of his claim?

Maybe by describing, as precisely and honestly as possible, the daily work of a judge in the GDR, Dr. Beyer must have thought. Maybe if he explains the concrete conditions under which he and his colleagues operated a Western listener will find it easier to empathize with their real dependencies than with those he might otherwise presume based on his ignorance and justified suspicion. An optimistic strategy, I tell myself. A disastrous strategy, as will very soon become evident.

Dr. Beyer begins his talk by stating the idealized premise of socialist adjudication with which I am by now familiar: 'independent of orders in individual cases, dependent upon society's overall expectations from a judge.' It was a job description 'which was accepted by most members of the judiciary.' But within this framework, Dr. Beyer says, two-thirds of East Germany's judges 'were far removed from Party politics.' Their workday was shaped by the labors and frustrations of an over-bureaucratized economy. They 'did not bend the law but carried it out.' In Dr. Beyer's forty years on the bench as a civil and family law judge, not one decision was the product of someone's interference from outside. 'If you will believe me . . .,' he adds, because he must have noticed the many doubtful faces in front of him. A slight collective restlessness in the room suggests that not many listeners believe him. Dr. Beyer makes a new attempt. Whatever forms of institutional interference existed, he says, were aimed at improving the quality of judicial decision-making. 'Findings had to be correct!' Hence the information network of the 'weekly reports' or the court's co-operation with their 'consultation partners.' Murmurs in the audience. Dr. Beyer ignores them, tries instead to illustrate the importance of effective consultation between lower and higher courts with the help of an example. Take the case of the skinheads responsible for the bloody brawl in the Zion Church in East Berlin in November 1988, he says. Their 'way too lenient' sentences were doubled upon the Prosecutor General's appeal. The district court judges had been taken by surprise: didn't we talk this over with the Regional Court and the Supreme Court? But no: it had been a case of inefficient communication and guidance!

Good heavens, I think. What possessed Dr. Beyer to pick this example? The socialist conviction that law should protect social welfare over individual rights is nowhere less acceptable to us than in the area of criminal law where—we think—punishment should match individual guilt as closely as possible. Why did Herr Beyer not stick with civil or family law cases where he could have explained the socialist state's interest in a trial's outcome in less compromising fashion? But Dr. Beyer continues to hack his way through the ideological thicket. Lower court judges valued the exchange of arguments which was part of the 'consultations,' he says. They asked superior judges for advice rather than turning to other counsel. They knew that the responsibility for each decision remained their own. 'I have myself participated in such exchanges hundreds of times!' he says. Guarded commotion among the listeners.

Things don't improve when Dr. Beyer admits that he has realized, since the momentous autumn of 1989, that consultations, too, can represent an interference with judicial autonomy. Derisive snickering when he reports that the practice has been discontinued. He undertakes one last attempt to pursuade his audience of his young Eastern colleagues' eagerness to learn and of their veritable hunger for the rule of law. These men and women have long recognized and accepted the collapse of socialism, says Herr Beyer. And, bravely ignoring the hostile silence in the room: 'I see no reason at all why their continued employment should endanger the functioning of a democratic judiciary!' He has come to the end of his talk. Reluctant and barely polite applause.

A fiasco. Was it avoidable? I am convinced that almost all West Berlin judges in this room assume that the tasks of East German judges were in essence not very different from their own but were carried out in a spirit of cowardice and political servility unimaginable in themselves or any of their Western colleagues. It might have helped had Dr. Beyer attacked this functional equation: judge = judge. He might have tried to explain to his audience that the tasks and mind-frames of civil or family law judges in the GDR in many ways resembled those of West German social workers. He might have compared the social profiles of West and East German judges: in the Federal Republic, middle-aged and middle-class gentlemen, who after many years of education and on-the-job training enjoy respectable incomes and high social status; in the GDR, more than half of the judges women, below the age of 35, with far shorter periods of schooling than their Western counterparts, and with the salaries of bus drivers or postal clerks. Judges in the two parts of Germany, it seems to me, did not share the same tasks, or shared them only partially. If admitted into the West German judiciary, formerly socialist judges would not simply have to switch political convictions (a change of color that must cause legitimate suspicion) but would have to learn many professional attitudes and techniques from scratch. The job of an apprentice may be harder than that of a turncoat. But it is also more honorable and more likely to elicit sympathy and support. Maybe Herr Beyer's audience might have been more willing to follow this line of reasoning. Maybe not.

In any case, as Professor Sendler now begins to argue for a welcoming policy towards the East Berliners, I realize that he, too, does not ground his plea on an understanding of the systemic differences between the two judiciaries but on the impulses of a warm and open nature. He does not try to analyze but to persuade and thus cannot appeal to his listeners' insight but only to their generosity. An even rarer commodity to come by? Let us keep our own fallibility in mind, Herr Sendler says. Remember that under similar conditions we would not have acted differently from those we now condemn. 'Integrate rather than exclude.' Ask yourself whether your rejection of the East Berliners might not be motivated by a desire to protect your turf. Don't force your colleagues from the East to seek solace from 'the wrong friends.' Everyone must be accorded 'a right to learn,' Professor Sendler says, 'morally as well as intellectually.' When he is finished, again only lukewarm and perfunctory applause.

And now the discussion. But nobody raises his hand. Is everyone in complete agreement? I cannot believe it. Nor can the chair of today's event: he suggests a ten-minute break to gather our thoughts. After the break, the same sullen, almost obstinate silence in the room. In the end, a few good-natured people do stand up to say their part, but their remarks do not challenge the conciliatory message of the two main speakers. West German guest judges need their Eastern colleagues to help them understand the social context of litigation in the new East German states, says a young judge from the Rhineland, now assigned to a court in Potsdam. Maybe an exchange of East and West German judges would advance both sides' understanding, says another West German guest judge, now working in Thuringia. Professor Sendler speaks up one more time. 'I would not dare to go to the wall for the incorruptability of anyone in this room,' he says emphatically. 'Myself not excluded!' Still no reaction from the audience.

I feel short-changed as I walk toward the station to catch my train.

23 November 1990

Making use of a trip to Hamburg, I decide to visit with Professor Hein Kötz, director at the Max Plänck Institute for Foreign and International Private Law, who last month was part of a group of about twenty scholars inspecting the 'Institute for Legal Sciences' at the Academy of Science in East Berlin. Under the Unification Treaty, all East German research institutions must undergo an evaluation procedure to determine their academic merit and viability in a united Germany. The *Wissenschaftsrat*, West Germany's

most prestigious independent scientific body, has been charged with organ-
izing the revision process. Under the socialists, the Berlin institute investigated by Herr Kötz and his colleagues had been called 'Institute for the
Theory of State and Law.' Last February, still under GDR rule, it changed
its name. Since then, the 'State' has vanished not only from the Institute's
title. It will depend upon Herr Kötz and his inspection team-mates' judge-
ment whether at least the Institute itself will have a chance of survival.

It is late afternoon and almost dark outside. A blue and white teapot and
cups are waiting in Herr Kötz' office. The warming candle under the teapot
flickers. But Herr Kötz' report on his inspection tour is anything but cozy.
He and his colleagues spent an entire day at the academy, and he gets
agitated just speaking of it. 'Awful,' he says; 'just awful.' The Institute's
work no good, and its research projects for the future not any better. They
want to do something on Japanese law, don't know the language, haven't
even been to the country! I want to know whether they speak any English.
'Better not ask!' Herr Kötz does not expect anything from the East Berliners. 'It'll have to go,' he says again and again. 'Everything will have to go!'

I have known Hein Kötz and his love of controversy and disputation for
years. So I contradict him: no reason to assume that IQs in the GDR were
lower than in the Federal Republic. Why shouldn't East German academics, too, be capable of useful work? Then let them look for jobs in East
German universities, says Herr Kötz. But he knows as well as I do that East
German universities now hire only people from the West! Well, he can't
help that.

I offer another reason for continuing at least some of the Institute's
members: shouldn't East German academics these days be given the benefit, not of doubt, but rather of hope? Socialism discouraged creative work
and fostered mediocrity. Don't GDR legal researchers now need a creative
pause to gather their thoughts, discover their own strengths, and show their
mettle? But Hein Kötz sees no reason to spend scarce public resources on
such uncertain prospects of future productivity. I find it difficult to disagree
with him. I only need to remind myself of the sterility of intellectual debates
in East Germany's legal literature: its constant repetitions of the most
recent political slogans; its dearth of disagreement and criticism; its lack of
precision, of empirical data, of practical examples, even of references to the
country's own case-law. No, East German 'legal science' does indeed not
look like a promising object for investment. Consider, for instance, what
counted as 'comparative law' in the GDR: the one or two pages under the
heading 'State and Law under Imperialism' published regularly in the '*Neue
Justiz*' (one of the two, or—if I count very generously—five law reviews in
the entire country) in which East German legal academics (including some
of those reviewed by Hein Kötz and his colleagues) in pieces entitled 'The
Historic Fate of the Doctrine of Separation of Powers' or 'Class Struggles

and the Dismantling of Union Rights in the USA' regularly predicted the inevitable fall of bourgois legal institutions. Or the little column 'Read Elsewhere,' again published in the *Neue Justiz*, a collection of press cuttings coming occasionally from fellow socialist papers like *Humanité* or *Morning Star* but more likely than not taken straight from the pages of the *Press and Information Bulletin* of the West German Government, where embarrassing facts about life under capitalism could frequently and conveniently be found.

Of course, there was also more ambitious work. But in East German academic publications, all independent thought had to be so carefully hidden between the lines that the creative energies of a writer seemed primarily taken up with trying to cheat the censor. As a result, an article's intellectual packaging often weighed far more than the bit of insight eventually emerging from the wrapping. East German legal academics, it had always seemed to me, at least in their writings, were busily piling up mattresses to prevent the Princess Party from discovering the pea of truth concealed at their very bottom. But even if the maneuver was successful, the writer, in the end, was left with nothing to show for all his troubles but a little pea.

And yet, I cannot agree with Herr Kötz's draconian remedy of 'everything will have to go.' This is, after all, a reunification: one of the new partners should not be held to standards that are not also applied to the other. How many West German research institutions—including the Max Planck Institute!—would not also reveal quantities of dead wood if submitted to a rigorous investigation by the *Wissenschaftsrat*? All, Herr Kötz admits. And then, I add, should we not bear in mind that these evaluations affect real human beings; that we are dealing with ten, twenty, thirty years of their lives; years that cannot be retrieved? From where do we take the authority to write off, in a single day, the entire lifework of others? Herr Kötz seems irritated. 'Should we have taken three days?' he asks.

2 December 1990

Election Sunday, the first in reunited Germany. We have been asked to tea by Professor Hermann Klenner and his wife in East Berlin. Unlike most of his law school colleagues, Professor Klenner should have few professional worries these days. His well-known past collisions with the Party now single him out like distinguished decorations. In 1958, at the infamous Babelsberg Conference, Hermann Klenner had been accused of 'revisionism' and for two years had been banned to the post of mayor in a forgotten village in the Oderbruch marshes. In 1968, after another political rencontre, another demotion: this time from the Humboldt University's law faculty to the Central Institute for Philosophy at the Academy of Sciences. Working in jurisprudence and legal history also helped Hermann Klenner to evade Party pressures for political compliance: at least on the face of it, he could pretend to steer clear of contemporary issues and seek refuge with the great spirits of the past. With most other reputations around him now collapsing, Professor Klenner is one of the small number of East German academics who have held on to their good name under the new age.

Not that he was a dissident. Like the particularly brilliant and rebellious child of lackluster parents, Hermann Klenner caused the Party much worry but was also its darling. Scolded and praised, punished and rewarded, he was now given, now denied permission to travel abroad, was assigned to important posts, kicked out of them, and in the end was even awarded the *Nationalpreis*, the highest honor for intellectual achievement in the land. With all the to and fro, Hermann Klenner managed to keep in better contact with Western colleagues and to preserve more of his intellectual independence than most other law professors in the GDR. In 1986, when he attended a conference at the University of California, Professor Klenner also spent a few days at my law school in Texas. One of my colleagues used the occasion to ask the exotic visitor to speak to the students of his con-stitutional law class. 'That was no socialist,' the host afterwards reported to me, pleased with event but also a little disappointed. 'That was an ordinary liberal!' Hermann Klenner would certainly have disagreed. Despite his altercations with the system, he was—in his own ascerbic way—also very much part of it. I remember well a conversation we had in November 1989, a few days after the opening of the Berlin Wall. 'What's going to happen to socialist law?' I had asked. 'Now we'll finally get going,' Herman Klenner said like someone flexing his muscles to pull the stranded cart out of the ditch.

The Klenners live in Prenzlauer Berg, one of the older parts of East Berlin, in a pre-war apartment house whose sparse and elegant *Bauhaus* lines are blurred by dust and peeling paint. In their apartment not a wall is unlined by bookshelves. In many places, the volumes are stacked in double rows. But he has a system for finding his way about, Hermann Klenner says.

Our talk turns to the Academy of Sciences. Herr Klenner is angry at the ruthless inspectors from the *Wissenschaftsrat*. How could Professor Dieter Simon from Frankfurt, its chair, only weeks before the investigation, pub-lish an article in the *Frankfurter Allgemeine* in which he demanded—ob-viously with East German legal academics in mind—that 'now redundant experts should not be allowed to hog scarce public resources by merely relabelling their area of expertise' and that 'any efforts to find new aca-demic posts for former East German scholars should best be avoided'? How could a review following such demands still be called impartial? And how could the inspectors, in a single day, arrive at their verdict? Obviously, its results had been determined in advance.

Although the Academy has, for more that twenty years, provided
Hermann Klenner with shelter in precarious political weather, he does not
seem to mourn its imminent demise. But he wants respect and justice for
those of its members—among the lawyers, in his estimate, about a third of
the staff—who even under socialism did interesting and solid work. He
disagrees with my suggestion that a moratorium of hope be granted even to
those scholars whose performance in the past was less than impressive. 'But
why?' he asks. Because good legal scholarship was virtually impossible
under socialism, I say, and because at least the young people now need time
to discover their own strength and to prove it to others. No, Hermann
Kenner won't accept that. Real talent will always find its way, he says. The
intellectual poverty of the past was no excuse for mediocre work. If worst
came to worst, one could always write 'for one's desk drawer.'
    I think he is mistaken. Good scholarship must be learned: through read-
ing, role models, discussions, criticism, disagreement, pride in one's own
success. That requires unhindered access to literature, public debates, critical readers, independent publishers—freedom of thought. I imagine a
young legal scholar working in East Germany on his dissertation—not, like
Hermann Klenner, in a relatively sheltered corner like legal history or
philosophy, but in a field close to the exercise of power: in criminal law,
administrative law, or law and economics. For this young man or woman,
many questions were taboo and many answers already settled by the Party.
In his university, Western literature could be found, if at all, only in the
library's 'poison cabinet' and could be obtained only with special permission. Trips to the West and contacts with Western colleagues were out of
the question. He knew that his dissertation's success would at least in part
depend upon its 'refutation of bourgeois theories' and its 'utilization of
Soviet experiences.' And he did not have to be told to wear the blue shirt of
the Free German Youth organization for the viva. How could he learn good
scholarship? From whom? I find it hard to believe that outside political
pressures could simply be shrugged off once you were seated at your own
desk.
    Even those scholarly articles 'written for the drawer' thus show marks of
what East German intellectuals describe as 'the scissors in the head.' Now
occasionally unearthed and published with many years' delay, these once
forbidden articles demonstrate how in an age of general timidity the
boundaries of courage are redefined. Hermann Klenner, too, had one of his
'drawer articles' recently come out: a piece called 'Legislation and Legality,'
written in 1956, in which he pleaded for more precise rules governing the
regulatory powers of socialist state agencies and for a clear-cut hierarchy of
different categories of legislation. *State and Law*, the East German law
review which once rejected the piece, now decided to publish it, thirty-five
years after its original inception and only months before the journal's own

demise. But reading this article or others of its kind reminds me of looking through an album of faded photographs that record long forgotten and now unintelligible happenings. Had I not been told in advance that I was about to read a dangerous and subversive text, I would not have noticed it. Even so, I have to read the pages twice to determine what exactly it was that at the time caused the misgivings of an apprehensive editorial board. True, Hermann Klenner's article wants to subject the socialist legislative process to formal rules and procedures. But his criticism does not go to the heart of the traditional weakness of legislatures under socialism. His proposed rules would not have allowed East German citizens to use the law for their protection against the state. He did not attack the socialist doctrine of a 'unity of powers.' Even Hermann Klenner at the time knew too well who was in control. If he now claims that 'quality' provides the magic formula for distinguishing good socialist legal scholarship from bad, this very claim, I think, bears witness to the fact that even socialists like Hermann Klenner cannot admit to the full measure of intellectual devastation wrought by the political system they believed in.

3 December 1990

Herr Beckert, the other day, had mentioned the names of two young colleagues from the Supreme Court who had recently opened a law partnership in East Berlin. I should go and see them. Of course, the telephone number is not yet listed. So I set out on foot to find their office in the Scharnhorst-Strasse, behind the Charité Hospital in an undecisively ugly part of town close to what is left of the Wall. I walk past construction projects, empty lots still reminiscent of wartime ruins, a few decaying socialist apartment houses and—a recent Western contribution to the quarter— a barrack housing a sex shop. A name-plate points to the side entrance of a low brick building. No further sign, no doorbell. I enter an empty hallway smelling of paint. From there a pencilled note directs me to the second floor. Finally, the right door, opened by a tall young woman who turns out not to be the receptionist but Dr. Ilona Maria Eichhorn, one of the partners, and who leads me straight into her brand-new office. Whitewashed walls, plain furniture, a poster on the wall, some plants. Everything looks inexpensive, fresh, and full of hope.

Dr. Eichhorn had not been with the Supreme Court for very long. Like many law students in the GDR, she had initially planned to become an attorney. Why? Because she admired the black robes of defense attorneys (worn not in East German courts but on West German television); because she was not interested in natural sciences and too ambitious to want to be a teacher; because her grades had been good enough to assure her of a place in law school even though her parents were members of the intelligentsia.

Law school had been easy. But then, as usual, the few available spaces in
lawyers' colleges had been over-subscribed, and the young law school
graduate had been 'directed' towards the judiciary. Three times, Frau
Eichhorn had tried to leave the bench for a job in industry or academics;
once, even got so far as to sign a contract for a post at Humboldt University.
But the Ministry of Justice would not let her go. There were not enough
judges in East Germany. So Frau Eichhorn eventually made her peace with
the Supreme Court; more easily so, since her contract with the Court
allowed for time off to finish her dissertation. She had been assigned to the
Family Law Senate, and there was lots to do. Not many contacts with judges
from the other Senates—'it was a weird collective,' Frau Eichhorn says—
but the work was interesting. The Court's ambitions were focused on improving the legal quality of lower-court case-law and Frau Eichhorn felt
comfortably settled in her job.

And then came Gorbachev; came the outrage and disappointment when
GDR leaders pooh-poohed his reforms as a mere 'change of wallpaper' in
a neighbor's home and when the Soviet journal *Sputnik* disappeared, as too
liberal, from East German news-stands; came finally the intellectual and
political upheavals of 1989. Was it a good year? No, a terrible year. So many
discussions, so much strife; the young people at the Court at war with the
older ones; the wretched rehabilitation cases now beginning to flood the
Court; worst of all, the growing realization that all those painful accusations
against their state which they at first had waved off as capitalist propaganda
and then, with qualifications, had just barely thought believable, were sur-
passed by an even more despicable reality.

They debated the urgency and scope of possible reforms; were pleased
with their own courage for leaving a copy of the *Neue Zeit* openly on their
desk; got so carried away by their political discussions that occasionally
arguments at the Supreme Court came close to fist-fights. And then it
turned out that their posts, which they had so heroically put at risk, were
lost anyway; that the political system they wanted to reform was long
beyond repair; and that they were not at the spearhead of a historic movement but had merely fought silly and useless private battles at its rear. In the
end, when most older justices had already left the Court, Frau Eichhorn had
stayed behind only because someone, after all, had to do the rehabilitation
cases. No, definitely not a good year.

I want to know what Frau Eichhorn thinks about the re-employment of
formerly socialist judges under the rule of law. Well, she does not want to
speak for others. But as far as she herself is concerned, Frau Eichhorn is
relieved no longer to be a judge. She had in the past so contentedly buried
herself in her work, had so readily excused the system's flaws as the personal foibles of a few old men, had so happily concentrated 'on keeping her
desk in order,' that she no longer trusts herself. Obviously, Frau Eichhorn

had not noticed injustices which were conspicuous even at the time. Who was to guarantee that she would show sounder political instincts and more backbone in the future? Much better be a lawyer. Hadn't she always wanted to be an attorney anyway? As of now, Frau Eichhorn still needs her official admission to the Bar. But her application is being processed. And courts are generous these days and admit her as counsel even though the final documents have not yet arrived. Clients are coming, too; the hospital's proximity turns out to be a real advantage. She and her partner are going to make it, she believes.

No, Frau Eichhorn has no quarrels with her fate.

4 December 1990

Public soul-searching at the Humboldt University's Law Faculty in East Berlin. Tonight is a meeting at which students and professors are scheduled to ask and answer questions about their past. It takes place in the University's Council Hall on the first floor, a room of quiet elegance: parquet floors, raised seats for the professoriat behind a balustrade of polished wood, a grand piano, greenery. The room is packed. The entire law faculty has come; so have research assistants and administrative personnel, guests from the Free University and the Technical University in West Berlin and above all a crowd of students, many of them only with standing room. Nobody sits on the empty professors' chairs behind the balustrade.

Professor Rosemarie Will speaks the opening words. She is the controversial dean of the Humboldt Law Faculty. Westerners distrust her because of her past: membership of the SED (East Germany's Communist Party); until its big financial scandal, also member of the PDS, the SED's much-berated successor; adherent of the 'Third Way', a group of Party outsiders who in the years prior to 1989 began to advocate the need for fundamental political change in the GDR; and after the *Wende*, when a separate East German state still seemed possible, participant in the round-table discussions on constitutional reform. In the eyes of her critics, Frau Will's present political stance reflects the ambivalence of her curriculum vitae. She is not prepared simply to write off the past. Rather, she wants to reject the bad, use what is still useful, learn from mistakes and, most important, wants to manage her faculty's intellectual and moral rehabilitation with the active involvement of all concerned. It is primarily due to Professor Will's amazing energy that law teaching at Humboldt has already undergone an almost total change. A new and staggered curriculum introduces formerly socialist students to West German law, providing the strongest doses of capitalist instruction to those who have the least time left to absorb it. Students in their fourth and final year, who next summer will be the last law students to graduate under GDR rules, have the most to catch up. They are almost exclusively taught by West German guest professors who at Frau Will's invitation now roam the corridors of Humboldt's law wing. East Berlin law professors assist their colleagues from the West, sit in on their classes, teach students from younger years, who started their education late enough not to require total intellectual remodelling, and concentrate on the school's less ambitious evening program. Older law teachers try to revive their acquaintance with the Civil Code of 1900, now again in force in all of Germany, which (although much amended) had also governed East German civil law relationships until the passage of the GDR's own Civil Code in 1975. And everyone reads, reads, and reads.

'Well, if it weren't for Rosi Will . . . ,' I hear everywhere where lawyers discuss the future of the Humboldt University. Sometimes the tone is weary: if it weren't for Rosi Will, life would be easier: less commotion, less of a struggle to seize the rudder and determine one's own course of reform. In the West, the tone is hostile: if it weren't for Rosi Will, East Berlin law professors could no longer succumb to the illusion (or get away with the pretense?) of wanting to pull themselves out of the morass by their own bootstraps. Among professors and students at the Humboldt University, the tone is also grateful: yes, if it weren't for Rosi Will, there would be no hope of professional survival, let alone a chance to straighten out a self-made mess through self-determined efforts.

Frau Will herself is often at her wits' end. She is operating on unfamiliar grounds; must constantly maneuver, push, resist, persuade, command, and mediate; and is always dependent upon the approval of the City's Senate Administration where almost no one watches her efforts with sympathy. And the rules of the game are new and confusing. 'I can't tell you what types of decisions in this new society can be controlled with money,' I heard her say the other day in response to a student's question that had suggested a link between the Senate's financial policy and its hostility towards the Humboldt University. Nor can she seek consolation in her past. '*Ach*, I went along like everybody else,' she once said, tired and depressed. But she does not believe that these past mistakes should now disqualify her from fighting for a better and fairer present. So she fights: determined, stubborn, with a down-to-earth sense for practicalities and and an almost childlike directness and lack of disguise which either leaves *Wessis* offended or wins them over to her cause. And now she sits in her familiar red sweater at the moderator's table and hopes that today's exercise in self-inspection will get off to a good start.

It does not look like it. The evening had been planned to give law students and teachers a chance to inquire into and reflect upon their faculty's close involvement with a dishonest and repressive political system. It should not be too difficult to come up with some questions on this score. What did you really believe in? Where did you compromise? How obvious were the consequences of your decisions? What were your rewards? What are you ashamed of? But no questions come. Finally, one of the Humboldt law professors raises his hand: he wants to make 'some very personal comments.' But the paper he pulls from his coat pocket and reads to the assembly is anything but personal. Instead, we hear a carefully composed text that does not speak of hopes and worries but of 'psychological states of being' and 'the subjective conditions of honesty.' Not: this is what I was afraid of; here is where I went wrong. Why so complicated? I ask myself. I know a little bit about the speaker; he was described to me as a thoughtful and decent man. I do not think he is looking for excuses. Maybe current events are too overwhelming to allow those caught up in them to call their guilt and *Angst* by its proper name. Maybe the speaker is still caught in the bilingual mode of socialist communication; does not yet manage to use his private human language in this public forum. In any case: he does not reach his audience. Towards the end, his text says something about 'the young people who were entrusted to our care.' The young people applaud, reserved and a little bored.

And now it is their turn. Will they be more outspoken? No. A young man rises and reads another prepared statement demanding that 'even the most painful questions must be asked.' But not here, everyone seems to think; not now, not by me. Finally, to break the silence, one of the West Berlin guest professors takes the floor. I know him well; only recently, he had confessed to me how much he preferred teaching at the Humboldt University to teaching at his own school back in West Berlin because here, people were open and involved and here, what he had to offer was really wanted. He is not the man to hide his views. 'I am intentionally blunt about things here in East Berlin,' he had told me, 'because attempts at sensitivity come too darn close to the tactfulness of an undertaker.' Today, as always, he is frank. He does not go for all this self-reflection, he says. The past can't be made over. Crimes are a matter for the prosecutor and political offenses should go to the University's Honor Tribunal, which will investigate a faculty member's possible misconduct under socialism. Beyond that, questions of 'character' are a private matter. He finds the students' moral condemnation of their professors quite embarrassing. The quality of a person's work should count. Performance is the only evaluation criterion with predictive value. About the past, one can talk later 'if one day we should have lots of time.'

At first, hesitant murmurs in the audience. Then lively applause. I am pleased that a student gets up to contradict my colleague: how can one deal with the future without first having faced the past? And by the way, not only the professors were to be blamed! The students, too, had every reason 'to eat humble pie.' It looks as if our discussion is up and running. But now Professor Heckelmann, the president of West Berlin's Free University,

speaks up and again steers the evening in the wrong direction. He has other
worries than the past: namely, the future relationship between the
Humboldt University and the Free University. If Humboldt should survive,
both universities, coexisting in the same city and under the authority of the
same Administration, will have to find some *modus vivendi*. How will the
Free University fare with the unexpected and uninvited bedfellow? It is
much richer than the Humboldt University and therefore will probably
have to suffer cuts for the benefit of the East Berliners. It is overcrowded
and therefore will want the Humboldt University to take its share of the
huge number of students now clamouring for an education. That means,
says Professor Heckelmann, that the Free University is very interested in
the kind of instruction offered by Humboldt. If the Humboldt University
deviates too much from Western taste, it will not attract West Berlin students. It must pull its load. But there's the rub: the East Berliners, complains
Herr Heckelmann, 'are not particularly co-operative.' Advice from FU
representatives did not seem welcome. The East Berlin curriculum, taught
largely by guest professors from West Germany (though not from West
Berlin) was at best a 'patchwork'; too many well-known names, not enough
basic courses! And the money, donated by the Free University in the
euphoria following reunification and intended to help the East Berliners to
restock their libraries, had been misallocated: 'way too few texts on administrative law; too many on co-operatives!'

   In other words: we Westerners know better, and you should have asked.
In one respect, I think, Herr Heckelmann's remarks do speak to our topic
tonight: namely, to the question whether the Humboldt Law Faculty can
take control of its own rehabilitation. Yes, Dean Will had said and had
invited those West German professors whose skills and philosophies corre-
sponded best with the faculty's self-perceived needs. No, Professor
Heckelmann says now: you can't manage alone and therefore had better
listen to us. And for the rest of the evening, this authority pattern, now
established, prevails: *Wessis* explain to *Ossis* what needs to be done. A West
Berlin professor, his voice stern and determined, insists that self-reflection
'is now a must' and warns against a repetition of that misplaced forgiveness
which Germans once before displayed towards former Nazi functionaries
('*Ach*, not again,' a woman sighs in the row behind me). Another Western
colleague criticizes the overambition of Humboldt's law curriculum: what
with day and evening classes, correspondence courses and a special program for unemployed lawyers, he says, it has bitten off more than it can
chew. A West German guest professor introduces himself as one of the
'patches' in the 'patchwork' viewed with so much disfavor by Herr
Heckelmann and defends the East Berliners: it is quite useful, he says, that
the Humboldt curriculum is still a little rough and unco-ordinated, because
it teaches the students that 'the right law' is not, as in the past, a simple

matter of state definition but something 'to struggle for.' Long and grateful applause. And none of the Westeners needs a sheet of paper to say his bit. All are articulate, witty, relaxed, with the poise and self-possession of victors. 'If only I could learn to talk like that myself,' each student in the audience must think.

Only a few of them have spoken up tonight. On one occasion, when a first-year student complains about knowing no more about the past of his West German than of his East German professors, there is lively applause. But most young people in the room, like their elders, stay silent and wait for what the *Wessis* have to say. The evening has almost come to a close when a third-year student finally gets up and says: 'We expected a different debate tonight.' He and his friends are worried. Are they learning enough? Why should their East Berlin professors now be qualified to teach West German law? How will the East Berliners ever qualify for their exams? And, addressing a representative of the City's Examination Board, who earlier had been introduced as a guest from West Berlin: will the Board pay attention to the fact that most of the older students' education had taken place under socialism? And if so: will they be able to compete with Western graduates? Or will theirs be 'a thalidomide degree,' evoking pity rather than respect? The man from the Examination Board explains and soothes the fears.

I, too, expected a different debate tonight.

7 December 1990

A visit with the Institute for Legal Sciences at the Academy of Sciences in East Berlin, the object of Herr Kötz' and his colleagues' recent inspection trip. I am curious to learn how the inspected themselves experienced the visit. Unlike the Academy's main building, the Institute does not border on the beautiful Platz der Akademie (about to be renamed, as in pre-socialist days, the Gendarmenmarkt) but lies in the Otto-Nuschke-Strasse (named after a former head of one of the GDR's non-communist parties and also likely to be soon rechristened), a dark and depressing side-street, where I have to climb over large asbestos heating pipes to reach an equally depressing office building, in which the Academy's legal section still has its refuge. In the shaky lift, the 'out of order' signs, often in use, are dangling from a precautionary hook. But today the lift is working.

I have an appointment with Roswitha Svensson: 40 years old; lawyer; 'A-dissertation' 1977; 'B-dissertation' (East Germany's version of the West German 'Habilitation' which like it qualified the candidate for a university career) 1986; in between, a stint at Party headquarters (a not atypical career move for ambitious academics); 1988 professor; since June 1990 deputy director of the Institute. In past weeks, I had encountered Frau Svensson's name whenever the conversation turned to the GDR judiciary: she heads a working group at the Academy engaged in an empirical study of the background and attitudes of East German judges. It involves the first and last opinion poll of socialist judges in Germany and is partially financed by the Ministry of Justice in Bonn. But we must talk about her judges some other time. Today, I have come to hear Frau Svensson's account of that ominous visit from the *Wissenschaftsrat*. How was it?

Dear me, how was it? They had received a preparatory list of questions about the Institute's structure, tasks, personnel, equipment, age profile, and the like, together with the request for a detailed description of their research plans. Someone from the *Wissenschaftsrat* had called ahead to order a room, coffee and sandwiches for the day of the 'visitation.' At nine o'clock on the morning of the dreaded day, the inspectors had arrived: about twenty people; not more than four or five of them lawyers, Frau Svensson thinks; among them Professor Simon, President of the *Wissenschaftsrat*, whose devastating article in the *Frankfurter Allgemeine* every member of the Institute for Legal Studies was bound to have read. Professor Kase, an economist, had headed the group.

He had shaken hands only with Professor Röder, the Institutes's director—nobody else had exchanged the greetings so customary under German rules of etiquette—and for two hours the visitors had withdrawn to the conference room put at their disposal. Then, at 11 a.m., the Institute's leading staff had been asked to join the inspectors: the Director, the deputy directors (Frau Svensson and Professor Hölzer, a specialist on European law), the department heads, and Professor Heuer, chair of the 'Academic Council,' the Institute's newly elected body of self-government. The Western visitors had been seated on one side of the long table, the East Berliners—fewer in number—on the other. Then came the questions. What made us think that we would be able to compete with Western scholars? Hadn't we forfeited the right to analyze our past? Was there any intellectual coherence in our research projects on East German legal history and sociology? Yes, Professor Heuer had replied; the projects all drew on our familiarity with legal developments in the GDR. And then Herr Kötz had said: 'Well, isn't that rather like making the goat the gardener?'

'That's when the stammering set in,' Frau Svensson says. No one among the East Berliners had known how to defend himself. No one had really dared. A few faint-hearted tries, easily parried by the *Wessis*. Two younger members of the inspection team had whispered and smirked behind hands held to faces. And no one from the Institute for Legal Science had stood up and in a flaming speech had thrown back into the inspectors' faces their freedoms, their privileges, their arrogance and their self-satisfaction. What could have empowered such an act of self-assertion? I can imagine the encounter: domesticated members of a species cornered by untamed and savvy relatives from the wild. They hadn't even reached a substantive discussion on the merits of their proposals.

Then came lunch-time. Did East and West Germans go to lunch together? No, no. The inspectors were led to their reserved seats in a restaurant by a young member of the Institute, who returned with a worried report on snippets of conversations overheard along the way. In the afternoon, the inspectors visited the Institute's individual departments to talk directly with its employees. Since Professor Svensson as leading staff was not included in these meetings, she knows this part of the program only from hearsay. Accounts varied. Some people reported open conversations and attentive listeners. Others felt that they had encountered condescension and hostility. As it turns out, the visitors had not only found fault with members of the Institute for Legal Sciences. Some Western colleagues, whom the East Berliners had been happy to win as collaborators on a number of projects, had also been the butt of disparaging remarks. How familiar it all seems to me: the nonchalance, the raised eyebrows, the contented smiles of professors badmouthing their absent colleagues. It is pleasant to show off even to losers.

Finally, after the individual conversations, one more common meeting between the inspectors and the heads of staff, at which the East Berliners had to justify the personnel needs for their different proposals. According to Frau Svensson's description, another disaster. Then—it was already 5 p.m.—the representatives of the Institute once more had to leave the room. The Westerners remained to talk behind closed doors until—oh, it must have been 7 p.m. In the end, a private conversation between Professor Kase and Professor Röder, the Institute's director. Frau Svensson knows of its content. The evaluation's outcome had been predestined from the very start, Herr Röder had said. Vehement denials by Herr Kase. Try to put yourself in our place, Professor Röder had added. What do we have left? 'That is the price we have to pay so our children can grow up in a free society,' was Professor Kase's reply. Yes, he had used the word 'we.'

That was it. After the inspectors had left, the members of the Institute, tired and worn out with waiting, had stayed and talked a while over wine and coffee. Frau Svensson had gone home around 8 p.m., not the last to leave. A week later, a meeting at the Institute to discuss the event. No one believed that the Institute could possibly survive. Since then, the group's unspoken motto seems to be: *sauve qui peut.*

Maybe last year's sudden and drastic political weather-changes help to explain why the Institute for Legal Science could disintegrate so fast and with so little resistance. The rapid transition—from rebellion to liberation and from there to new dependencies, from confusion by way of wild hopes to new worries and fears—has left many of the protagonists cynical and exhausted. But the Institute had always been a disconnected place. Law was a relatively new addition to the Academy of Sciences. The first 'working group on legal science' was established as late as 1967 under Professor Hermann Klenner, only to be dissolved the following year after Klenner's supposedly revisionist fall from grace. Next, a three-year pause to ensure ideological disinfection. In 1971, the present Institute was founded, then called 'Institute for the Theory of State and Law.' Its first director was Professor Wolfgang Weichelt, chairman of the People's Chamber's Committee on Constitution and Legislation and all his life a loyal servant of the system. Professor Weichelt seems to have viewed the sixteen years of his stewardship primarily as a political and administrative job. Academic ambitions came second. The Institute did *Grundlagenforschung*: 'basic research' reaffirming the primary political tenets of the Party. Empirical work 'conflicted with security concerns.' Criticism and debate were tolerated within the Institute's own four walls—enough of it, says Frau Svensson, 'to enable us to swallow other things'—but were on no account allowed to penetrate to the outside. 'Nothing ever budged,' Professor Hölzer, one of Frau Svensson's colleagues at the Institute, later confessed to me. And: 'We had almost no impact on any decision-making processes.'

But Gorbachev's rise in the Soviet Union brought a change of weather and an influx of younger people eager to challenge old habits. Discussions livened up; research stirred with new ambitions. Not all new undertakings bore fruit. An opinion poll of judges, planned in 1985, was called off by the Minister of Justice and did not progess beyond the stage of questionnaire. A 'Study on Deputies,' submitted in the fall of 1988 to the Central Committee's Department of State and Law, never reached the department's executive. Professor Weichert, already ill with cancer, was personally summoned to come and retrieve the hapless document. 'In the interest of a harmonious work-place I prefer not to have seen it,' someone at the Central Committee had told him.

But even failures were useful. Even if a research project foundered, it was difficult to retreat beyond the point its discussion already had established. Without anyone taking much notice, the boundaries of what was thinkable at the Institute expanded. The 'Study on Deputies,' rejected by the Central Committee, was discreetly circulated among colleagues 'if they were reliable.' 'Please, don't get me wrong,' Professor Hölzer, who told me of the story, had added immediately. 'This had nothing to do with political resistance. We all thought of ourselves as good socialists. But we were dissatisfied socialists.' They did not want to undermine but to improve the system. Still, as if wakened by rain after a long drought, even the Academy of Sciences, here and there, began to put out new green shoots.

And when the *Wende* came, at least some members of the Institute were eager and ready for change. Frau Svensson's project on the judiciary began to take shape in the last months of 1989; since January 1990, it has been running at full speed. The new empiricists, finally unshackled, threw themselves enthusiastically into their work. Short of funds, they paid for part of the preliminary work themselves. When the questionnaires were first tested in other towns, they spent their nights on the sofas or floors of friends and colleagues. A working-group on criminology, which like Frau Svensson's group was established in January 1990, began to draw up a 'criminal profile' of the GDR and to work out a sophisticated framework for an analysis of East German criminal policy. Institute members sought contacts with West German and foreign scholars. Old administrative hierarchies were replaced by new democratic structures: a new director appointed, an 'Employee Assembly' voted in, a 'Scientific Council' elected to debate the Institute's research plan, which in the past had been determined by the Director, the Deputy Heads and by 'those higher up.' In the spring of 1990, the new council met almost every week.

Nearly everyone at the Institute welcomed the turnabout. But even in the excitement of new and unheard-of possibilities, most members wanted not a revolution but a transition. The vote on the 'Academic Council,' Frau Svensson says, produced some astonishing results. Twenty-five candidates had competed for fifteen seats. Some of the old department heads did not make it. Most votes went to the 'moderate reformers,' those people who could be expected 'not to turn everything upside down.' Professor Röder, who had been the only candidate for the office of director, was elected because of his authority, his poise, his experiences in the outside world— not because of a particular scholarly philosophy. People wanted to start anew but not to cut off and deny the old. Transplanted trees need an established root system. Their past might not be something to be proud of; nevertheless, most members of the Institute of Legal Sciences wanted to keep it.

There were enough new lessons to be learned. The confusion of literature! The academic controversies! The competition! And, above all, the exercises in democracy! The other day, Herr Klenner recounted an incident that had happened at the Academy of Sciences' Institute for Philosophy. A meeting of one of the many new committees engaged in self-government. One is about to vote. 'Openly or in secret?' someone asks. 'Well, let us first have a vote on procedure,' someone else suggests. 'No, no,' says a third committee member, 'if only one of us wants a secret vote, we have to do it in secret.' They do it in secret.

But already in the summer of 1990, rumors begin to spread. There is talk of impending evaluations by Western experts—scarier yet, of the possibility that the entire Academy of Sciences might be closed down. The word *Abwicklung* (closure) is mentioned, first just an unfamiliar technical term, but soon a synonym for everybody's fears. At the Institute for Legal Sciences, members begin to wonder which of their research projects is most likely to find favor in West German eyes. There is furtive and not-so-furtive infighting for survival. In September 1990, the Scientific Council appoints a 'Curatorium' of mainly West German and foreign academics meant to advise the East Berliners on research projects and to back them in their upcoming encounter with the *Wissenschaftsrat*. The Curatorium develops plans for cutting and streamlining the Institute's research projects to ensure at least its partial survival. And what had the inspectors thought of these attempts? They had picked the 'wrong advisers,' Professor Simon had told Frau Svensson and her colleagues. Now the *Wissenschaftsrat* would have to take the trouble to knock down what others had taken the trouble to build up.

What next? Frau Svensson does not know. There is no official word yet on the results of the evaluation. Their budget extends only to 31 December. Since reunification, collaborative undertakings with Western colleagues have fizzled out: the East Germans are no longer considered interesting. Anyone at the Institute who can find outside work is leaving. As to be expected, the best people are the first to go. At the Institute, many offices are empty; the corridors deserted. All outside telephone lines but one have been disconnected. By and by, the building in the Otto-Nuschke-Strasse is taken over by West German attorneys. One of them, Frau Svensson says, does nothing but bankruptcies.

11 December 1990

Back again at the Institute for Legal Science to continue where I left off last week: with a study of the 'Report in Response to the Questions Posed by the *Wissenschaftsrat*,' the Institute's scholarly self-portrait and plea for survival. The director is ill and I am allowed to use his office; a friendly secretary brings coffee. The room could be anywhere: a modern conference table, a couple of comfortable armchairs, a desk, a safe. Outside, snow is falling against a dark sky.

What do you do that others could not do just as well or better? the *Wissenschaftsrat* had asked the East Berliners. Are there important reasons for letting your projects survive at the expense of others? A disquieting question that I would not like to have to answer for myself. Three or four hours, I sit in the grey quiet of Herr Röder's room and pore over the answers, interrupted only by a quick lunch of roll and Wieners in the building's cafeteria. What could the *Wissenschaftsrat* learn from these pages? What can I learn?

My first impression is one of scarcity, if not outright impoverishment. The East Berliners had to make do with very limited means. Even the report presents itself in modest garb: three cardboard folders in faded yellow, the paper rough and porous, the print greyish and unassuming. The Institute's financial balance sheets remind me of the extraordinary privilege of American academic life. The Academy of Science's law library subscribed to 282 journals and newspapers—the Law Library of the University of Texas receives 6,020. Each year, 37,000 marks were spent on acquisitions and subscriptions in East Berlin—my Law School in Texas spends $855,000. The university-trained employees at the Institute, from the young law school graduate to the Institute's deputy director, earned between 1,400 and 2,880 marks a month—before taxes! I am embarrassed to compare these sums with my own salary.

Financial restraints were compounded by geographic restrictions. Sixty per cent of the Institute's associates were so-called 'travel cadres': people allowed occasional excursions to the West. But even they had to reapply for a specific permit before each trip—and hard currency was in short supply. That meant that most travelling professionals went to the East. If someone attended a learned conference abroad, more likely than not it took place at one of the sister academies in Eastern Europe. Professional contacts with colleagues in capitalist countries were subject to strict constraints that only in very recent years seemed to relax a little. Only the Institute's international lawyers sustained halfway reliable ties with the West: attended meetings abroad, held memberships in international organizations and occasionally published in English.

But to most members of the Institute of Legal Sciences, the world at large was out of bounds. And even life at home seemed pretty far removed: sponsored research, requested and financed by specific clients and geared to the solution of practical problems in industry or administration, did not exist—at least not in the immediate sense of the word. That all research at the Institute owed loyalty to its only sponsor, the state, went without saying. Again, only the international lawyers maintained some contact with real-world affairs and occasionally did expert opinions for the Foreign Ministry. But by and large, most members of the Institute were only scholars, working only in the GDR, focusing only on topics and using only literature acceptable to the powers that be. Political, geographic and financial constraints imperceptibly overlapped and blended into one and the same condition of dependence. I am reminded of a conversation many years ago with a pastor in Weimar. 'What is worse,' I had asked, 'the lack of freedom or the fact that there are no oranges or bananas in the stores?' 'It's the same,' he had replied. 'The worst is that you never have a choice.'

What else can I learn from the Institute's report? That like all other academic institutions of this world—my own not excluded—it has a staff of very mixed ability. Some members rarely publish. Here is someone who wrote forty-four pages during the last five years, and here is someone else, who in the same time-span produced twenty-one pages and a chapter in a book. At DM 1,430 a month, the output should, perhaps, not come as a surprise. Frau Svensson had already told me that it was quite possible 'to take life easy' at the Institute. With luck, unproductive colleagues could be 'praised away' and might move on—maybe to the Humboldt University or the Academy of Social Sciences. Realistically, they could not be fired. At least, not for reasons of incompetence. But even someone who two or three years before the *Wende*, during the opening debate on a departmental research project, had suggested a comparison between socialist and fascist law (A madman? A hero? Somebody who just didn't care anymore?) had not been fired—he had been 'transferred' to the library and kept busy until he finally received his exit visa to West Germany. Some colleagues came to the Institute because, for whatever reason—political, professional, personal—they had reached an impasse in their former lives. In a close country, such career moves could temporarily gain a person a little space. And finally, I find in these pages the long-familiar names, often encountered in the literature, of those whose productivity nobody could possibly dispute: the Institute's true scholars.

Can the report tell me something about the quality of their work? Of course not: to judge that, I would have to sit down in earnest and read. But even reading, I have found, will not always allow me to evaluate the writer's merits. I can tell from a piece whether its author is learned or smart or whether he can write. But I find it very difficult to draw from it conclusions as to the writer's creativity. In part, because the boundaries of the permissible were so narrowly drawn in the GDR that the most interesting debates did not take place in print but in oral conversations: at conferences, office meetings, or over lunch in the faculty cafeteria. In part, because intellectual and academic conventions differ widely from place to place. In many years of reading, I only very rarely encountered an article in an East German law review that made me want to take my hat off to its author. But I also discovered that my intellectual tastes are no longer the same as those of many of my West German colleagues. What they praise as being solid and thorough, I often find boring. If they are annoyed by inconsistent or unsystemic legal constructions, I am annoyed if a particular interpretation does not shed light on underlying social realities. In the GDR, where the German penchant for meandering abstraction was reinforced by the socialist bent toward conceptual rigidity and compounded by most authors' attempts to hide behind political platitudes, the outcome was a legal literature so tenuously related to real life that I have difficulty discovering any social meaning between its lines.

Could my lack of comprehension also be due to the different scholarly paradigms under which I and my East German colleagues operate? Even free academics may be caught behind their garden fence. Here is an example. A few years ago the Critical Legal Studies Movement, a group of American and European left-wing legal academics, decided to meet not, as usual, in the United States, but at the University of Bremen in West Germany. All members of the group shared basic theoretical convictions; most knew each other; many were friends. Indeed, the meeting had been planned to demonstrate intellectual openness and transnational solidarity. It turned out to be an exercise in cultural dissonance. The Americans smiled incredulously at the conceptual concoctions of the Germans; the Germans shook their heads over the naïve eclecticism of the Americans. I would have loved to be there to catch the little squibs and snide remarks when members of each group—once safely amongst themselves—poked fun at the other. But since everyone, after all, was friends, the event was later redescribed on both sides of the Atlantic by some unspoken agreement as an important mutual learning experience. Here in East Berlin, at the collision of East and West German styles of legal scholarship, only the East Berliners have to do the learning.

Will they be able to? To judge by their research proposals, there are many other capitalist skills still foreign to the East Berliners, such as the art of pleading for money. Clearly, the members of the Institute have not yet learned to sell their projects. Even under socialism, it was crucial to convince those higher up of the importance of your work. But while in the GDR reports for the Party bureaucracy had to be optimistic, loyal, and politically correct, grant proposals submitted to potential West German sponsors should be critical, well documented, and precise. Many of the projects I find listed on the sheets before me are far too vague and unsubstantiated to convince a Western critic. But they address important issues, particularly those projects focusing on the growth and decay of law and legal scholarship in the GDR, which arguably should not be dealt with by the East Germans alone but which could never be handled without the full involvement of those who have known and experienced socialist law from the inside. But what had Professor Simon said about Frau Svensson's project on the judiciary? 'You're done, aren't you. The questionnaires are all in.' At my school back in Texas, we view the fact that someone just completed a good piece of work as the most reliable guarantee that he will continue to do good work in the future. That prediction implies, of course, that he is allowed to have a future.

Evening

Another debate on the integration of East Berlin judges into the *Rechtsstaat*, again organized by the West Berlin Association of Administrative Judges and taking place at the same venue as last time, the Plenary Chamber of the Administrative Court in West Berlin. The introductory talk is given by an official from the Documentation Center on SED-Injustice in Salzgitter, West Germany, which for the last thirty years has collected victims' reports on their encounters with the East German machinery of law enforcement. It is a depressing litany of border shootings, secret police surveillance, and the repression of dissent at home. But when the speaker has finished, the tragedy, as in ancient Greek theatre, is followed by a satyr play. The association's chairman gets up and provides a little addendum to our last meeting on 25 October, when to my surprise the same contentious topic as today's had not resulted in a meaningful discussion. We now learn why. The audience's silence last October had not meant that most people in the hall agreed with Dr. Beyer's and Professor Sendler's plea for generosity towards the *Ossis*. On the contrary: immediately after the meeting, a dozen or so disgruntled listeners—all West Berlin judges—had gotten together and in a letter to Professor Limbach, the Senator of Justice, had complained about attempts to include into their fold 'people without that independence, authority, and strength of character' which are 'the distinguishing qualities of a *Rechtsstaat* judiciary.' But why had they not spoken up at the meeting itself when, Lord knows, they had plenty of opportunities to have their say? Because they had not dared to contradict the President of the Federal Administrative Court, because their own superior judge had also been among the audience, and because they had wanted to hide disagreement within their own ranks from the East German visitors. I am reminded of a remark one of the judges at the Littenstrasse courthouse once made when we were discussing the relationship between West Berlin judges and the judicial administrators in City Hall. 'Just another case of power relations,' she had said in that cheerful and down-to-earth Berlin dialect that in West Berlin is the trade mark of taxi drivers but that in East Berlin you are just as likely to hear from judges or prosecutors. Just another case of power relations? From everything I know about Herr Sendler and his court, the diagnosis does not fit. More likely just another case of 'scissors in the head', it seems to me.

19 December 1990

It is now official: the Humboldt University will be taken over by the State of Berlin but not in its entirety. Those departments particularly steeped in Marxist-Leninist ideology will either be closed down (like the notorious Institute for Criminology) or—if their subjects will be kept in the curriculum—will be closed down only to be reopened in reconstituted form and with new staff. Whether this second form of institutional purification conforms to the Unification Treaty strikes me as doubtful: the Treaty allows only the *Abwicklung* (closure) of those East German institutions whose services are no longer needed in a market democracy. If a department's subject continues to be taught at Humboldt University, it would seem that the department, too, preserves its *raison d'être*. Faculty members whose involvement in past repression makes their continued employment unconscionable can, of course, be fired. But under the Unification Treaty, these would be individual dismissals, requiring in each case proof of misconduct. At least on the face of it, the Treaty does not allow the convenient wholesale exchange of staff—West for East—at institutions that otherwise continue to function.

If such legal objections were ever raised in the debates preceding yesterday's decision, they certainly were not heeded. The Senate's resolution is unequivocal: *Abwicklung* not for the Humboldt University at large but only for certain objectionable departments. Which of the departments must go (and which must die only to be born again in Western guise) will be determined in the next few days. Rumor has it that besides History and Economics, the Law Faculty is considered beyond moral and political rehabilitation and therefore likely to be closed. Coming Saturday, at a second special Senate meeting dealing with Humboldt's fate, the rumors will be confirmed.

20 December 1990

In the 'movie room,' one of the large lecture halls at Humboldt University. The teacher's union has called a platform discussion on 'Union responses to the *Abwicklungs* decree.' About seventy people have come. They sit dispersed throughout the auditorium, on threadbare velvet seats; most of them older, all with worries written on their faces. The woooden table-top above my knees carries a carved message: 'I want out!' Someone must have taken at least an hour for the job. I wonder whether the outcry referred—pre-1989—to the GDR or—post-1989—to a particularly boring lecture.

At the long table on the dais sit union people, a lawyer, a few student representatives. It does not take us long to move from general complaints about the lopsided character of Germany's reunification to the specific problems of each employee now fearing for his job. A union man gives tactical advice. If, as is likely, faculty and staff of the doomed departments are offered temporary extensions of their contracts—after all, classes must go on and it will take the Senate Administration some time to revamp whole faculties—one should carefully weigh the options. Accept the offer? It demonstrates, after all, that a particular function is still needed and thus weakens the Senate's legal case under the Unification Treaty. Reject the offer? Since the Administration is now faced with the difficult task of securing an uninterrupted teaching schedule without permanent staff, a unison refusal of 'closed down' faculties to play along may put pressure on the Administration and improve the University's bargaining position.

But can a lecturer or secretary who is offered an additional nine months' pay afford to reject that offer? Can he or she rely on others doing the same? From the questions that follow, it is soon obvious that whatever solidarity might have existed at Humboldt prior to the *Abwicklungs* decree now crumbles under its weight. 'This is the worst thing that could happen to us,' says a member of the *Personalrat*, which represents the university's employees. 'It depends on all of you whether we can develop a strategy. You must push us!' he says. But nobody does. Instead of suggestions for concerted action come accusations against others. An employee complains about 'professors concentrating on saving their own skin.' Applause. Someone else criticizes the University's governing body for having held an emergency meeting rather than joining students and staff for a protest demonstration at City Hall. Applause. 'We must talk about the future!' says a union speaker imploringly. Here in the 'movie room' most people seem to worry less about the institution's future than about their own.

Many raised hands. A young man asks for 'concrete instructions': what shall we do if after Christmas they won't let us back into our offices? An old man wants to know whom he can sue: 'The University Rector?' The magic word has fallen, password to the new rule of law: 'to sue.' Of course, an employee could also sue his employer under socialism. But it was rarely necessary. In an economy in which labor was scarce and dismissals next to impossible, most employees had little reason to fear their boss and most bosses were more inclined to overlook their workers' failings than to withhold benefits which were their due. If a disagreement should ever escalate into litigation, an employee could count on lenient colleagues (most labor disputes were adjudicated by lay tribunals staffed with fellow workers), benevolent judges (should the case be appealed to the district court), and the charitable rules of the Labor Code. East German labor law adjudication could be annoyingly didactic. But the process was not threatening. Reading its case-law, I occasionally had the feeling of watching spoiled children trying to get the better of well-meaning and indulgent parents. I remember the case of someone who, having repeatedly missed work, been drunk on the job, and insulted his superiors, managed after several lawsuits to settle for a voluntary discharge with back pay until the Supreme Court finally put its foot down and quashed the settlement 'for concealing the factual and legal issues at stake.'

Under capitalism, labor litigation takes place in a colder climate. There is union support, and there are often solicitous labor court judges. But now, the employee's lawsuit must suddenly defend a job that under socialism rarely was at risk. And now, an employee suing his employer can no longer rely on the support of his collective. In the old days, when firings were unheard of, most GDR labor litigation took place with the worker still securely ensconced at work. But in West Germany, an employee suing his employer has almost always lost his job. By the time he comes to court, he has already been separated from his colleagues. A lawsuit will intensify his isolation: it does not focus on collective issues but only on the plaintiff's

individual rights and obligations. American rules of procedure are not quite
so egocentric: they allow 'class actions,' in which a group of plaintiffs with
similar complaints can join rank to defend a common cause. But under
German law, only personal rights can be pursued in court. However similar
his fate might be to that of others, each employee turning to a court for help
will be strictly on his own. *Chacun pour soi—Dieu pour nous tous.*

Here in the 'movie room,' people recognize and fear the de-solidarization
process which was initiated by the *Abwicklungs* decree and which can only
be accelerated by attempts to defend this or that job through individual
litigation. One of the union members on the podium tries to get away from
legal responses to the crisis and to reinstil politics into the discussion. The
Senate Administration has 'the liveliest interest' in securing the temporary
help of those dismissed, he says. 'Don't go along! Organize union meetings
to co-ordinate your strategies! Schedule the meetings late enough to maxi-
mize time pressures on the Administration!' 'Those guys know that they
need you!'

But everybody in this room also knows that he needs work. I can see that
there will be no common strategy. People do not yet trust either themselves
or their new freedoms. 'That's written in the constitution,' one of the West
Berliners on the podium says at one point. '*Papier ist geduldig*,' mumbles
the woman next to me—'paper is patient.' Like she, it is the recipient of
messages, not their author.

3 January 1991

Again in Hamburg, where I once more visit Professor Hein Kötz at the Max
Planck Institute to ask a few additional questions about his and his colleagues' inspection trip to East Berlin. Since our last conversation, it has
occurred to me that the Max Planck Institute, too—like all big research
facilities jointly funded by the West German Federal Government and the
states—must occasionally be subject to inspections. I am curious to find out
how the periodic review of Professor Kötz' own institute differs from that
which he and his colleagues carried out at the Institute for Legal Science in
East Berlin. Here is the upshot of my inquiry.

Yes, every Max Planck Institute is monitored by an 'Academic Council'
of German and foreign scholars. Herr Kötz and his Hamburg colleagues
nominated their Council's representatives themselves. Council members
regularly receive the Institute's publication list, visit every year or two to
talk to the directors about its work, and write a report. Most of these
visitations, says Herr Kötz, are 'relaxed.' Without an aggressive chairman,
the Academic Council functions mainly 'by way of acclamation.' But their
own chairman 'is quite a hard-nosed fellow,' he adds with an undertone of
collegial respect, who at times 'had given them real grief.' How had they

gone wrong? A publication project had taken much longer than originally scheduled. Had the Academic Council also criticized the project on its merits? No. Hein Kötz' reply is short and matter-of-fact. To go so far as to meddle with the substance of other people's work would seem to violate elementary rules of academic etiquette.

I also learn that the social atmosphere at evaluations tends to be much more civilized in Hamburg than it was in East Berlin. The inspectors of the Max Planck Institute make do without the institutionalized suspicion considered natural at the Academy of Sciences. They do not interview the employees and certainly would never do so in the absence of department heads. Inspectors and inspected go together to lunch and, after a little evening reception at the Institute, to dinner. No need to feel apocalyptical about the event. Does it never happen that an institution's funding is at stake, I ask. Yes, when the Criminological Research Institute in Lower Saxony had been reviewed, it was to determine whether the Institute should be closed down or continued. As in East Berlin, that evaluation had taken place under the auspices of the *Wissenschaftsrat.* 'They played a different tune' on that occasion, says Herr Kötz. The inspectors were scholars with no connection to the Institute. But even there, the directors had been present at all conversations, and both actors and potential victims had gone to lunch together.

And I discover yet another difference between East and West inspections: all members of the Max Planck Institute's Academic Council are legal scholars. Things were different at the Institute for Legal Science in East Berlin, where only about a third of the inspectors had legal training. Did the non-lawyers play an active role in the deliberations? Oh yes, 'they joined the fray like everybody else.' 'But they lacked expertise,' I say. No, they didn't. Even people from outside the field can judge a research project's soundness and promise as long as they are scholars themselves. That depends, I say. Maybe an economist or historian can evaluate whether a legal research project is well argued, consistent, or methodically sound. But he will not be able to tell whether it asks the right questions. To do that, you have to be familiar with GDR legal institutions and case law, know something about the country's legal history, have a sense for social context. Whether it is wise 'to make the goat the gardener' is, I am sure, a question over which scholars of all fields could join in vigorous debate. But it is not a question of the East Berliners' scholarly qualifications.

Why not, says Herr Kötz, surprised. Because it is a political and moral question, I say. The image of 'the goat as gardener' suggests that East German legal scholars were so deeply entangled in the political system of socialism that they can now neither muster the honesty to question its legal implications nor legitimately participate in an investigation of their own history. Whether the members of the Institute for Legal Sciences can indeed be accused of aiding and abetting injustices of the past and whether—even if we assume their guilt—each survivor of socialism should not be given the chance to change his mind and start anew is a question of political ethics, which in extreme cases should be adjudicated by a court and otherwise must find its answer in the political process and in the consciences of all concerned. In any case, the Unification Treaty had authorized the *Wissenschaftsrat* only to assess the East Berliners' scholarly capacity to perform. The inspectors had no mandate to evaluate the likelihood of their colleagues' moral rehabilitation. That means that the non-lawyers in Herr Kötz' evaluation party had not been entitled 'to join the fray like everybody else.'

We finally agree to disagree.

10 January 1991

A day-long colloquium in honor of Hermann Klenner's sixty-fifth birthday at the Institute for Legal Sciences in the Otto-Nuschke-Strasse. It meets in a large, unexpectedly elegant room on the ground floor of the building before an elegant academic public from East and West: grey-haired gentlemen in grey suits; a few ladies, equally sedate in dress; some young people. The room is very hot. Its large windows, facing the street, are barred.

The morning's topic is 'The Philosophy of Law and the Law of Philosophy.' I arrive late, unfortunately have missed the laudation, do not know the speaker, and discover to my surprise that even after several minutes of careful listening I cannot guess whether he comes from East or from West Germany. Apparently, the lecturer is interested in the relationship between legal philosophy and legal theory. He delineates categories and sub-categories, classifies and compares, but I find nothing in his talk that I can confidently hold on to. This is just how I have felt for years about much of East Germany's legal literature. Legal theory in the GDR seemed further removed from real life than its materialistic provenance would have led one to expect. Even if, lost in the pages of a law review, I would occasioually pinch myself to remind me that topics like 'The Mandatory Character of Law' or 'The Identity of Law Formation and Impact' also had veiled political significance, the veil was so opaque, the arguments themselves were spun in such intricate and fragile patterns that, to my mind at least, they virtually never succeeded in pulling together legal theory and social practice. Above all, East German legal theory did not reflect—let alone explain—anything that happened daily in East German courtrooms. It appeared to take no note of the parental character of socialist law; paid no attention to the pampering, the tutoring, the cruel rejection of its children. As a result, I often learned more from court decisions or from reports in which lay assessors or members of social courts described, in bumpy syntax, their experiences with the law than from the academic literature; learned more not only about law in action but also about socialist conceptions of justice. 'The things you read!' GDR colleagues would say with puzzled condescension when I referred to my unimpressive sources. People with intellectual standards did not waste time on them.

Meanwhile my whispered question to a neighbor has revealed the speaker to be Professor Dreier from Göttingen in West Germany. The discussion following his talk addresses the issue of whether legal theory is indeed a genuine legal discipline. Does anything turn on the answer? How German all this is, I think. How comfortably socialism fit into German heads. America is far away. Some people in the audience, by the way, look rather sleepy. I, too, have to struggle to keep my eyes open. Although those window bars must have been intended to protect us against rebellious forces on the outside, I feel as if all of us together were trapped behind them.

But things liven up in the afternoon when Professor Karl Mollnau, from the Institute of Legal Science, presents his paper on the infamous Babelsberg conference. The conference, convened by the Central Committee, met in April 1958 at the Walter Ulbricht Academy of State and Law in Babelsberg, on the outskirts of Berlin, before an invited audience of five hundred guests. It was a milestone—tombstone might perhaps be the more fitting word—in East German legal history. In Babelsberg, as Professor Mollnau is now about to tell us, began the irresistible decline of legal scholarship in the GDR.

Not that legal developments in East Germany had not taken unpleasant twists and turns before. But after the unfocused search for a new beginning during the immediate post-war years and after that mixture of ruthlessness and deception that characterized much of the legal policy of the newly founded German Democratic Republic, East German legal scholarship seemed ready to take stock and to discover its own voice. True, much that was said and written in this period was simply a carbon copy of Soviet teachings. But there were also attempts to develop new and authentic ways of thinking and talking about law. Strangely enough, in the first decade of the GDR, the boundaries of intellectual discourse extended further— despite Stalinist repression and the Cold War—than in later and seemingly more moderate and open years. A colleague at the Humboldt University once explained to me why this was so: because there still existed some real hope that socialism would indeed be able to create a better and more just society. People who believe in what they say are more likely to defend their views, criticize others, engage in meaningful debates. After the Twentieth Party Congress in the Soviet Union, East German legal writers also began discreetly to look to bourgeois legal scholarship for inspiration. Perhaps the political thaw would eventually have allowed some blending of bourgeois and socialist elements to create a new and hope-inspiring model of law.

This is exactly what the Babelsberg conference set out to prevent. As Karl Mollnau now tells us: the conference was meant 'to contain and roll back' the process of de-Stalinization that threatened to liberalize East German legal scholarship. East German law, that had just begun to assert some modest independence from the Party, was to be brought back under its firm control. Walter Ulbricht himself, First Party Secretary, presented the conference's main paper entitled 'Marxist-Leninist Theory of the State and its Application in Germany.' His central message: law cannot exist independently from the state. Nor can there be any distance or tension between state and law: law is nothing but an instrument of the state to steer and transform society according to its plans. It is the task of legal scholarship to enhance and refine the law's capacity to serve the state: 'The scientific soundness of our theory of state and law is measured by its usefulness to the practice of socialist construction.'

Ulbricht's paper in Babelsberg came in large part from the pen of Karl Polak: Ulbricht's ghostwriter, legal mentor, comrade, fellow war exile to the Soviet Union and the evil spirit of East German legal scholarship until long after his death in 1963. It is useless to speculate about what Ulbricht could have achieved without Polak, or Polak without Ulbricht. Both complemented each other like hand and glove. Ulbricht wanted power and a socialist state on German soil. Polak hated bourgeois law; hated its separation of individual and society; hated the rule of law, which to him was only a deception shoring up the rule of capitalism. In Polak's view, the juxtaposition of citizen and state, so crucial to a capitalistic society, had been obliterated and transcended by socialism. Since a citizen no longer needed protection against his state, state and law could without scruples be treated as identical. More: they *were* identical. Law was the will of the state; both were as inseparable as heart and heartbeat.

In Polak's writings, 'state and law' are always mentioned in a single breath. Polak refused even to think about their interaction. To ask about the relationship of state and law revealed a world view that saw both as 'separate entities,' he wrote. The question was 'meaningless, antimarxist, anti-scientific.' Polak's work is filled with absolutes and extremes: there are 'fundamental facts,' 'fundamental differences,' 'fundamental changes.' His argumentation makes no compromises and knows of no concessions. His world is separated into light and dark: right stands against wrong, new against old, objective against subjective, consciousness against spontaneity, friend against foe. 'The issue boils down to an either/or' is one of Polak's favorite expressions.

Reading his work today, I find Polak's refusal to check his theory against political realties no less German than the anti-empiricism of other legal scholars in the GDR. Still, this is a very different theory from that which I have encountered for decades in East German law reviews. Polak does not engage in strained and scholastic ideological exercises. His language is straightforward and unambiguous: I may disagree with what he says, but at least I always know what he means. There burns a different fire in these texts than those little flickerings of conviction anxiously nourished throughout most other East German legal writings. I do not know what fed the flames. Herr Mollnau once told of an occasion when, as a student, he had been given a lift in Karl Polak's car. The famous man had during the entire trip spoken of nothing but his own ideas. A man possessed? It seems certain that Karl Polak spent at least a few weeks in a mental institution. Or was it the exiled Jew, who had turned Stalinist because he hated everything which could result in Hitler's Germany? The farmer's son from Lower Saxony, who had earned a doctorate with a thesis on existentialist legal theory and whose ideas had finally gone to his head? The professor, drunk with power?

Perhaps a little bit of all of them. In any case, Karl Polak could produce the perfect intellectual justification for what Ulbricht wanted in 1958: a legal system that would be not a watch-dog over political authority but rather its faithful servant. But it is depressing to see how readily East Germany's legal academics who had just timidly begun to find their feet, played along in the vicious game. All those gathered in Babelsberg in those days must have known what to expect. The conference followed in the wake of the thirty-fifth Plenary Session of the Central Committee of the SED in February, at which Ulbricht had managed to outmaneuver an internal Party opposition group led by his deputy Karl Schirdewan. The lawyers would be next. Ostensibly, two in particular had attracted the attention of Party ideologues: Hermann Klenner, who four days earlier in an article in *Neues Deutschland* had been accused of revisionism, and Karl Bönninger, who taught administrative law in Leipzig and who, in a Festschrift article the year before, had argued in a manner suspiciously close to *Rechtsstaat* reasoning. Professor Bönninger was present at the conference and listed among its speakers. Professor Klenner was absent: someone had come to reclaim his printed invitation because Klenner's presence among the guests might have been too offensive to Comrade Ulbricht. But did the singling out of two black sheep imply that everybody else was safe? Hadn't they, too, on this or that occasion, said or printed things which could be interpreted to reflect sympathy for the rule of law? How would they fare in Babelsberg? It must have been a company of very worried people who gathered on 2 April 1958 to listen to Walter Ulbricht's speech.

Even today, a generation later, reading the minutes of the Babelsberg Conference will send ripples of cold fear along your spine. With a few abbreviations, the record could be turned into a macabre script for a film on Stalinism in Germany. The setting: the Academy of State and Law in Babelsberg, a heavy and imposing building in polished sandstone, coldly elegant, and sufficiently oppressive to have served as Nazi backdrop in the film *Mephisto*. The star: Walter Ulbricht, armed with Karl Polak's phrases, who talks not only about law and political power, but—omnipotent and omniscient—about any other topic raised during these two days: the statutes of agricultural co-operatives, legal education, labor law. Twenty-two times Ulbricht intervenes in the discussion. Sometimes with threatening undertones: Didn't Klenner once sympathize with the Imre Nagy government in Hungary? 'How come nobody noticed?' he shouts. 'You were together with him, were you not?' Sometimes in the concerned and caring voice of the local squire. Someone in the discussion mentions a village teacher who has refused to leave the church. 'Give him a little time,' Father Ulbricht counsels from his seat. 'Things don't always work out so fast. And no deadlines!'

And then there are the bad guys: Karl Bönninger and Hermann Klenner. Karl Bönninger does not do justice to his part. He has not even noticed that he is in the middle of a political cleansing campaign with himself as the object. Instead, he seems to take the meeting in Babelsberg for a scholarly conference: contradicts Ulbricht's interjections, does not even apologize, insists on his viewpoints and in the end complains that the interruptions distracted him from properly pursuing his topic. Not a hand stirs in applause when Professor Bönninger finishes his talk. Since Hermann Klenner plays his role *in absentia*, he can more easily be cast as an anti-hero. A man 'who has no idea what socialist law is about,' says Walter Ulbricht. The other speakers eagerly agree. 'Embittered and silent,' says a colleague, and with 'an inclination to separate the theory of state and law.' Someone 'who doesn't like Comrade Ulbricht's leadership of the Party,' says another. I have to admit that Hermann Klenner is quite convincing in his part as intellectual anti-Stalinist. And finally, the rest of the cast. Many subdued and silent walk-ons. As bit-players, a couple of local Party secretaries, who raise their hands to assure everybody that they at least are not the ones to blame. For light relief, some local administrators who in plain and straightforward words talk about village problems. And in supporting roles, the many law professors who do most of the talking and who surpass each other with self-criticism and declarations of allegiance.

Readily, they admit the error of their ways. They allowed 'an atmosphere of compromise' to pervade their departments, in which discussions could be governed by 'academic rules of etiquette.' At Humboldt University, they had seriously debated 'whether it was justified to segregate certain types of legal literature or whether these books should be put back on to the shelves of the main reading room.' At the University of Jena, law school exercises in administrative law had included hypotheticals from police law: that is, instructors at Jena had not only conceived of the possibility of conflict between individual and state but had even encouraged their students to study such conflicts! And academic publication standards had gone to seed. 'It is truly scandalous,' says a lecturer from Leipzig University, that the contributions to a Festschrift honoring the fortieth anniversary of the October Revolution were simply collected and printed without any prior political discussion. 'That was a disgrace for which we all bear responsibility . . . and of which I personally feel ashamed.'

Whose fault was it? One's own, of course. But actually, others were even more to blame. 'Comrades, we have gone wrong,' says, in one or the other way, almost every speaker. One confesses to inner struggles. 'I have to admit that I found it extremely difficult . . . to understand the legitimacy of these criticisms,' someone proclaims. One tattles. Comrade Steiniger is 'politically indecisive,' one of his colleagues reports. Comrade Bönninger at a discussion in Berlin has called law 'the juridic corset of politics,' another informs the audience. Comrade Klenner has made 'cynical and provocative remarks about Comrade Walter Ulbricht,' somebody else reveals. 'This is not the place to go into details,' he adds, darkly. And one demonstrates political vigilance with cat calls. 'You've got to deal self-critically with the problem!' a colleague shouts during Professor Bönninger's presentation.

And at the end of their little speeches, always the promises to reform. 'I want to assure you, comrades,' says Professor Hochbaum from Jena, who only two years ago had proposed administrative appeals to buttress the individual's protection against the executive—'I want to assure you that we will do everything to overcome the shame we have heaped upon ourselves.' Shouts of 'Bravo!' and applause. What had Ulbricht accused them of? 'Some of our comrade scholars have not yet understood that they must do their research in their capacity as Party members.' Now his audience knows what is expected of them. 'Today, comrades, I have realized that even as theorists, we are above all Party functionaries,' Professor Hochbaum says. A student *apparatchik* from the Babelsberg Academy puts it in even plainer language. Now we will be much better at answering the decisive question, he says: 'What helps the Party and what harms it?'

Until the last days of the GDR, East German legal academics have not forgotten that question. Right after Babelsberg, Karl Bönninger and Hermann Klenner were put on probation, as it were, and demoted to posts in local government: Bönninger as secretary of a rural council near Leipzig; Klenner as mayor of a forsaken village in the Oderbruch fens. At the Humboldt law faculty in Berlin, the marble busts of famous bourgeois scholars were removed from the library and stowed away in the basement. Lectures on the 'history of political and legal theory' were struck from the GDR law school curriculum. Eventually, the icy weather would break.

After a couple of years 'at the base,' Bönninger and Klenner were allowed to return to their teaching posts. In May 1962, the journal *State and Law* published a manifesto of ten scholars, among them Hermann Klenner, which in fifteen 'theses' argued that even Socialist legal theory could gain from the study of Germany's 'progressive' bourgeois heritage. Nothing much happened either to Professor Klenner (who, judging by the diction of the 'theses' had a decisive hand in their composition) or to the other authors involved, beyond the relatively mild reproach that they had obviously not yet grasped 'the full thrust and meaning' of the Babelsberg conference. And although many other legal scholars in the years to come 'after numerous bows to Babelsberg continued to pursue well-trodden paths,'—as Karl Polak puts it sarcastically—they usually did not find their way blocked by the Party.

But the Party never renounced its claim to the loyalty of legal scholars which it had raised so ruthlessly in Babelsberg. Nor did those scholars ever dispute it. No one told the truth about Babelsberg. I must admit that I have no idea how one could have managed to do so. A 1988 article in which Professor Karl-Heinz Schöneburg (who had reason to be dissatisfied with his own conduct at Babelsberg) tried to revive the topic by gently criticizing the 'contradictions' and 'one-sidedness' of the conference was not accepted for publication—there had been objections at the Central Committee. And since no one stood up to challenge it—not in law faculties, not on the editorial boards of law reviews, not in Party circles—the evil spirit lived. As late as 1985, when Karl Polak would have celebrated his eightieth birthday, a memorial article in *State and Law* praised his 'unconditional Party spirit' and the 'impressive actuality' of his work. As late as 1987, 'Babelsberg' was the magic word which someone fallen into disfavor with the Party would use to plead for reacceptance. Perhaps if, in the years of socialism, someone had found the courage to address the specter by its true name, it could have been exorcized. Today—fourteen months after the *Wende*, three months after reunification—GDR legal scholarship is beyond help.

17 January 1991

War in the Gulf.

I spend the entire day on *Abwicklungs* matters at Humboldt University. At nine o'clock in the morning, a meeting arranged by the Law Faculty's student council, at which the Senator of Justice, Frau Limbach, speaks about the Senate's plans for the University. It is not her portfolio, and—as becomes obvious from her talk—not a policy she would have favored herself. But she does her best to demonstrate solidarity with cabinet decisions. A couple of accusations ('You know that lawyers in the GDR before, during, and after their studies had to support the state'; 'citizens here complain because nothing changes'); a couple of catcalls ('You don't have to tell us what our citizens complain about!'); the usual arguments (the old Party networks are alive and well; too little has happened in one year; you can't pull yourself up by your own bootstraps); the usual tensions between accusatory *Wessis* and defensive *Ossis*. Then a flaming speech by Professor Wera Thiel, Humboldt University's labor lawyer: fast, feverish, spoken in one breath against 'subjection then, subjection now.' We must bring about our own transformation, she says; don't expect changes overnight, 'you will have to make do with the heads you find.' A half-hearted commentary by Frau Limbach, who basically seems to agree. Then, a third-year student rises to proclaim that, speaking for himself, he is only interested in the timely conclusion of his studies. Whatever the politicians plan for Humboldt University, they must ensure that the required number of classes can be taught. Apart from that, 'I won't lose sleep over the *Abwicklungs* decision.' This self-centered statement sufficiently enrages one of the West Berlin cameramen—as usual these days at Humboldt, the meeting is filmed for the evening news—to forget his role as observer. 'You students were just as cozy with the Party as your professors,' he shouts excitedly from behind his tripod. 'You should show some solidarity with them!' Stunned silence in the room.

After lunch, in the same Lecture Hall 2002, a plenary meeting of the Law Faculty to bring everybody up to date on the situation. As usual, the meeting is public; almost everything takes place in public now at HU; even occasions which at my faculty in Texas we prefer to keep behind closed doors. The Dean, Professor Will, reports. The University has indeed decided to contest the closure of its five 'ideologically contaminated' departments in court. If— as seems likely—the Senate Administration nevertheless proceeds with the liquidation, the University will also sue for an injunction. The first court hearing has been scheduled for February. The entire litigation may take years. Given the uncertainty of its outcome, it will be difficult for the University to engage in a vigorous process of self-reform over which it might soon lose control.

But Frau Will is not inclined to show undue deference to a Senate policy which she believes to be in violation of the Unification Treaty and which she hopes will soon be crushed in court. Despite present uncertainties, she wants at least the faculty's professional and moral self-review to proceed as planned. To this end, the Law Faculty's new personnel review commission should take up its work as soon as possible. The Commission—its cumbersome German title *Personalstrukturkommission* is usually condensed into a handier 'PSK'—is based on a resolution by the University Council of last December, under which every HU department is to elect a mixed body of East and West German representatives to investigate each University member's political involvement and possible corruption under the old regime. A central personnel review commission (*Zentrale Personal-strukturkommission* or ZPSK) co-ordinates the review process throughout the University, and hears appeals. Each employee who hopes to continue in the employment of Humboldt University must submit himself to the review of his departmental PSK. Based on a candidate's record and a hearing, the PSK will then decide whether he or she is sufficiently 'professionally competent' and 'personally qualified' to be kept on. To judge from my own experiences back at the University of Texas, it will be hard enough for committee members to agree on their colleague's professional competence. But even more troublesome are the 'personal qualifications.' Yesterday, at a student strike meeting to protest the Berlin Senate's *Abwicklungs* decision, a student asked the University Rector, Professor Fink, to put a figure on that share of university employees who in his view were not compromised by their association with the SED regime. 'There is no one in this University who is untainted,' was Professor Fink's reply. If that is true, how will it be possible to distinguish between the trustworthy and the incorrigible?

I am not asking an academic question. As it happens, I am myself a member of the Law Faculty's PSK. When Frau Will persuaded me to add my name to the department ballot, I could see no risk: the list was long enough. But then the unexpected withdrawal of two other candidates suddenly propelled me from the safety of the sidelines right into the renewal process of the HU. What can I do to extricate myself? I want to say something about 'too much work,' remember what the daily work-load of Frau Will must look like, and fall silent. She knows, too, how to defeat my reluctance to get involved. 'Just think of all the things you will learn for your book!' says the dean. I let myself be bribed.

Only a few hours later, at 6 p.m., the first session of our PSK. We meet in one of the collective offices of the law department (no one here has an office all to himself); a nondescript and crowded room where only the 30-foot ceiling reminds you of the former glory of this university. There are eleven of us: a secretary, three students, three assistants and lecturers, four professors. Tomorrow, we will be joined by four external committee members, all of them senior academic dignitaries from West Germany. Since the 'externals' teach elsewhere and cannot be expected to make more than the occasional visit to East Berlin, they will participate only in our most important meetings. I am one of the 'internals,' since Professor Will, to raise the Committee's reputation in the eyes of distrustful West Berlin observers, insisted that Western candidates, too, be listed on the faculty's PSK ballot. There is a second *Wessi* among the four professors of our group: Professor Nordemann, attorney in West Berlin, part-time professor at the Free University and presently guest professor at Humboldt.

We quickly agree on a timetable and various matters of procedure. Dr. Tatjana Ansbach, a lecturer in international law, is elected Chair: a lively, intelligent and round young woman, who—as I will soon learn—is also straight as an arrow and, if necessary, can be sharp as a knife. Personally, I know only one of the other committee members: Dr. Felix Posorski, senior lecturer at the HU Institute for Public and International Law, whom I met a couple of years before the *Wende* to talk about social courts in the GDR. Come to think of it, it must have been more than a decade ago. I remember that we talked in a cafeteria on Alexanderplatz, because it would have been folly in those days to try for a meeting at Humboldt University. Today, we smile and shake our heads over the amazing way in which history has made our paths cross once again.

The University resolution establishing the PSKs mentioned no evaluation criteria other than a faculty member's 'professional competence and personal qualifications.' Our committee cannot take up its work without first agreeing on the meaning of these standards. Difficulties start even sooner than I feared. We can't arrive at a common definition of 'professional competence.' An East Berlin colleague suggests 'soundness and creativity of scholarship.' I try to explain, as tactfully as possible, that Westerners are unlikely very often to discover these qualities in the ex-GDR's legal literature. A West German reading an East German law review will be struck, above all, by the monotony of Party-controlled opinion; by the ritualistic repetition of Party quotes; the phoniness of Party eulogies. GDR readers, familiar with the time and place of writing, see more: the hair's-width deviations from the current Party line; the risks involved in a particular choice of topic; the carefully muted undertones of disagreement. And they know an article's author not only from his written work but also from many oral encounters, where he could show truer colors which now, alive in an Eastern reader's memory, will also cast their hue over a colleague's written work. But what should count: the work itself or its social and political context?

We agree on 'exhausting available room to maneuver' as a significant criterion for evaluating the quality of scholarship. I feel a little apprehensive about future meetings.

24 January 1991

Today I have an appointment with Dr. Ursula Rohde, who less than three-quarters of a year ago was still presiding judge of the GDR Supreme Court's panel for family law. We are to meet in the City Bar at the Hotel Unter den Linden, at the corner of Friedrichstrasse. For the price of a pot of coffee, the City Bar offers comfortable armchairs and enough peace and quiet to talk, if you want, for hours. I have used it repeatedly for interviews in recent weeks; the waiter and I nod to each other like old acquaintances.

Although I am on time, I find Frau Rohde waiting. She looks like someone used to authority. An intelligent, guarded face: 'a lady,' my mother would have said. I feel underdressed in trousers and a sweater. We begin by talking about the main stations in Frau Rohde's professional life: law school; at 23 (the lowest age permissible), entry into the judiciary; at 30, family judge at the Supreme Court, just at the time when the GDR's new Family Code was drafted and first tested in judicial practice. 'Those were extraordinarily constructive years,' Frau Rohde says.

Family law is one of my own fields, too, and I am eager to learn something about the relationship between law and politics in the Supreme Court's family-oriented case-law. I know, of course, that the family law of the GDR was in many respects 'apolitical'—leaving aside its early years, that is, and always provided that such leaving aside is permissible. But it did not take GDR family policy very long to discover that even under socialism the family can serve the state only if healthy, and that healthy families require a measure of internal autonomy. Decisions lying outside the immediate family circle were another matter: the Party had no qualms about imprinting its world-view on children in schools or in the practically mandatory Free German Youth organization, for example. But although East German legal literature was full of talk about the family's obligations towards society, personal relationships between family members were in practice left private. Family legislation, too, reflected growing political abstinence from intra-family affairs. While, for instance, the Marriage Decree of 1955 allowed divorce only if a marriage had lost its meaning 'for the spouses, the children, and society,' the Family Code of 1965 added two little words to this description, authorizing divorce if a marriage had lost its meaning 'for the spouses, the children and *therefore also* for society.' Instead of forcing social notions of happiness upon the family, GDR family legislation and case-law accepted private happiness as an important prerequisite for the family's social functioning.

All of which is not to say that family law in the GDR was not, at the same time, also highly political. The principle of 'equal rights for women,' for example, an age-old socialist war-cry, influenced East German case-law far earlier and far more decisively than West German case-law—despite the fact that the West German Constitution, too, contains an equal rights provision. Radical gender equality led to other important legal consequences in the GDR, such as the principle that women should be fully integrated into the work process. And from women's supposed professional equality followed, in turn, the legal demand that divorced women, like divorced men, should be able to support themselves and that alimony— once understood as the innocent and injured wife's compensation for the

loss of her former husband's support—could now, under socialist conditions, only be the rare exception.

Some of these views have, by now, also found limited acceptance in West
German family law thinking. The issue I want to pursue today concerns a
GDR-specific variant of the equal protection policy for women which led to
the unequal treatment of husbands and wives in custody disputes at divorce.
To lighten working women's dual burden of job and household (and to raise
the country's sluggish birth-rate), East German mothers were entitled to
spend the first year in their baby's life away from work at home, at the
state's expense. If the parents should later divorce, the mother's close
contact with the child during the 'baby year' would favor her in any event-
ual custody dispute. But since the law also wanted to encourage women's
professional advancement, it did not allow frequent physical absences to be
held against a mother, who, instead of taking primary care of her child,
decided instead to further her career. The rule which naturally applied to
fathers claiming custody—we're sorry, but being away at work, you did not
spend enough time with your child—thus did not apply to working mothers.

This doubly preferential treatment of mothers meant that it was virtually
impossible for an East German father to obtain custody against the wish of
his former wife. Only if a mother had no interest in her child or if she was
drastically unsuitable to take care of it could there be hope for the father.
True, West German or American courts, too, will in most divorces award
custody of a couple's children to the mother. But East German case-law on
this matter was more rigorous and more rigid than that of other countries.
It was by no means undisputed in the GDR. Frau Eichhorn, for example, in
our conversation last December, had mentioned her uneasiness about the
preferential treatment of women in East German custody disputes. Her
former colleague at the Supreme Court and present law partner, Dr. Heidi
Gacek, whom I interviewed a week later, had shared those misgivings.
Already in November 1989, a fortnight after the opening of the Wall, when
in a conversation with two attorneys in East Berlin I had enquired about the
most immediate legal changes to look out for under rejuvenated socialism,
'custody for fathers' had been included in my conversation partner's list of
imminent reforms. It thus seems likely that the official judicial hostility
towards fathers was not shared by many family law experts in the GDR and
was not necessarily of the judges' own making. There must have been
political influences to explain it.

If so, what was the Supreme Court's role in the events? It had further-
reaching powers than Western courts: in particular, its right to issue 'Guidelines' (which gave authoritative interpretations of current law and, if
necessary, filled gaps in existing legislation) and its 'cassation' jurisdiction
(that is, its right to review and quash even final court decisions in the
interest of a uniform and politically correct approach to social issues). In

many areas of family law, the court never bothered to exercise its cassation powers: for example, it left the question of whether and at what point a marriage was sufficiently disrupted to warrant divorce based on breakdown entirely to the decision of the trial courts. But the question I am interested in today—under what conditions fathers could claim custody of their children—had been considered so important by the court that it chose several times to quash lower-court decisions by way of cassation, always in favor of the mother.

What had moved the court to intervene in these cases? Its own omnipotence? Or did the Party have a hand in the decision? I had already posed the question to Frau Eichhorn and Frau Gacek. According to their reports, the Party's views on custody disputes were known at the court at least on those occasions when a letter had arrived from Inge Lange, head of the Women's Commission at the Politburo. As they recall, that might have happened three or four times during their years with the court. The Central Committee's occasional demand for something that Frau Gacek called 'flow-back' also betrayed interest of the higher-ups in family law decisions. Besides Inge Lange, both women also mentioned Margot Honecker (Minister of Education and, in that capacity, Head of Youth Services) as someone to be reckoned with in these matters. But the exact nature of Inge Lange's and Margot Honecker's relationships with the court remains obscure. As a lower-ranking judge, 'I could avoid controls,' said Frau Gacek. In politically touchy cases, when a 'discussion' at the Central Committee was called for, it was always Frau Rohde who went. She was irritated on those days 'but not afraid.' 'I'm sure she held up her end of the conversation,' Frau Gacek said. 'She got stuck with those things no one else wanted to do.' That applied, too, to a custody dispute in which Frau Gacek had wanted to award care of the child to its father, a pastor. She had been outvoted on the family law panel. The father had lost custody not for being a pastor but for being male. Now, someone had to write and inform him that his petition to the Supreme Court (asking for a cassation of the lower-court decision, which had also gone against him) was denied. 'I won't do it,' Frau Gacek had said, annoyed at the case's outcome. In the end, Frau Rohde herself had written the dreaded letter.

Now, sitting across from her in the bourgeois plush of the City Bar, I am reminded of the description by a former colleague: 'Not a comfortable person. Not a yes-sayer.' Nevertheless, Frau Rohde seems unwilling to talk about her relationship with those to whom she, too, must on occasion have said yes. She does not deny that, like others, she disapproved of the preferential treatment of women in custody disputes. But when I ask about the mechanics of the process by which political decisions in the GDR were translated into Supreme Court case-law, she becomes evasive. How influential was the Women's Commission at the Politburo? It did not have 'much of a reputation,' Frau Rohde says with undisguised contempt. How about Inge Lange and Margot Honecker? She never had contact with either, says Frau Rohde. Were there occasions when the Party leadership recommended certain lower-court decisions for Supreme Court cassation? There was 'the iron rule' at the court that judicial matters were only for judges to decide. Any Party involvement in the production of guidelines and directives by the court? The last two family law guidelines, dealing with child support and property division after divorce, had been submitted to the Central Committee's Department for State and Law 'for information.' But the department had made 'no suggestions' in response. Why were the drafts submitted in the first place? And why should the Central Committee be entitled to 'suggestions'? Frau Rohde will not let herself be drawn into an argument. The decisions of her family law panel were not determined by any outside political influences, she says. How then can she explain a custody case-law far more hostile to fathers than the East German judiciary itself apparently felt? Again, Frau Rohde waves the question off. 'You will not get much out of her,' someone had prophesied when I had mentioned our upcoming encounter.

But why the reticence? What is it that Frau Rohde defends? Not the reputation of the political system she once served. Frau Rohde seems honestly aghast at the many instances of socialist injustice now daily surfacing on television screens and is 'appalled at our willingness, at the time, to swallow them.' She recalls her 'horror' at the revelations of Stalin's crimes at the Twentieth Party Congress in the Soviet Union, echoes of which spread even through the GDR. And she remembers a vague feeling, after the Babelsberg Conference, that 'something really bad had happened'—a reaction that showed more political sensitivity than was common in those days, especially coming from a young judge busy enough with finding her footing in a new career.

And yet, no word about the interactions which must have taken place between her and someone, somewhere at the Central Committee. Why not? Because our conversation circles around her own life's work, I think, and because she is not willing, at least not now, to let this work be damaged by suspicious questions. 'My entire life was family law,' she says at some point. I know a little bit about her work. The Supreme Court's guidelines on family law issues, produced under Frau Rohde's auspices, are solid, professional attempts at tackling those problems which occupy family lawyers the world over: how to bolster family stability, how to achieve justice between warring spouses, how to protect children who always, everywhere, are the first to suffer.

Not that legal experts won't disagree about the fairness or utility of this or that aspect of the Supreme Court's guidelines and decisions on family law. And there is no denying that at least early guidelines contained enough

vague and partisan provisions to invite political misuse. But if the last two
family law guidelines of 1983 and 1986 did not occasionally mention terms
like 'polytechnical high school' or 'socialist property,' a Western reader
would not even notice that he was looking at the texts of a legal system
foreign and objectionable to his own. Even Guideline Number 25 on custody issues, which dates from 1968 (not a good year) and contains a number
of dangerously loaded passages, insists that 'the development of the child is
best furthered in stable, continuous family relationships'—a principle that
even the most conservative bourgeois family expert could easily subscribe
to. How did the Court handle family law conflicts in which politics played a
direct and obvious role, I want to know from Frau Rohde; let's say a
custody fight between parents of whom one had managed to escape to West
Germany? In those cases, we would really do our best to make 'a tip-top
impression,' she says. At first, because the GDR had not yet gained international recognition and then, after the Helsinki agreements, because it was
important to avoid 'unnecessary embarrassments.' So the Supreme Court
insisted on 'good-looking' decisions in these matters. 'We must come up
with judgments that could equally apply to parents in Rostock or Suhl'
(who had never fled the country) was the Court's motto in cases involving
parents in the West. I can think of no published family law decision in the
GDR which gives the lie to Frau Rohde's description.

Once again: no scandalous discoveries. I understand why Frau Rohde
seems so annoyed by my questions. Instead of focusing on the important
and impressive chapters of her biography, I rummage through some tangen-
tial issues in the apparent hope that they might yield some information
about Frau Rohde's political dependence. Compared to the bulk of her
achievements, the occasional preferential treatment of mothers in custody
disputes is of little weight. And who says that the decisions—even if they
should have been swayed by Inge Lange's communications from the Politburo—are therefore necessarily wrong? Didn't American family law, too,
for a long time follow the 'tender years' doctrine under which custody for
younger children almost automatically went to the mother? Didn't women
in the GDR, too, suffer from so many social disadvantages that there was no
reason to get all worked up about the rare discrimination in their favor? Do
my questions serve any purpose other than to cast a shadow over someone's
respectable and hard-won life achievements?

I almost expect Frau Rohde at this point to accuse me of political self-
righteousness and a distorted and biased view. But she does not. She is hurt
by my questions, tries to evade them, but does not dispute their legitimacy.
Whatever happened in those 'discussions' which Frau Rohde so reluctantly
attended at the Central Committee must have contaminated the Supreme
Court's work even in her own eyes. And 'custody rights for fathers' cannot
have been the only family law topic of interest to the comrades at the

Central Committee, either. There must have been other issues considered worthy of Party intervention. I wonder whether Frau Rohde is thinking about them now.

Does she feel she has suffered injustice after the *Wende*, I ask. Yes, says Frau Rohde. The answer comes without hesitation. However clean or tainted her professional conscience, Frau Rohde does not believe that she deserves the total exclusion from the law which is now her lot. Sometimes, she talks about events as if they were some geological occurrence: an earthquake, a continental drift, something free of moral undertones. 'Whatever happens, happens,' she says three times during our conversation; 'there is nothing you can do about it'—superficially referring to the Gulf War but clearly with her own life's course in mind. Sometimes she speaks of her sudden change of circumstances as of an illness from which she now must recuperate. She talks about the discomfort of her office in the Littenstrasse courthouse: no sunlight at all; even in the summer, she would always have cold feet. 'If you want to be a little kind to yourself, you'd better quit now,' she had told herself. So she had left the Court by the end of June 1990, three months earlier than needed. 'I didn't want just to be tolerated for a few more weeks,' she says.

There, I think, is the key: Frau Rohde's pride. It does not allow her to let some itinerant US professor investigate the rifts and detours in her personal history. She evades my questions but does not break off our conversation; she wants to continue it on her own terms. She does not give, but neither does she let go. She will not say things but does not want to leave them unsaid. We both know that there is enough to talk about, but we are too far from one another (and perhaps in some respects too similar?) to bridge the abyss between the winner and the loser after the *Wende*. It is useless. And so, to finish our conversation, I ask one final question: 'Did you make any particular mistake in your life which you now regret?' 'Yes,' is the answer, 'when I entered law school, I should not have gone to Humboldt University but to the Free University in West Berlin.'

'*Ach*,' I say, disappointed; 'that is the same answer I got from Herr Toeplitz, too.' Dr. Heinrich Toeplitz, from 1960 to 1986 President of the GDR Supreme Court and Frau Rohde's boss most of her working life, had consented to talk to me a couple of months ago. During the three long hours of the interview, I learned nothing that advanced my understanding of law and justice under socialism. In an attempt to get beneath the slippery surface of our conversation, I had finally asked whether Herr Toeplitz could recall any significant mistake in his career. My question did not aim for a political confession; I had only hoped that the admission of this or that mistake might throw some light on the man himself and on the energies that kept him going. 'Yes,' Dr. Toeplitz had replied, 'in 1950 I should not have joined the GDR Ministry of Justice but should have started out as an

attorney instead. Then I would not have to worry about my pension today.'
That was the worst error he could think of after having served for twenty-
six years as the country's foremost guardian of legality.

I explain the parallel to Frau Rohde. Now she is really angry. 'At least I
don't ask you these kinds of questions,' she says. Then she does it anyway:
'And what mistakes do you regret having made?' The question is legitimate.
I owe Frau Rohde as honest a response as I can muster. But as hard as I rack
my brains, I cannot think of a professional decision which now burdens my
conscience. My personal life is quite another matter: I have no difficulty
recalling instances in which I was not as generous or altruistic as the situation had called for. But in my work? If here or there I have said or written
something wrong it does not matter because in my line of work questions
are more important than answers. I did not kowtow because there was no
need to fear those above me. I did not lie because the truth was not
dangerous. I did not toe the line because in Western academic careers,
unorthodoxy is as likely to be rewarded as punished. I did nothing wrong
because I was not obliged to do right: I could almost always follow my own
rules.

Of course, all this comes to mind way too late for me to do justice to Frau
Rohde's question. And she, in turn, cannot muster the moral energy to be
as open and honest with me as she might wish herself. For a little while, we
continue to talk around and past each other with growing irritation. Then,
we give up.

As we leave the hotel, the waiter gives us a friendly nod. 'Homework all
done?' he asks. That's what he said some weeks ago, too, when after
another interview in the City Bar I had left with another East German
colleague: 'Homework all done?' We had laughed and responded with
some harmless pleasantry. But Frau Rohde is too hurt and too angry to
engage in cheerful banter. 'We don't need to do homework anymore,' she
says sternly. Although it would be nice, I think, if like untidy homework, we
could rewrite certain passages in our life for a better grade.

At the hotel door, we take our leave with a politely hostile handshake.
On my side, it includes a measure of respect.

29 January 1991

A conversation with Professor Karl Mollnau at the Institute for Legal
Sciences. Herr Mollnau is—or was—head of the Institute's section for
Legal Theory. I am not quite certain whether the Institute, whose funding
extended only until last December, legally survived into the New Year. But
at least it has preserved the physical presence to allow our appointment in
the Otto-Nuschke-Strasse. I want to find out how a legal scholar could
function under socialism. Our interview takes place in an office that seems

to have housed several Institute members: its multiple desks and filing cabinets make it look crowded and impersonal. I could swear that the plastic ceiling tiles contain asbestos. Herr Mollnau and I sit, as in a railway waiting-room, on two haphazardly placed chairs facing each other. Only towards the end of our conversation, when Karl Mollnau searches in one of the desks for a document he wants to show me, do I realize that this room once must have been home to him.

He comes from a family of small-time farmers. In 1952, he began to study law at Humboldt University—at first without any thoughts of a future academic career. But then he caught fire: he liked the law's historical bent, and he liked its abstractness. And so he stayed: first at Humboldt University and later, when the then 'Institute for the Theory of State and Law' was founded in 1972, at the Academy of Sciences. My first question today goes to the planning of research in a system which abhorred creative spontaneity: how exhaustive and how confining was the plan? But Herr Mollnau's level-voiced and placid description of the relationship between central and institutional research plans suggests that planning did not represent a significantly greater threat to East German academics than bureaucratic constraints pose to the members of many Western state-run universities. At least in the area of law one could apparently influence the drafting of plan targets, could reinterpret them to suit one's needs or could otherwise manipulate the process in a way that made it possible to pursue personal research interests within the parameters of the plan. All right: if not the plan, what were the most important determinants of Herr Mollnau's work?

The constant push and pull between different academic factions vying for influence, for example. Conflict divided even the Central Committee, where the Department of Academic Affairs worked 'with all due care' against the ideologically more rigid Department of State and Law. At the Institute for Legal Science, tensions existed between the Director—a loyal *apparatschik*—and some of the sections, and were replicated within the sections themselves. The litmus test was the conference at Babelsberg. Basically, legal scholars in the GDR came in three groups, Herr Mollnau explains: the heirs and disciples of Babelsberg (like the director of the Institute for Legal Science, Professor Weichelt), a small band of 'anti-Babelsbergers,' and a solid middle group 'placing its bet on the safest horse—namely, on positivism.' The groups were divided by the same dispute which the Babelsberg conference had intended to settle once and for all: the fight over the proper domain of law under socialism. The 'Babelsbergers' saw law as a creature of politics. The 'anti-Babelsbergers' argued for a limited autonomy of law. The positivist middle watched, waited, kept a close eye on the political weathervane, and hoped for a west wind.

This, then, was the setting for the obscure and sometimes barely perceptible debates which marked the development of legal scholarship in the GDR like veins in rock. In the past, I had occasionally followed these debates in the legal literature, but had rarely attributed more than aesthetic significance to their outcome. Now, listening to Herr Mollnau's descriptions, the discussions appear more urgent and more real than when I only read about them. I realize that the shadows boxing on the screen had been cast by the encounters of real-life people. Even if the combatants had no impact on social and political developments in the GDR, their struggles left personal scars.

After the Babelsberg conference, Karl Mollnau—then research assistant to Hermann Klenner—learned so himself. Supposedly 'led astray' by his mentor, he was ordered five mornings in a row to appear before a Party meeting at the University to answer questions. After one of the interrogations, he went home, pulled a number of books from his shelves, and burnt them in the wash-house in his garden. I am curious to know the titles. Mostly Russian theorists from the 1920s: Trotsky, Bukharin, Stutchka. Plevier, too.

That year Karl Mollnau himself was left unscathed. His turn came ten years later in the wake of the so-called 'theory debate' of 1967–8, which concerned plans for an East German textbook on socialist legal theory. Together with Hermann Klenner (who by then had returned from his Oderbruch exile and become head of the new legal research group at the Academy of Sciences), Karl Mollnau had drafted the prospectus for a book which would not, as before, focus on public law (or, in GDR terms, 'state law') but on economic and labor law as the core and center of gravity of East Germany's socialist legal system. In other words, a repetition of those mistakes which had already been criticized in Babelsberg: disregard for 'the power question,' revisionism, and—as Attorney-General Joseph Streit explained at the Nineteenth Plenary Session in October 1968 to the comrades at the Central Committee—a 'massive attempt . . . to propagate a supposedly value-free theory of law.' Hermann Klenner's working group at the Academy was dissolved; Klenner himself—after initial suggestions that he might be unfit for any other work than a job in the library—found refuge at the Central Institute for Philosophy at the Academy of Science. Karl Mollnau, at the time already a professor and Associate Dean of the Humboldt Law Faculty, lost his deanship and had to break off work on his 'habilitation' thesis, now also judged 'revisionist.' Although 'marginalized,' he was allowed to continue to teach.

Not every collision between 'Babelsbergers' and 'anti-Babelsbergers' was equally dramatic. The 1981 controversy over the publication of Pashukanis' writings in the GDR, for example, was so low-key that it might not have been political at all. Evgenii Pashukanis, the most brilliant legal theorist produced by socialism, in his book *General Theory of Law and Marxism* (Moscow, 1924) explained all law as a necessary product of market relationships. Since his theory not only rejected the usefulness of law under socialism but also—turning the argument around—characterized present Soviet law as a typically bourgeois phenomenon, Pashukanis was arrested in 1937 and disappeared: Stalinism had no use for 'legal nihilism' but needed instead a theory that could legitimate the purposeful and ruthless use of law as an instrument of power. Pashukanis' writings disappeared as well and remained invisible long after the demise of Stalinism. In 1956, Karl Mollnau had been lucky to find a copy of the *General Theory* in a second-hand bookstore. Twenty-five years later, he and his colleague Professor Karl-Heinz Schöneburg decided to try for a new edition in the GDR. Surprisingly, the project failed not because of irate Party opposition but for lack of paper—an excuse that might not have been valid at the time but that in any case sounded convincing. Since Pashukanis' book is not what you would call an armchair read, it is also quite possible that no one at Party headquarters had actually read it.

There was another 'full-scale battle' at the Institute in 1986: this time, over the question of whether the one and only GDR textbook on legal theory (already once an object of contention) should be reissued in a new edition or whether it needed total remodelling. The combatants had aligned themselves in the by now familiar formations: Professors Klenner, Mollnau, and Schöneburg on the side of reform, the Party bureaucracy on the side of those who saw nothing wrong with the old edition. 'It was basically another fight over Babelsberg,' says Herr Mollnau. The final fight over Babelsberg happened in October 1989, when at a Party meeting at the Institute, members discussed the legitimacy of the brutal police interventions during the demonstrations of 7 October. 'I should have called for the resignation of the Institute's director,' Herr Mollnau says, still dissatisfied with his own performance in that battle. Not that it would have mattered any more.

So, there were real debates among East German legal scholars. I accept the point. But how were they fought? What were the rules? Did struggle over legal theory affect not only the combatants but also those in power? How, for instance, did one show courage? By one's choice of topic, says Herr Mollnau. Not only what you said about an issue but whether you decided to talk about it in the first place sent a signal. Take Hermann Klenner's book, *Marxism and Human Rights*. It appeared in 1982 and now that he mentions it, I remember in particular the book's appendix, which provided GDR readers with a long list of documents reminding them of their rights, beginning with the Magna Carta and ending with the latest UN convention. But according to Herr Mollnau, Klenner's own text also contained carefully camouflaged attacks on human rights shortcomings in the

GDR. The passages on Spanish scholasticism in this respect had been 'sheer
artistry,' Karl Mollnau says. He, for his part, in a review of the book, had
stressed its sections on national self-determination. Why? Because he
wanted to remind readers of the GDR's dependence on the Soviet Union.

'It was a code language for the initiated,' Herr Mollnau says. And, of
course, 'a language of slaves,' he adds. 'Hardly courageous, when viewed
from today's perspective.' And, from today's perspective, no longer comprehensible at all. I recently decided to take another look at Hermann
Klenner's book on human rights. I found its passages on Spanish scholasticism. But even with the best of intentions, I could detect no ulterior meaning in the text besides Klenner's (by no means politically subversive)
criticism of the missionary human rights obsession of American foreign
policy. Whatever coded critique of socialism Karl Mollnau may have found
between the lines must have come not from Klenner's text but from Karl
Mollnau's own thoughts and from his familiarity with his mentor's real
political beliefs. Political resistance as wishful thinking? The real trick was
to expose the Party in a way it would not notice, Herr Mollnau says. Then
your criticism was built to self-destruct, I say from the safe distance of
another time and place.

You had to disguise your message '*um sie herüberzubringen*,' says
Herr Mollnau—'to carry it across.' Nowadays, I often hear the word
herüberbringen in conversations with East German academics—'to carry
over,' 'to get across.' It reminds me of contraband. Herr Mollnau tells me
about one case in which his smuggling was successful, though what was
'carried over' might not have been worth the trouble after all. In the 1980s,
he had been asked to write an article about 'the socialist *Rechtsstaat*' for the
Party daily, *Neues Deutschland*. The suggestion had originated at the Central Committee. Herr Mollnau wrote his piece—'it was no good,' he says—
but among the usual flow of words it contained a sentence meant to be
taken seriously: something about law's being 'the gauge of power.' The
editors at *Neues Deutschland* smelled the rat and wanted the sentence cut.
But, then, somebody at the paper (maybe himself not averse to traffic in
illegal substances) had made use of his connection to someone higher up
and somehow or other had defused official worries. A secretary called Herr
Mollnau at the Academy: 'it has been approved.' Even officials at the US
Consulate in East Berlin had gotten wind of the affair. But 'it was a lousy
article,' Karl Mollnau says again. Maybe people at the American Consulate
took note of one of its sentences, but nothing suggests that it had any impact
on public or private behavior in the GDR. 'Basically, the piece served, once
again, to stabilize the system,' its author says today.

Whereas the anti-Babelsbergers thus had to speak in code, the
Babelsbergers saw no need to mince their words. More or less open threats
fell during the discussion about the new edition of the textbook on legal

theory. The rebels pushing for a new approach were told to expect Party disciplinary proceedings: 'This will be the end of the Institute,' the hard-liners announced. It was a drawn-out battle: about fifteen meetings concerning the correct approach to the teaching of legal theory in the GDR, two of them in the presence of delegates from the Central Committee, although fortunately from the CC's more moderate Department of Academic Affairs. The Department of State and Law—'a bunch of real cement-heads,' as one of Karl Mollnau's colleagues had once told me—was not directly involved in the affair—'but I am sure Herr Weichelt kept them well-informed,' Herr Mollnau says.

Meetings like these were part of a system of intellectual controls that worked far more smoothly and thoroughly than any central censor could have done. 'I always had a censor: myself,' Karl Mollnau says. The 'internal censor' was backed up by a multitude of outside assistants. There were your colleagues, with whom you usually discussed your work. 'No, you can't do that,' one of them might say. There were the filtering mechanisms of the publication process. Before articles went to print, they were submitted to the Institute Director, together with a little explanatory note—'For your info. To appear in *Neue Justiz*' perhaps. Professor Weichelt would respond with a simple 'OK' or with the request for a 'discussion.' 'We mustn't make waves,' he might say in the ensuing conversation. Plans for a book had to be 'defended' in collective debates at the initial and final stages of a project. Then came the negotiations with the publisher. 'That's when the fun began in earnest.' Publishing house and editor searched for whatever 'flea in the ointment' they could find and in turn tried to forestall criticism of their own ideological watchfulness by gaining prior approval of a project from those above them—the Central Committee, the Department of the Interior, Lord knows whom else. 'That was the worst,' Herr Mollnau says, 'that the censor was not someone you could get a grip on.'

'What were your ambitions in those days?' I ask. 'To limit power through law,' Herr Mollnau says. He hoped to do it by way of legal theory. 'I wanted legal theory to receive the recognition that was its due.' The farmer's son who, like that very different farmer's son Karl Polak, believed in the power of concepts. Maybe that was where things went wrong, I think: that so many legal scholars in the GDR sought refuge in a theory sizzling in its own bland juices. I had always believed, Karl Mollnau says, that quarrels about the proper role of law 'involved the problem of dogmatism. That was a mistake. I should have stuck with materialism.' And: 'The other side maintained control for so long because they catered to real needs. Those of the *apparat*.' I am reminded of the myth of Antaeus, who loses all his strength when lifted into the air by Hercules. How about the Babelsbergers, I ask: did they have both feet on the ground? No, not really. Nobody took note of the true state of the East German economy.

Actually, Karl Mollnau recognized the surreal quality of much of what was going on in East German legal scholarship sooner than many of his colleagues. In the early 1980s, he began to focus his interests on the implementation of legal norms. The effectiveness of law was also the subject of two legal theory symposia organized by Karl Mollnau which in 1985 and 1987 were held at the Academy of Sciences in Berlin. Three volumes of conference papers bear witness to the participants' attempts to come to grips with social realities in the GDR. But today, these contributions look strangely anemic. Even after reading a sentence twice, I am often at a loss as to what the author meant by it. Yes, I can see what many of the conference members wanted to 'get across': more respect for procedure, more participation rights for citizens, more legal controls over the administration. But the reality, of which their papers speak, comes almost entirely from the shelves of libraries. The writers' language hides more than it reveals. With very few exceptions, I find in these volumes no statistics, no case studies, no observations of legal practice and, of course, no opinion polls. And no one mentions the real shortcomings of socialist law: its failure to protect political freedoms, its discrimination against outsiders, its environmental enforcement deficit, the helplessness of its economic law.

Karl Mollnau concedes that one of the greatest weaknesses of socialist legal scholarship was its lack of interest in anything empirical. 'We took far too long to recognize the sociological component' of legal scholarship, he says. It was not just a lack of insight: theory was safer and more comfortable. 'We were no heroes, heaven help us!' Professor Mollnau says, relating one more story about a collision with the political bureaucracy. But even more debilitating than their fear, it seems to me, was my East German colleagues' hope. 'I believed that socialism could be made more democratic,' says Herr Mollnau. 'There were always times at which we thought that things might move a little.' 'To move something,' 'to create some movement' are also expressions I often hear these days when talking with East German colleagues about their ambitions under socialism. Nobody dreamt of creating something radically new, of coming up with ideas that would stun the academic community. In a petrified world, 'movement' was all you could hope for. And had his legal theory 'moved something,' I ask. There were 'microscopic changes,' Herr Mollnau says. Legal theory contributed to 'the shift of climate.' I raise the obvious objection: wasn't it rather the change of weather in the Soviet Union that affected meteorological conditions in the GDR?

What do you think will remain of socialist legal theory? I ask as I stow away notepad and pencil. 'There was no "socialist" way of thinking about law,' Karl Mollnau says. I do not have the impression that the admission comes hard to him. Are you a socialist? 'Not any longer.' But 'it doesn't feel as if I had lost something of great importance.' Maybe whatever hope remained after almost forty years of legal research and writing in the GDR had worn so thin that it was easy to discard. Herr Mollnau worries about practical problems lying ahead of him but does not fear any ideological void. For a scholar, the loss of faith must also come as a relief, I think. 'I want to have an unobstructed view of reality,' Karl Mollnau says.

III

Sitting in Judgment

20 February 1991

Bad news for Humboldt University: it lost the first round in its legal battle against the Senate Administration's closure of its five 'ideologically tainted' departments. Today, the Seventh Chamber of the administrative court in Berlin denied the University's plea for an injunction. The University will appeal.

3 March 1991

A bright blue Sunday morning. I must leave the house earlier than I would wish to catch a timely city train to East Berlin. This morning, the Faculty Council of the Humboldt law department will decide on the recommendations of its Personnel Review Commission. Yesterday—Saturday—our PSK had, after an endless session, voted on each of the candidates we had examined: twenty-eight professors, forty-three lecturers, eleven research students and twenty-four non-academic staff members. And it is only six and a half weeks ago that we met for our first session! The pace is frightening. In less than seven weeks, we have supposedly determined who among 106 members of this once-socialist university is suitable and deserving to continue to work in a cleansed and democratized academy. Whatever the outcome of our efforts, it can at best be an approximation of the truth. We have made decisions because decisions needed to be made—not because we or anybody else might have been particularly suitable or legitimated to make them. And our tempo! But I can see why the University Rector and the Law Dean pushed for quick results: a new beginning requires a reckoning with the old, which in a drawn-out process of self-examination would have become increasingly difficult and futile. For the candidates, too, speedy decisions were better than months of uncertainty and worries. All—examiners and examinees—after weeks of meetings, telephone calls, conversations, rumors and sleepless nights are finally glad to have reached the end of the road. May those whom we have done injustice forgive us.

Not every member of the Law Faculty has been included in the vetting. Nine professors and eleven lecturers, for whatever reason, decided not to submit to the examination process. Practically speaking, this means that they will have to leave the university. Not that our commission has the power to retain or fire those it investigates. All we do is submit recommendations to the Faculty Council. The Faculty Council will either accept or reject them. The final decision lies with the University Administration and, beyond that, with the Berlin Senate. Uncertainties are compounded by the litigation over the Senate's *Abwicklungs* decree. Although the University lost its initial suit to enjoin the Administration from the immediate execution of its decree, that decision does not prejudice the overall outcome of the case nor does it rule out a later injunction on appeal. Years will pass before the legal dispute will be settled. In the meantime, the Senate Administration may or may not honor our committee's decisions. Thus, even a positive evaluation by the PSK does not ensure continued employment at Humboldt University. But either a negative vote or the absence of any evaluation will almost certainly result in a person's dismissal from the university.

How does one go about evaluating the entire life-work of 106 men and women in a few weeks? Every candidate had to submit a curriculum vitae, a complete bibliography and reprints of his or her work to our commission. He had to fill out a questionnaire with the usual inquiries about Party posts, contacts with State Security, a license to carry a weapon (I learned to my surprise that important functionaries in the GDR were entitled to be armed), travels abroad, decorations, and the like—questions which hopefully would help us to separate big fish from little. And he had to go through an interview with one of the three sub-committees which we had formed to manage the onslaught. The PSK did not investigate a person's background at its own initiative—even with more time, we had neither the staff nor the expertise to play detective. Our decisions are thus based entirely on information provided by the candidates themselves.

Even so, we could not have managed the work-load without subscribing, from the outset, to a fairly narrow definition of our mandate. The university decisions establishing the PSKs had also authorized them to submit suggestions on ways to improve their departments' research and teaching and thus to contribute to the general reform debate at the university. But we soon realized that discussions about curriculum reform, hiring policies, or research priorities would have severely overtaxed the commission's strength and would have distracted us from our most important job. We decided to ignore those issues. The next step was to resolve which aspects of our candidates' past we should investigate. According to the university guidelines, the PSKs were to review not only each candidate's 'personal integrity' but also his or her 'professional qualifications.' How could we tackle the latter task? 'We have to photocopy people's writings, send them around, make inquiries with colleagues in the field, and read as much as we can manage ourselves,' said I, who just had come from her faculty's appointments committee at the University of Texas. The suggestion was obviously absurd. Given the number and condition of photocopiers at Humboldt

University, even the first step in my program was impracticable. And who was to do the reading? Outside experts from East German universities might well be biased and from West German universities would be hard to find, reluctant, slow (and possibly biased as well). Our external committee members were busy people who had not bargained for more time-consuming work than the occasional meeting. The internal committee members included specialists in international law, family law, comparative law, administrative law and intellectual property. Why should these people single-handedly pass judgment on all scholarship in their respective fields? Who should speak for those branches of the law not represented on the committee? And how—burdened down with reading—would we ever reach the point to make decisions?

Besides, there was another difficulty. The bibliographies attached to people's curricula vitae often ran surprisingly short. Sometimes, they were missing. Reprints were submitted in far smaller numbers than I had anticipated. One or two candidates claimed they could no longer remember everything they had ever published in their life. It seems likely that to most members of the Humboldt Law Faculty the memory of this or that article they once wrote is something they would rather not dwell upon today. But there is another reason, I believe, why we found so few reprints in our files. In an East German university, writing was not nearly as essential as in the 'publish or perish' climate of an American university. I very much doubt that anyone at Humboldt, as I do at the University of Texas, keeps an up-to-date publication list in his desk which is not only meant to reflect his standing in the academic world but will also be an important factor in the determination of his annual salary increase. In its universities as elsewhere, the GDR was not a society geared to performance. Obviously, there were scholars whose talents, energy and ambitions drove them to perform. But you did not have to follow their lead. Other things counted besides a person's scholarship, such as political loyalty or willingness to carry out dreary collective chores. Teaching counted, too, which in an institution obsessed with academic reputation and glamour may often come second.

And so, being unmanageable, our commission's task of evaluating each candidate's 'professional qualifications' soon slipped out of focus. Instead, we concentrated on a person's ability and willingness to adjust to the demands of a bourgeois legal system. How could an academic who for decades had taught East German 'state law' now be expected to teach West German public law? Could someone who had studied and taught civil law at a time when the old German Civil Code was still in force in the GDR, and who later, after the passage of the East German Civil Code in 1975, had switched to the teaching of 'socialist' civil law, really still profit from his youthful exposure to a legal system that had changed considerably in the intervening years? Should our confidence in a candidate's ability to function under the new system be rather bolstered or shaken by the fact that he had written his dissertation on 'the suppressive functions of West German civil law'? In these and similar cases, the commission placed less weight on a person's actual knowledge than on his hunger for knowledge. What had he or she done to retool: registered for classes, attended conferences, established contacts with West German colleagues in the field? 'I have been reading so much this year that I have simply had no time for writing,' a candidate explained to the commission. Yes, we could understand that. If anything, it spoke in our eyes for rather than against a candidate if he did not want to return to writing before he could be sure of what he wanted to say.

Before long, the professional aspects of our investigations had merged imperceptibly with the personal ones. The commission's third task—to examine 'the personal integrity' of each candidate—moved center-stage. A few more times, I would take reprints home from our meetings and read until late at night my eyes glazed over. But those were reflexes from another life. I began to accept that our PSK had not been brought into existence because the quality of legal research in the GDR might not conform to international standards. It existed because of Babelsberg, because of the Stasi, because of the court decisions denying *Ausreiser* requests or imprisoning 'parasites' for failing to show up for work. It existed because of the eagerness of socialist law to serve those in power. Legal scholarship and teaching had played an important role in the law's corruption. And so, it was right to focus our investigation on the question of whether erstwhile servants of the system could now plausibly be integrated into the new *Rechtsstaat*.

Two sets of standards guided our answers to that question: a long list of evaluation criteria developed by the Central Personnel Review Commission of the University, and a similar list issued by the Berlin Senate Administration to serve as yardstick for the hiring and retention of public employees. Although the Senate standards did not bind our commission, we decided we had better take note of them to forestall possible later Senate criticism of having overlooked important moral issues. All these criteria could be applied by looking either to the past or to the future. We could ask: where did someone go wrong in his previous life? Or we could ask: what is the likelihood that he will make better choices in the future? To our commission, the second question seemed almost more important than the first. But our attempts to predict the seriousness of someone's future commitment to the rule of law raised another problem: what to do with candidates of pre-retirement age, who had only a few years of university employment left? According to the Senate guidelines, prognostic decisions concerning older employees 'were not advisable.' Decisions as to their employment therefore had to be based entirely 'on an evaluation of the applicant's past behavior.' Was that supposed to mean that older candidates were automatically presumed to be incapable of change? Did the Senate guidelines authorize a summary approach to the evaluation of pre-retirement personnel—maybe, as practiced in many other East German institutions now trying to fend off the axe, by offering older faculty members short-term contracts coupled with early retirement—in order to make positions available for the retention of younger personnel? I could see that to some commission members the thought was tempting. Mandatory early retirement for some would increase everyone else's chances of survival. But it would be a bad way in which to begin our work, we decided, if we were to subject individual interests, once again, to those of the collective. The commission resolved: no summary treatment of pre-retirement personnel. Everyone was entitled to be judged on his or her own merits.

So much for principles. Of course, we also had to contend with numerous practical problems. Mail from East to West Berlin would take forever. Telephones lines were open only very early in the morning or late at night. As a result, communication between Eastern and Western commission members was chancy at best. Sometimes, third parties could be used as relay stations. And what about our creature comforts? During weekend meetings, when the University cafeteria was closed, it was hard to find food in the vicinity of the University. To treat ourselves, the commission decided to meet one weekend in the law offices of our colleague Professor Nordemann in West Berlin, where telephones and copiers would work, and where, in the presence of freezer and microwave oven, we would not have to worry about going hungry. 'Objection,' said a commission member from East Berlin. Was it permissible to remove the files from Humboldt University? Why not, said the *Wessis*. Because of data protection! said our *Ossi* colleague. The stringent reputation of West German data protection law had once before caused trouble, when some of the people to be vetted insisted that their files should not be read by any commission member without another's being present in the room. Was it because the investigated viewed the commission with the same suspicion as any other political institution which until now had controlled their lives? Because the legal protection of privacy was still so foreign that the protected could not tell what kind of secrecy made sense and what didn't? In any case, we managed to calm the fears. For one Sunday, the commission met in capitalist opulence in West Berlin.

Finally, the week of the hearings. Each sub-committee was responsible for one-third of the interviews, that is, for twenty-five to thirty people (excluding non-academic staff members, like secretaries or telephonists, whom we decided to question only in rare circumstances). Originally, we had scheduled half an hour per interview. Of course, that time turned out to be much too short. Despite our familiarity with a candidate's file, even the hour that we usually took was not enough to sustain the illusion that we had actually understood what made the person tick. But prolonging conversations wrought havoc upon our timetable. Again and again, we had to send an emissary to those waiting outside the door: 'Could you please come back in another hour?' After each conversation, a short discussion among committee members, a vote, a summary scribbled for the record, and 'the next one, please.' Obviously, meals had to be eaten on the run. On weekdays, a friendly secretary would occasionally bring coffee. Commission members learned not to leave home without a bar of chocolate in their pocket. Between interviews, we shared whatever one or the other member happened to have brought. In the evenings, it took an effort to lift our stiff and weary bodies from the chairs in which it seemed that we had spent half of our lives.

But how much harder than for us must this week have been for those whom we interrogated. Each candidate's behavior seemed to reflect a conscious choice of pose: hostile, eager, disciplined, open, macho, deprecatory. Some appeared intentionally formal; some, intentionally relaxed. Despite the fact that all had consented to the vetting, all candidates, I think, distrusted the commission. Why should two *Wessis*, coming from another world, and a number of colleagues whose lives and careers were just as much in shambles as their own now be in a position to select those who should be allowed to keep their jobs and those who should lose them? What legitimated us to make such life-shattering decisions? I almost think that the examined would have found it preferable to be judged by a commission composed entirely of Westerners. The victors' verdict would have been easier to swallow and easier to shrug off. Untrained in democracy, the members of the Humboldt University Law Faculty seemed more irritated than pleased by the absence of any hierarchy in the relationship between examined and examiners. To most, I think, the fact that they themselves had elected the commission members by secret ballot simply was not enough to legitimate our authority.

What did we want to know from the examinees? Understandably, most questions turned on people's relationship with the Party. Everybody had been something: secretary of the Free German Youth organization, group agitator, member of the Basic Party Group leadership, member of the Departmental Group leadership, discussion leader at ideological training sessions, Basic Group secretary, head of the university militia. Without the explanations of their Eastern colleagues, the Western members would never have penetrated the ranking of the many posts. Who occupied the more important functions? Often the best people: they were more likely to be asked and found it harder to talk their way out of an offer that pretended to be flattering. 'You'll learn something,' the recruiter would have told them. 'I was never one to stand aside,' someone adds as he describes his office. I find it difficult to decide whether the explanation speaks for or against him. Like the church in the Middle Ages, it was the Party in the GDR that provided the structures in which capable and ambitious people could prove themselves. In every society, success takes place in preordained and socially acceptable patterns. Only someone who needs no outside help to realize his calling can do entirely without social acclaim. Maybe you can be a poet without, or even against, society. But to write prose, it seems to me, would already be difficult for someone totally removed from that web of social relationships which also forms the cloth from which he cuts his figures. And to be a lawyer against the legal system under which you operate is hard to imagine. So, it can come as no surprise that virtually every Law Faculty examinee in one or another fashion participated in Party life at the University. The rare candidate who had escaped all recruitment efforts usually appeared also to be a loner, an odd man out, who under any social system would have marched to a different drummer.

Since almost everyone held some Party office, it became important to understand in what spirit that office had been filled. Someone explains that he became Secretary of the Law School Party group only to 'protect the Faculty against the District Party leadership.' Well, did he? Somebody else, describing his unanimous election to an influential grass-root post, tells the commission about his satisfaction over 'this important demonstration of trust.' Whose trust? Some tasks, now reviled, were automatically part of a job. Every bit of foreign mail, for instance, had to cross the Dean's desk before it could be passed on to the proper addressee. 'What did you do with it?', we ask the man who was Humboldt's Law Dean for many years. 'I initialled it,' he says. Was there a better way? Occasionally, even committee members are persuaded that Party posts can serve praiseworthy functions. Someone uses her membership in a Law School Section's party secretariat to develop a program under which every research student in the section is provided with a specific timetable programming step by step the timely completion of his thesis. Back at my law school in Texas, we have a special committee attempting something similar. Everywhere in the world, young scholars need encouragement and feedback.

How varied are the careers I now get to know! There are the big shots, those in whose lives everything went according to plan: punctual first and second dissertation, rapid promotion, good connections to the Party, significant appointments. Since they have been driven from influential and envied posts, they are now worse off than others. They have not yet gotten used to the loss of their own importance. Then, there are those whom socialism threw off course: Dr. Rudolph, for example, lecturer at the Institute for Intellectual Property and Copyright and member of my PSK sub-committee. He lost his job at the Patent Office of the GDR because he had refused to break off contacts with his wife's mother, who lived in West Berlin. 'I couldn't deprive my children of their grandmother, could I,' he says like someone explaining something that really needs no explanation. So he was kicked out of the Patent Office. Although 'kicked out' is something of a misdescription since people at the Patent Office would have loved to keep Dr. Rudolph and were happy that a refuge could be found for him at Humboldt University. The intellectual property section at Humboldt could barely function without him. But Herr Rudolph never became a professor. Professors—like officials at the Patent Office—were not allowed to have 'West contacts.' Had Dr. Rudolph stayed at the Patent Office, he would not have become a professor either. He is not angry at Humboldt University. I have never heard him say a bad word about any of his colleagues. If he speaks up, it will always be in favor of a candidate.

Some of the examinees have simply had bad luck. We interview an intelligent, articulate young man. He wrote his 'A-dissertation' on a legal topic that has since ceased to exist. Because no lectureships in his field seemed likely to open up at Humboldt University in the then foreseeable future, he moved to another university of lesser reputation. At his new school, 'big topics' were frowned upon. So he wrote his 'B-dissertation' (now called 'Habilitation') on a 'small' topic which like the first has since been stricken from the academic canon. He completed his thesis in the spring of 1989; all three outside readers had given their stamp of approval. But with the political commotion in the late summer and autumn of 1989, it took a while to arrange for the viva. In March 1990, he failed it. He had not known how to handle some questions on West Germany's Civil Code and the topics of his two dissertations had only fueled worries about his ability to function under the new law. Here is someone with ambition, interests, brains, and a love of learning. The old academic system served him badly. Chances are, the new one will not even have him.

Once in a while, there is a golden boy or girl among the candidates. Someone to whom everything comes easy. Who was sufficiently well placed to be successful under the old regime, and smart enough not to allow himself to be sucked in by it. Who did fine before the *Wende*, would have continued to do fine without it and who no doubt will make his way under the new order. Not because he is a turncoat but because intelligence, critical distance, charm, and a healthy sense of what is feasible will serve you under any social system. Shall we begrudge it that in the general misery around him he does not feel miserable himself? Of course he passes.

Yesterday, with all interviews completed, we met for our final plenary session. The 'external' commission members, too, had travelled to Berlin for the occasion: all of them, smart, influential, grey-haired gentlemen who know their rank but on this occasion draw no attention to it. The decisions we are about to reach are of such existential significance to those affected that there is no room for personal vanities. All are resolved to do the best they can. Now and then, the distance between Eastern and Western members of the PSK is illuminated in a flash of cultural dissonance. It is primarily a matter of speech: the brisk, precise, cool language of the *Wessis* at times outpaces the direct, concrete, and human language of the *Ossis*. One name after the other is read out from our list. The sub-committee who interviewed the person explains its recommendation, there is a short debate, and then a vote. Occasionally, a particularly complex case requires a lengthier discussion. Finally, all results are settled. Of the twenty-eight professors of the Humboldt Law Faculty, ten have been found to lack sufficient 'personal integrity' to warrant their continued employment. Among the lecturers and research students, the percentage of 'unsuitable' candidates is lower. None of the non-academic personnel has been found unworthy to continue in his or her job at Humboldt University.

Today, our commission will explain and defend its recommendations before the Faculty Council who will then accept or reject them by open vote. Our meeting takes place in Room 2103, once home to the Humboldt University Party Secretariat. You can still tell from the padded double door. We sit around a long, U-shaped row of tables: the Dean, the members of the Faculty Council, the PSK members, a representative from the Senate Administration of Justice, a few delegates from the University's central administration, one or two other guests. I note with relief a coffee-cup at every place. Just as yesterday, one name after the other is read to the assembly, we explain our verdict, there are comments, a debate, and then the Faculty Council's vote. If the next name on the list belongs to someone present in the room, he or she waits outside until a decision has been reached. Most of our recommendations are accepted.

But occasionally, there is a stumbling block. A name is read. One of the people from the University administration interrupts: 'Didn't you know?' Apparently, rumors are going around concerning the candidate's relationship with the *Stasi*. At my own university, I would find it beneath my own and my colleagues' dignity to listen to rumors of this kind. But this is a different place and a different time. No, we didn't know. The decision is postponed, the person's name passed on to the University's Honor Tribunal.

Another delay when the discussion turns to one of the staff members. Usually, it does not take long to deal with these cases: office personnel, secretaries or clerical staff cannot be made responsible for what went wrong at Humboldt University. But this a special case. It concerns a young woman, historian by training, who once held a research position in the University's Department of Marxism-Leninism. When after the *Wende* her department was closed, she found work for DM 800 a month in the Law Faculty's main office where she organizes class schedules and room planning. Not an easy job, but one she is managing to everybody's satisfaction. But the Senate Administration has ordered that all employees of the former Department of Marxism-Leninism be dismissed. The PSK members understand that Marxism-Leninism, or at least that version of it taught at Humboldt's Department of Marxism-Leninism, is now definitely a thing of the past. But does that mean that the Department's former members should forever remain unemployed? A well-functioning timetable is an important and useful contribution to the Law Faculty's attempt at self-reform. It has nothing to do with the sins of the deceased Department of Marxism-Leninism. Apart from her association with the Department, the candidate has not been accused of any other failing. The PSK will not declare her morally unsuitable to carry out her present job.

Frau Ansbach, who as chair explains the commission's verdict to the meeting, speaks with passion. We will not repeat the errors of the past, she says. The rule of law requires respect for the individual. Lump-sum justice violates a person's dignity. I can see tears in her eyes. Silent reflection in the room. All of us know how much the University depends upon the goodwill of the Berlin Senate Administration. These days, in particular, it does not seem wise to reach decisions that run directly counter to Senate orders. But the discussion that now follows makes it obvious that everyone around the table agrees with Dr. Ansbach. A West Berlin colleague, guest professor at Humboldt and member of the Faculty Council, asks to speak. 'Do what you think is right,' he says. 'But do it unanimously.' Unanimously, the Council votes: no objections as to the young woman's personal integrity and competence. Weeks later, I learn that upon Senate instructions, the University dismissed her anyway.

The session continues. Occasionally, there are questions. One of our decisions in particular baffles a Council member. She wants to know how we could possibly have reached it. 'What were you actually looking for?' she asks, irritated. A good question: what were we looking for? For the misuse of political and intellectual authority, of course. But no less, it seems to me, for the right mixture of guilty feelings and self-confidence. We became suspicious if someone too breezily identified with his former self. 'I don't have a bad conscience,' he might say at the interview. 'I always did the best I could and see no reason to say otherwise today.' Honest though it sounded, I did not like to hear that kind of statement. We thought it implausible that someone who had taught law under socialism should never have done, said, or written anything that he would not have to regret today. But we also mistrusted the over-eager candidates, those who had, without ever looking back, crossed over to the rule of law with flying colors. Their eagerness might have been authentic coming from a botanist, perhaps, or from a linguist. But from a lawyer? Did their enthusiasm not suggest that they had never noticed how thoroughly socialism had affected their thinking? Did it mean that they had always set their sails to the political wind and therefore had no problem changing their course?

We looked, I believe, for people who took the present political transition the hard way—but not too hard. For signs of trauma, combined with the capacity to heal. For those who, acknowledging the burden of the past, nevertheless turned full of anticipation towards the future. We looked especially for projects, ambitions, hopes. A young research associate is asked whether he intends to go for his 'Habilitation.' 'Well, yes,' he says 'if the Faculty will so direct me. . . .' We laugh unhappily. No more outside direction as to how you should lead your life. Now you must seize the initiative yourself. I noticed during this week of interviews how little time it had taken my lawyer's instincts to fall silent. What we were after had nothing to do with law. With justice? Although I hope so, the hope seems presumptuous. We were trying to assist at a departure for new and promising shores.

What carried weight with the commission? It is easier to say what did not carry weight: political pressures, old boy networks, self-promotion, vanity, revenge. The PSK was the least conventional of all the academic committees I was ever part of and also the best. No one threw his weight about. Everyone listened. Differences of opinion were articulated, discussed, and settled. All focused on the task before us: to acknowledge past injustice, not to belittle past achievement, to honor true changes of the heart, to respect the individual. I am not pleased with the results of our labor. But I do not see how we could have done a better job.

All this I try to explain to the questioner, get muddled, start anew. But then I think of an argument that might help to persuade people of the admittedly ambiguous justification for our work. The evaluations of interviews in our sub-committee were almost always unanimous, I say. I cannot confidently define what we were looking for, but we almost always knew whether we had found it or not. The questioner nods, still skeptical, but not without some sympathy for our efforts. She does not know herself how else one could have gone about the task.

It is late afternoon by the time all the names of our list have been marked off.

25 April 1991

Two new decisions affecting the fate of my colleagues in East Berlin: one, half a victory; the other, nine-tenths a defeat. Yesterday the Federal Constitutional Court in a case involving the suspension of former GDR public employees held among other things that East German institutions may be closed down, *abgewickelt*, only if their former functions also will be discontinued. To shut down an institution only temporarily in order to restaff it with 'untainted' (and largely Western) personnel amounts—says the Court—to an illegal circumvention of the Unification Treaty. If former socialist public functions continue to be useful and in demand under capitalism, those who carried them out may not be summarily dismissed but must, instead, be individually vetted and, if warranted, fired for cause. Humboldt University's case against the temporary closure of its five departments, presently before the Administrative Court of Appeals, looks pretty good.

And today I learned in a telephone chat with Frau Svensson that the results of the *Wissenschaftsrat*'s evaluation of the Institute of Legal Science are finally available. As everyone predicted, the *Wissenschaftsrat* recommends closure of the Institute. Two working groups with three researchers each (from Criminology and International Law) are to receive continued funding, preferably by way of integration into some existing academic institution. (Which?) The report also suggests that five members of the Institute should be given the chance 'to apply for individual funding.' It does not mention where that 'individual funding' might come from. And since the report does not name those supposedly praiseworthy five researchers either, nobody at the Institute can draw attention to an 'honorable mention' by the *Wissenschaftsrat* to make his job application elsewhere more persuasive. Where could a former member of the Institute of Legal Science find work anyway? West German universities hire East German academics neither as professors (because they are held to be unqualified) nor as lecturers or research assistants (because they are over-qualified and often too old). East German universities, now run almost exclusively by emissaries from West German patron universities, follow the same rules of thumb. Professor Hölzer, one of Frau Svensson's colleagues at the Institute for Legal Science, recently told me that his job application to the East German University of Greifswald had produced a rejection letter from the West German University of Osnabrück. Since no one needs the *Wissenschaftsrat*'s permission to apply for funding, its recommendation for the nameless five strikes everyone as something of a mystery. Why not recommend ten researchers or—more realistically—none at all? In the old days, the usual response to enigmatic orders from above was 'well, the comrades must have had their reasons.' It is not an easy thing to say when your own professional existence is at stake.

So, there reigns 'quite a panic' at the Institute for Legál Science. No information yet as to unemployment benefits or possible retraining programs for those dismissed. Frau Svensson will become a lawyer; now she is glad to have applied for admission to the Bar under the old GDR rules. Will she ever return to academe? She doesn't know. 'No use being stiff-necked about your goals these days,' she says.

8 May 1991

At the Senate Administration of Justice in the Salzburger Strasse in West Berlin only two minutes away from City Hall. It is housed in an attractive art deco building with a rounded front and a complicated entry hall which like the prints of M. C. Escher leaves you wondering whether its staircase is actually leading up or down. A row of leaded windows in pink and terracotta shows signs of the zodiac. The effect is pleasantly theatrical: half maze, half temple of fortune.

It is 6 p.m. I have an appointment with Councillor Klaus Ritter, Deputy Department Head at Justice and in charge of the vetting process for the 369 East Berlin judges and prosecutors who have applied for admission into the Berlin judiciary. These days, Herr Ritter practically lives in his office. Even on weekends, a telephone call is more likely to catch him at work than at home. He heads a task force set up at the Ministry to investigate each applicant's political and professional suitability. Besides the approval of the Senate Administration, a candidate will also need the endorsement of the so-called Judicial Selection Committee, an independent body elected by the Berlin legislature upon nominations by the political parties, the judiciary, and the Bar. Under the Unification Treaty, both authorities—the Senator of Justice (advised by Herr Ritter's task force) and the Judicial Selection Committee decide 'together' on the re-employment of each applicant. The no-vote of either authority inevitably spells defeat.

But it is Herr Ritter's committee that organizes the vetting process and that, coming first and thus prejudicing its outcome, sets the tone of the inquiry. It is here that the personal files of the applicants and all those questionnaires filled out last autumn are collected and evaluated. Although the committee intends to interview at least the plausible candidates personally, I learn that, until now, few hearings have been held. Rainer Hannemann, the young judge from East Germany's former contract court, is the only one among my conversation partners from last autumn who has been questioned by the Senate Committee. Right now, we are concentrating on the ambiguous cases, says Herr Ritter. I am puzzled. Herr Hannemann, 'an ambiguous case'? What are the Senate Administration's criteria for determining who among the candidates is acceptable to the *Rechtsstaat*? There are no written criteria, says Herr Ritter. He corrects himself almost at once: at least 'there is nothing I can give you.' Why not? Doesn't each applicant have the right to know the standards under which his fate is settled? Herr Ritter's answer makes clear that the Senate Administration does not operate on the assumption that former socialist officials, just on account of their erstwhile offices, have many rights. Legally, the Justice Administration views a candidate from East Berlin no differently from any other candidate for the judiciary: an outsider applying for a job who is entitled to no more than the non-discriminatory exercise of administrative discretion. If the Senate Administration takes so much trouble over the selection process, it is out of sheer political generosity and not because their former posts would give East German judges any kind of head start over Western competitors.

Nevertheless, some clues as to Herr Ritter's method of selection emerge from our conversation. There is, first of all, the written record of each candidate: his personal file and the questionnaire. Already, trouble. In February 1990, the post-Honecker reform government under Hans Modrow (shortly before it was ousted in the first and only free elections in the GDR) in a decree 'safeguarding privacy in employment relations' had ordered the cleansing of all East German personnel files. The decree authorized all employees to view their files and to remove from them 'all records and documents no longer relevant.' Only a person's 'most recent' work evaluation was to be retained. It seems that East German judges and prosecutors, who for the first time in their lives set eyes on their own employment records, followed the decree's invitation with a vengeance. As a result, Herr Ritter's task force must now search for clues to an applicant's character in moth-eaten files which may omit the very information the committee is most interested in. And although applicants were asked to restore their records by reinserting the missing sheets it is not always easy to tell whether they actually did so. Two weeks ago, I talked about the problem with Joachim Rössler, presiding judge at the Berlin Court of Appeals, whose task it had been in the autumn and winter of last year to retrieve all information available on East Berlin judges and prosecutors and to prepare the materials for use by Herr Ritter's committee. Among the files submitted by the East Berliners, Herr Rössler told me, those of older judges are often skimpier than those of younger ones. The personal file of one of the justices of the former Supreme Court had contained all of eight pages. Since older GDR records are paginated, it is easy to discover gaps. In the case of more recent files, one 'can only presume the worst.' 'They managed all right to pull the wool over our eyes,' Herr Rössler said.

His hurt and disdainful tone of voice betrayed the extent of damage caused by that unfortunate Modrow decree. Whyever was it passed? Herr Oehmke, to whom I posed the question, attributed the decree to East German fears of a 'witch-hunt.' 'If they were bent on finding fault with us,' he said, 'we were not about to provide the ammunition.' But the decree was passed only three months after the collapse of the Wall. Did East German politicians at that time already worry about West German lustration plans? At least in part, it seems to me, the decree must have been motivated by the wish to facilitate new beginnings by erasing memories of a distasteful past. So many data in the files now were indeed 'no longer relevant': information about a person's 'West contacts,' for example, or about relatives in Party offices, which were kept up to date by the requirement that everyone had to submit a rewritten curriculum vitae every couple of years. Why keep those records? True, the Modrow purge of employment files served those with something to hide better than those whose slates were clean. It is safe to assume that many of the present applicants for judicial office removed documents from their files which would today cast a shadow on their political integrity. I have also been told of instances in which superior judges removed negative evaluations from the files of their subordinates—not to protect them but to cover up their own shameful readiness to inform on those below them. Under the decree, nothing but the bare bones of a person's employment record was intended to be kept. Frau Schomburg once showed me a page she had removed from her own file: an evaluation by her presiding judge characterizing her as 'unsuitable for leadership positions.' Too many run-ins, it appears, with her superiors. But to a Western reader, the criticism she had duly removed would rather have helped than harmed her. Herr Ritter tells me that many of the applicants seem to have restored their files as best they could, including documents that in Western eyes must speak against them. Still, nobody knows for sure. The files remain unreliable. What did Herr Oehmke say? The East Germans wanted to prevent a witch-hunt. Now West Germans call it 'vetting.' And it is the very dishonesty of the files that nourishes Western suspicions and thus the possibility that the vetting might indeed come dangerously close to resembling a witch-hunt.

What other information do Herr Ritter and his colleagues have for judging the applicants? If they can be found, the candidates' own judgments. If, that is. A handful of successful candidates have passed, by now, and in each case the committee had roughly twenty of an applicant's decisions to judge from. But often, there are fewer. One source of information has been the infamous prison in Rummelsburg where West German investigators have collected files, photocopied judgments, and added them to the application documents of the judges involved. The other likely source of information, the Documentation Center on SED Injustice in Salzgitter, unfortunately does not yield useful material for Herr Ritter's committee: its reports are based on the victims' narratives from memory and lack reliable identification marks like file numbers or even names. Some judgments, Herr Ritter says, have also been found at the Littenstrasse courthouse. But overall, it is largely 'a matter of chance' how much and what samples of a candidate's judicial output are available to the committee.

And what, in particular, are they looking for? Criminal decisions, to begin with. The most offensive judgments in the GDR usually concerned political matters—cases in which the possession of subversive leaflets or contacts with the West German Permanent Mission in East Berlin earned the offender several years in prison—and were rendered by special panels of judges, the so-called 'Ia Senates,' whose former members will now know better than to apply to Herr Ritter's committee and who, in any case, would have very little chance of passing the review. But since 1985, 'border violations' under section 213 of the Criminal Code—that is, attempts to flee the country—were adjudicated by ordinary criminal law panels and so Herr Ritter and his colleagues are looking for convictions under section 213. And they look for arrest warrants under the same provision, which were issued not only by criminal law judges but on holidays and weekends were signed by the 'judge on duty' who could come from any field. Even family law or labor law judges in the GDR could not always distance themselves from the country's most corrosive bane, although it was entirely a matter of luck whether those miscreants arrested on a weekend would include a 'border violator' or not. 'How many arrest warrants must an otherwise inconspicuous civil or family law judge have signed to be discredited for judicial office?' I ask Herr Ritter. Three? Five? Well, five arrest warrants would definitely give him pause, Herr Ritter says. If an applicant had signed a total of five arrest warrants, he would want to hear some explanation. Usually, arrest warrants were issued at the request of a prosecutor. Maybe it had not been necessary for the judge on duty to comply? But under GDR criminal procedure, suspects were to be detained if it seemed likely that they would otherwise try to escape, I say. Wouldn't potential refugees automatically fit that description? No, Herr Ritter does not know of any case in which a prosecutorial request for an arrest warrant had actually been denied.

All right, then. Let us assume the committee decides that a particular candidate lacks the qualifications for judicial office. What will happen next? He will receive a standard rejection letter, containing some general remarks about his unsuitability. After all, 'we don't want to insult people,' Herr Ritter says. Insult them! A candidate must know what elements of the decision he might want to challenge in court! Well, if someone complains, the committee will add more detailed reasons, Herr Ritter says. But at the initial stage at least, they will not invite objections by providing a rejected applicant with a detailed list of his failings.

Anyway, there have not been very many final decisions until now, says Herr Ritter. Since September of last year, most of the East Berlin judges whom I interviewed last autumn have not heard anything about their applications. Why did they not receive at least an interim reply? 'No time,' Herr Ritter says. Let them make inquiries. 'We need active people' in the judiciary. 'Those who stay put and wait just about prove themselves to be unsuitable.' It sounds as if Herr Ritter is approving of what might be called administrative Darwinism to add an element of natural selection to his vetting efforts. Will it sort out the weak, the timid, those not willing to stick their necks out? Even under the old GDR petition decree, I recall, administrative officers were set time-limits for responding to citizens' requests and—if decisions were delayed—had to provide an applicant with an interim response.

But I realize from our conversation that Herr Ritter obviously does not measure his committee's work by the procedural yardstick he would usually apply to West Berlin administrative practice. The East German applicants, it appears, are not yet part of the rule-of-law community. They are huddling in its antechamber, waiting to be let in. Even if untainted by political corruption, they have no right to regain their former offices. They have no right to be notified of the committee's selection criteria, no right to a speedy decision, to interim responses, to reasons should their application be rejected. Although Herr Ritter would consider it improper to inquire about a Western applicant's political affiliation, he takes it for granted that being a member of the PDS, the Communist Party's ostracized but nonetheless perfectly legal successor party, should probably disqualify East German applicants. To do him justice, I notice a little embarrassment on this point. It seems the Committee takes trouble not to ask a candidate outright about his membership. But it will try to find out indirectly, with apparently harmless questions like 'when did you leave the Party?' I recently spoke with a candidate who had been asked that very question in her interview. It had taken her an effort, she admitted, to reply truthfully. But since she was resolved not again to let her life be dominated by political fear, she gave the answer that Herr Ritter had been looking for: 'I have not left the Party.' And his reaction? Well, a candidate's membership in the PDS is cause for serious worries, Herr Ritter says. The Senator of Justice herself will want to decide those cases. To him, PDS membership probably suggests that the person in question 'has not yet faced up to her past.' But what about the Constitution, I say, which provides in Article 21 that every political party is considered constitutional unless the Federal Constitutional Court specifically states the opposite? Herr Ritter takes no note of the objection.

And yet, I am convinced that the Senate Committee does not take its responsibility lightly. Herr Ritter seems wrapped up in his job. Like 'a good examiner,' he claims to look not for ignorance but for knowledge; not for hostility but for loyalty to the constitution. These interviews are conversations, he says at one point, 'not interrogations.' Nevertheless, I suspect that, to the candidates, his unstructured and leisurely approach to the vetting process must look strangely familiar. The Senate Administration does not act as if a democratic balance between applicants and Committee were even desirable. Instead, it presumes a natural hierarchy between the participants—a right and proper gradient of power, with the Senate Administration on top and the new citizens at the bottom. Citizens? Rather—and hence, I believe, a sense of *déjà vu* among the applicants—rather petitioners than citizens. As under socialism, they have no legal entitlements but are dependent upon the good will of the decision makers. Even the committee's demonstrations of patience and concern fit the old picture. Herr Ritter tells me that he twice postponed decisions and counselled the candidates to reapply in three months' time because they apparently 'had not yet come to terms' with their involvement in socialist injustice. But I wonder how the two took the solicitous advice. 'Unsatisfactory grades: probation'—was that the message that had come across? At their second interview, both candidates 'had made an even worse impression,' Herr Ritter says. He seems surprised. Not all the applicants react to the vetting process with hurt defiance. Some of my conversation partners from last autumn are worried: 'I haven't had a word from them yet,' someone might say. 'What do you think: is that a good sign? Should I just wait? Will it hurt my chances if I push for a response?' New dependencies, new attempts to adapt. The victors do not appear in the roles of liberators.

How could it happen that the vetting procedures degenerated into an administrative process second class? I sense among the examiners enormous suspicion toward their examinees. Considering the daily revelations of miscarriages of justices under socialism, the suspicion can come as no surprise. The hapless file-cleansing decree under the Modrow government also must have done its part. But the main cause for the West Berlin distrust of anything related to the East Berlin judiciary is, I believe, the *Wessis'* incapacity to understand and place their Eastern colleagues. Two weeks ago, Herr Rössler had complained to me: even if you actually got hold of a respectable sample of a judge's decisions, it would not necessarily help you to make up your mind. There would often be no rhyme or reason to a person's judicial output. It wasn't that in the case of border violations, for example, political opportunists had rendered harsh decisions while judges with some backbone had let defendants off with lenient sentences. The same judge, in cases with apparently very similar fact patterns, might on one occasion have given a fugitive six months with suspension, and on another, two or three years without. Herr Rössler explained the discrepancies as the results of different orders from above: judges would do whatever they had been told to do at the most recent 'judges' conference.' 'Their idea of a judge simply cannot be compared to ours,' he said.

I also notice how the vetting process itself has poisoned communications between examiners and examinees. The East Berliners 'change their arguments from month to month,' Herr Rössler said, 'depending on the Senate Administration's knowledge of East German judicial practices.' Today 'they use different forms of camouflage' from yesterday. At first, the examiners were told: 'We've never heard of the practices you describe.' Then, when the evidence could no longer be disputed: 'We've heard of that but we have never done things that way.' And then, all applications from East Berlin 'look so alike.' That, too, causes suspicion: maybe the candidates have synchronized their stories? West German applications to the Berlin judiciary all look different, says Herr Rössler, more individualistic and one not exactly like the other.

But what does he expect? West German judges who are considering a move to Berlin come from different parts of the country, different positions, and are motivated by very different personal reasons. East German judges all come from the same cornered existence. A life under siege. Many are unemployed or have found at best some temporary occupation. Almost all know each other. All are waiting. Everybody asks everybody else: have you heard something? Was it your turn already? What did they ask you? Those who just had their interview must tell their stories; those who just failed it 'must by collective effort be coaxed out of their depression.' News spread like brushfire, like that account of yet another judge who had feared that her PDS membership might come to light during her interview. 'What did you find most liberating after the collapse of socialism?' had been one of the very first questions of the committee. 'That nobody will ever again ask me about my party affiliation,' was her clever reply. But she had failed the review anyway: too many arrest warrants. Still, her story circulates to everyone's delight: one tiny triumph.

It would be amazing if in this hothouse climate the applications to Herr Ritter's committee did not all look alike. And it is quite conceivable that at least some of the East Berliners learned of certain unsavory judicial practices in the GDR only through current rumors. Moreover, I am certain that they consulted with each other before filling out their questionnaires and submitting their applications. Who wouldn't in their place? Incidentally, it is not just the East Berliners who talk and act like people in a common boat. Members of the Senate Administration use expressions and arguments which suggest that, like soldiers huddling in the trenches, they too rehash the same old issues over and over again. Herr Rössler's phrase—'they pulled the wool over our eyes all right'—I heard verbatim from two other Justice officials. In the current vetting war, both camps fear to be outwitted by the other.

So here they are again: the old Cold War reflexes we thought we had finally outgrown. If anything, the West Berliners—whose self-importance makes them vulnerable to disrespect—are even more afraid of being duped than are their socialist counterparts. The East Berliners seem torn between the desire not to lay themselves open to Western attack and a hunger for candor that for so long had to go unstilled. 'I thought they wanted frankness,' I was told by the judge whose PDS membership had gotten her into trouble. So, asked by the committee about the most formative influence during her law school years, she had replied 'legal reasoning and the theory of socialism.' Herr Ritter, whom I now ask about that particular interview, remembers it differently. He was struck not by the young woman's earnest attempt to acknowledge and understand her past but by her, as he saw it, unwillingness to dissociate herself from the transgressions of the Party. In my own conversation with the judge, we had also talked about the PDS affair. 'Why ever did you stay a Party member,' I had asked. 'Were you not afraid that your PDS affiliation would hurt your chances of re-employment?' 'Of course, I was,' the judge had answered. 'That's why I stayed.' She had once, as a law student, been ordered by State Security to sever contacts with some West German law students met on a holiday in Prague and since she had cared more about her career than about her new-found friends, had reluctantly complied. Today, she is ashamed of the memory. 'I did not want to give in—again—to political pressures,' she had told me. And there had been another reason for her sticking with the PDS. 'I felt that, as a Party member, I had participated in getting us into this mess and now want to participate in getting us out of it,' she had explained. 'I did not want to quit.' None of this had come out in the interview with Herr Ritter's committee. I wonder what he and his colleagues would have made of it. Smelled another subterfuge? Herr Ritter admits that the examinees will often 'not lie intentionally.' 'Many candidates believe the stories that they tell us,' he says. It is obvious that he does not.

Will his incredulity assure that the East Berliners won't 'pull the wool over his eyes'? Already on my pre-*Wende* travels through the GDR—that is, in times in which truthfulness could equally spell trouble (although for different reasons than today), I found myself faced with the question of whether to trust my conversation partners or not. I decided that you probably come closer to the truth believing everything than believing nothing. For a lawyer at least, believing nothing seems to be the more appropriate reaction. But believing everything or—not to throw caution entirely to the winds—believing almost everything, will do more justice to the complicated social truth which I and Herr Ritter are looking for. It is not a yes or no affair. Each player's glimpse of it depends upon his position in the drama. All of us—*Wessis* and *Ossis*, examiners and examinees, Herr Ritter and the young PDS judge whom he mistrusts—have their facets of truth to offer. One day, we might be able to see the entire picture from a common vantage point. In the meantime, distrust would only make us lose important pieces of the puzzle. Distrust is costly for other reasons, too. For one thing, most people are more likely to respond to questions in good faith if they feel accepted by the questioner. And if you disbelieve them, you must fill the gaps left by their repudiated testimony in other ways: through speculation, hearsay, other people's stories (why trust them?), or your own guesswork—none of them necessarily more reliable than the evidence which you have just discarded, and none representing your rejected informant's particular perspective. No, I fear that Herr Ritter's disbelief is more of an obstacle than an aid to his search for justice.

Toward the end of our conversation, I learn something that throws me into doubt myself. I am about to leave; Herr Ritter and I chat for a little while, I put on my coat in the office of his secretary (long gone home), and I tell him about my own vetting experiences at Humboldt University. As it turns out, Herr Ritter's and my own committee are more similar in working style and philosophy than I would have thought. Like the members of my PSK, Herr Ritter and his colleagues are interested in the process of reflection and self-inspection by which the candidates approach their past. As in my PSK, the votes in Herr Ritter's Senate committee are almost always unanimous. Are our different results simply the product of our different sets of prejudices? Should not my Humboldt personnel review commission, too, have tried to approach its task with more respect for procedure, in colder, more precise, more legal fashion? Now I recall what an administrative court judge in West Berlin once said to me: 'You really have to labor at the rule of law.' I am afraid that neither Herr Ritter's committee nor my own labored enough.

15 May 1991

An early-morning appointment with Frau Fischer at the Hotel Unter den Linden. The City Bar is buzzing with the sound of vacuum cleaners. Last time, I met Frau Fischer in her office at the Littenstrasse courthouse. Since then, she has passed a crash course for insurance salesmen and in the meantime is waiting to hear from the Senate Administration of Justice. I want to know how she herself views those decisions which Herr Ritter's committee will very likely chalk up against her.

Frau Fischer joined the judiciary in 1983. Although she worked primarily as a family court judge, in seven and a half years of office she is bound to have signed a number of arrest warrants for 'border violations.' Her memories of those occasions are vague. They would be: those were matters of routine. If someone tried to flee the country, the 'danger of escape,' which was the primary legal prerequisite for an arrest, could always be assumed. Had there been special Supreme Court directives or instructions issued at 'judges' conferences' telling her how to handle arrest warrants? Frau Fischer is not certain but assumes so. Whatever those instructions ordered her to do, she would have done. Everybody else would have done so too. That was the way things worked.

Like almost all civil law judges in the GDR, Frau Fischer, on occasion, also sat as a criminal court judge. She recalls two border cases that she had to deal with. The first concerned a young man whom she had met in her court once before: at his divorce trial, when Frau Fischer—in her family judge capacity—had unsuccessfully presided over a conciliation meeting trying to save his marriage. Now he popped up again: this time as a criminal law defendant. After his divorce, the young man's life had apparently gone to pieces, and he had tried to flee the country in an attempt to escape the misery back home. Frau Fischer sentenced him to nine months in prison, less than the young man's own attorney had dared to ask for. She was a little worried: would the sentence stand? The defense counsel had been particularly pleased: maybe this meant that next time he could ask for a lesser sentence, too? Like Frau Fischer, he had been young and new to the game; neither had yet developed a sense for what was feasible and what wasn't.

The other case had also happened during Frau Fischer's early years with the judiciary. Another young man, this time a homosexual who had hoped to join an aunt in West Germany. Frau Fischer can no longer remember her sentence: a year and a half at least, she says; that was 'the going rate.' Maybe even two years. But why? 'He knew perfectly well that he was violating the law,' Frau Fischer says. But that law should never have existed, I say. Why didn't she give the poor fellow nine months, as she had done in that other case?

Frau Fischer seems baffled by my question. Her face is blank. 'I don't know,' she finally says. I don't let go. You would yourself have loved to travel to the West, I say. If the matter had been put to a public vote, you would have voted for open borders. 'Yes,' Frau Fischer says. She is still searching for an explanation for her harsh sentence. Maybe I gave him what the prosecution asked for, she says. As a young judge, you often followed the prosecutor's lead. She knows herself that the explanation is unsatisfactory. But she cannot come up with anything more persuasive.

So here we have one of those instances Herr Rössler complained about: the same judge, the same offense, widely divergent sentences. But Herr Rössler's explanation—different orders from above—does not solve the riddle. Frau Fischer, too, seems mystified by her own behavior. In the case of the second refugee, she did not think—that much is obvious. But why not?

Days after our conversation, a possible explanation occurs to me. The young man trying to run away from his own misery was no stranger to Frau Fischer. She understood his problems, could imagine herself in his place and, since a human relationship existed between the two, could react to his troubles in as humane a fashion as the system would allow. No common experience tied Frau Fischer to the second defendant. Homosexual acts between consenting adults were no offense under East German criminal law. But like all those marching to a different drummer, homosexuals did not fit in with socialism. They seemed out of place among the cheerful, victorious, and uncomplicated musclemen conjured up by the fantasies of socialist realism. As a result, homosexuality in the GDR remained largely invisible. One did not talk about such things. It was not until August 1987 that the Supreme Court finally took note and declared that homosexual citizens, too, were 'no outsiders in socialist society.' But at the time Frau Fischer rendered her decision, she very likely shared the bewilderment and distance most East Germans felt when faced with homosexuality. She told me about a detail of the case which had stuck in her memory. The defendant had purchased color-coordinated equipment for his planned escape: red torch, red pocket knife, a matching belt. 'Weird,' Frau Fischer said. And that 'weird' found an echo in a sentence that showed no human empathy between judge and defendant.

In all societies, it seems to me, decision-makers will be able to break with routine only if some voice interrupts them in the mechanical application of rules and reminds them that there are other ways. Frau Fischer's first decision showed that she, too, knew and listened to those inner voices. Her conscience slept in the second case because the voice that might have awoken it spoke an unfamiliar language. But even in a *Rechtsstaat*, I need to think only of guest-workers, of people of color, of Jehovah's Witnesses and, yes, of homosexuals, too, to remind myself that it is never easy for a judge's conscience to take note of voices pleading their cases in foreign accents.

And another thing. East German judges were products of the system not only in their dependence but also in their opposition. I am thinking of a divorce case someone recently told me about. The daughter of some Party big wheel, after only six months of marriage, wanted a divorce because she had become involved with another man. Her father made it known to the court that he expected a speedy decision. The judge who handled the case, however, took offense at the suggestion. Wasn't she supposed to be independent? So she decided on a 'work to rule' approach. Remembering the Supreme Court's instruction to thoroughly investigate the condition of the marriage to be dissolved, she summoned the wife's new partner to testify on his lover's adultery. At this point, the wife's father must have contacted the Supreme Court to complain. In any case, Frau Rohde telephoned the trial judge: was the new boyfriend's testimony really so essential? 'Is this a recommendation or an order?' asked the clever judge. 'You know perfectly well that I cannot give you any orders,' replied Frau Rohde, as the judge had known she would. And so the summons stood: the wife's new lover had to testify. My conversation partner told the story to demonstrate that if only they wanted to, East German judges could, without great risk, preserve their judicial independence.

But I, who come from a different world, also discover dependence in this story. I am less troubled by Frau Rohde's attempt to influence the trial judge's management of her case than by the latter's decision to insist on highly invasive testimony not because it mattered for the case's outcome— the divorce was certain—but because she wanted to impress the participants with the authority of the court. The husband had not been opposed to the divorce. He had not asked for custody of the couple's child. The boyfriend's testimony was compelled for no other purpose than to embarrass him and his lover and to provide the court with the occasion for a sermon on socialist marriage morality. The trial judge proved with her summons that she had the guts to withstand illegitimate interference from above. But she also proved herself to be embedded in a legal culture that did not grant the individual a right to be left alone. Both—Frau Rohde, presiding over a family law senate that had authorized the thorough investigation of marriage breakdown, and the trial judge, using that authorization to the hilt— ranked the court's pedagogic tasks above the respect for privacy. Neither saw anything wrong with the state's parental guidance of its citizens. Thinking back on this story, I realize that Herr Ritter and his colleagues will never find what they are looking for: immaculate candidates, untouched by the society that bred them.

Afternoon

Lunch on a windy bench on Alexanderplatz. After that, an appointment I have been looking forward to for quite a while: I am to view the huge attic of the Littenstrasse court building, which houses its archives. But first I must explain.

Shortly before Christmas, I saw a performance of *The Broken Jug* at the *Deutsches Theater* in East Berlin: Heinrich von Kleist's famous nineteenth-century comedy whose questionable hero, Judge Adam, a lazy, corrupt, and self-indulgent magistrate in a little Prussian village, is finally brought to his downfall by a combination of his own inept venality and the investigation of a travelling circuit judge. When I bought my program, I also received a little pamphlet containing, as it turned out, four pages of photographs of the Littenstrasse archives. Chaos incarnate! A slanted attic filled with haphazardly placed shelves, some toppled, others pushed aside, whose contents had apparently spilled and never been picked up again. Piles of documents and papers on the floor, some roughly tied in bundles, like waste paper to be recycled, others in mounds of loose sheets, shoved into a corner. Next to the pictures excerpts from a *Spiegel* article describing the obstacles to bringing the rule of law to the former GDR. 'The chaos was discovered by the director of a West Berlin county court when he came to supervise the clean-up work in East Berlin's palace of justice in the Littenstrasse,' the article said. Added to that, a couple of literary paragraphs on 'Kleist's view of justice in the *Broken Jug*' and something critical about the Prussian court system. The pamphlet's message was obvious: the slapdash corruption of Judge Adam pales in comparison with the chaotic state of East Germany's administration of justice.

I looked at the pictures and knew that there had to be something wrong with the story. Very unpleasant things had happened in the courthouses of the former GDR. But the colossal mess depicted in these photographs

could not have been typical of its administration of justice. After all, I had
seen the statistics. In 1989, almost three-quarters of all first-instance civil
law disputes and more than 80 per cent of all labor law disputes had been
decided in less than three months. Courts can work that fast only if they
keep order. So where did the chaos in the pictures come from? Studying
them again at home with the help of a magnifying glass, I discovered that on
the covers of one of those dossiers strewn about the floor the word *Akte*
(file) was spelled not with the modern 'k' but with the outdated 'c'. Ever
since that evening in the theater, I had asked around: who might possibly
know something about the archives in the Littenstrasse? My questions
finally led me to a young woman in West Berlin: Maria Latzel, law graduate
and doctoral candidate at the Free University. It is she who this afternoon
will be my guide in the Littenstrasse attic.

The former *Stadtgericht* is filled with the sound of hammers and the smell
of paint. Next month, the courthouse is scheduled to reopen. I follow Frau
Latzel up to the third floor, down a corridor, up again a little staircase that
seems to lead nowhere and suddenly find myself standing in the immense
attic. Beneath our feet the building was once divided between the Berlin
Stadtgericht, two district courts, the Procuracy, and the Supreme Court. Up
here it is united in a gigantic loft that leads around the building's central
courtyard, so that an inspection trip will eventually leave you where you
started out. Bordered on one side by the slanted roof, the huge space is
criss-crossed by innumerable beams and subdivided by a maze of supporting walls. Here and there, an invisible opening in the roof allows some light
to fall into the dusk. Most areas are filled with bookshelves, now properly
aligned and accessible. An occasional pile of papers on the floor, not yet
reshelved, reminds one of the former chaos. Some knocked-over chairs;
crumpled lunch bags; in one corner, leaning against a wall, a large cardboard emblem of the former GDR. And everywhere the smell of dust and
mortar. Frau Latzel tells me what she knows about the attic and its contents.

It was she who shortly after the *Wende* 'discovered' the attic for the
outside world. Maria Latzel is working on a dissertation on family law in
the Third Reich and had difficulties finding court records on her topic in the
archives of West Berlin. She could not believe that all family law records
from the Nazi years could really have vanished. When the Wall fell, she
extended her search with bicycle tours to the courthouses of East Berlin.
One day, she knocked at the door of the *Stadtgericht* in the Littenstrasse.
Since so many different institutions shared residence in the huge
courthouse, nobody knew for certain what Frau Latzel would find in its
attic. But she was allowed to go up to look for herself and discovered an
immense accumulation of court files, most of them stacked away without
discernible order, all filthy, of which the earliest dated back to the 1830s.
Hence the archaic '*Acte*' on the files pictured in my theater pamphlet.

With the support of Uwe Weitzberg, then director of the district court Berlin-Mitte (one of the Littenstrasse occupants) and with the permission of the GDR Ministry of Justice, Frau Latzel began to take stock of her treasure trove even before Reunification Day. Protected by face masks and overalls against the dust, Frau Latzel and a colleague first had to 'liberate the bookshelves' often stacked too tightly for access. Then came the ordering and reshelving. In the summer of 1990, when news of Frau Latzel's discovery had spread to the Free University, she and two other doctoral candidates were hired to inventory the attic's contents. I have seen her list and added up its different sub-categories. Calculated crudely by shelf space, of a total of roughly 3,150 meters of court records, about 12 per cent date from last century, 18 per cent from the years between 1900 and 1933, and 7 per cent from the Third Reich. About 60 per cent of the files are GDR court records from the 1950s to the 1970s. Of the decisions, 3.3 per cent are post-1980.

West German court archives operate under detailed rules establishing the length of time for which each written product of the judicial process must be preserved: requests for payment—two years; documents on the execution of judgments—five years; injunctions relating to real estate transactions—ten years; criminal sentences—thirty years, and so on. Under West German auspices, most of the files in the Littenstrasse attic would thus have been destroyed long ago. Theoretically, similar preservation rules applied to East German archives. But courts lacked the personnel to carry them out. Since the huge attic offered sufficient space, it was easiest simply to carry all non-current documents upstairs, add a new shelf if needed, and forget about them. But, unfortunately, the Littenstrasse attic was not as safe a storage place as it might look. The building's roof was in bad repair and its system of ancient heating pipes, weaving across the entire attic, was close to collapse. In one particularly disastrous month in the 1980s, Herr Oehmke later told me, there had been no fewer than sixty-two instances of burst pipes in the Littenstrasse court building. 'If there is water running, you can't expect people to carefully rearrange bookshelves.' The plumbers and roofers who came to repair what had broken once again, pushed shelves aside if they were in the way and did not bother to pick up the documents that toppled in the process. Splashes of their mortar covered the records already strewn about the floor. From time to time, on those socialist occasions of collective service euphemistically called 'judges' days' or 'student summers,' one of the courts domiciled in the Littenstrasse would send 'volunteers' upstairs to bring a little order into chaos. Once in the 1980s, one hundred bags of the more ancient records had been thrown away. Frau Fischer had on three occasions sorted files in the attic: once—for pay—as a student and twice—without pay—as a judge at the *Stadtgericht*. The last time Littenstrasse judges had tried to clean the Augean stables had been on

11 November 1989, two days after the opening of the Wall, and on a Saturday to boot, when everybody else in East Berlin had gone to marvel at the bright lights of West Berlin's Kurfürstendamm. Had it been up to him, Herr Oehmke would have ordered one more clean-up action last September, before he handed the courthouse over to the *Wessis*. But at this point, his judges refused to play along.

They would not have made much of a difference in any case. The mess was long beyond the weekend efforts of reluctant 'volunteers.' And so it happened that Frau Latzel found her treasure covered in dust but otherwise largely intact. She had been working in the attic on the very day the *Spiegel* photographer had come to take pictures. One of the shots included in my theater program Frau Latzel can even locate for me: it shows a bookshelf crammed with wills from the 1850s. I have encountered other pictures from the same series of photographs in later *Spiegel* issues. The most recent carries the caption: 'East German court files: the prosecutors are buried under work' and is used to illustrate an article about the victims of SED injustice. For this one, I do not even need a magnifying glass to recognize that the heading 'Acte' on one of the files is spelled with a 'c.'

But could it be that there is some truth to the *Spiegel* pictures after all? Obviously, the unquestionable chaos in the Littenstrasse attic has nothing to do with the unquestionable injustices suffered by victims of the SED regime. Still, there must have been quite a few documents up in that attic which under GDR rules of record-keeping should have been preserved. They were of course preserved. But if a GDR citizen, let us a say in an inheritance matter, had required access to a divorce decree of 1986 (according to Frau Latzel's catalogue, the most recent year of files found in the attic), it might have been very difficult to locate it in the jumble. Nevertheless, I do not think that the disorder seriously hindered East German citizens in the pursuit of their rights. It seems likely that court officials had least trouble finding the newest records, since they only recently were stored away. Moreover, those cases which require the most meticulous record-keeping in the West—real estate transactions—were of little significance in the GDR. Claims for social benefits, which in West Germany, too, occasionally require proof of past events, in East Germany involved little legal hassle. There cannot have been many cases in which the chaos in the Littenstrasse archives stood in the way of someone's realizing his rights. The condition suggested by the *Spiegel* photographs—a judicial administration so slovenly that it in fact amounted to an obstruction of justice—did not exist.

Still, East German record-keeping left a lot to be desired. West German judges working in Potsdam in the neighboring state of Brandenburg (where lustration practices are less drastic than in Berlin and where former GDR judges continue to staff the courts) have told me of their East German colleagues' conscientious and even 'finicky' working style. But all those court functions which in the GDR were not handled by judges but belonged in the domain of secretaries, para-legals, bailiffs, and the like were severely afflicted by East Germany's chronic shortage of staff. We managed to do a lot to reduce delay at the adjudicatory stage, said Herr Oehmke, but when it came to the execution of judgments, 'Lord-a-mercy.' Three-quarters of all the complaints submitted to GDR courts concerned the work of para-legals; half criticized the sluggish enforcement of court decisions. Enforcement, too, is a crucial ingredient of justice. The GDR judicial system, proud of its proximity to the people, tried everything to overcome the problem. There was the 'same day completion' campaign, there were the occasional successes of some courts (like the 'Fürstenwalder model') announced with great fanfare for everybody else to follow—'we struggled like anything,' said Herr Oehmke. If there was so little to show for all the efforts, it was not because of procrastination and neglect but because of the country's poverty. Despite its many deficiencies, East Germany's administration of justice was far removed from Judge Adam's slapdash, lazy, Epicurean corruption.

So why did the public relations people at the *Deutsches Theater*, in publishing the *Spiegel* photographs in their playbill, endorse a critique which is so far off the mark of what was really wrong with East Germany's judicial system? I do not accept the explanation that East German citizens are now eager to believe the worst because they mistrusted their country's judges all along. The system's outcasts did—the *Ausreiser*, fugitives, and dissidents—and for good reason. But the silent majority—or, rather, the muttering, mumbling, and grumbling majority in the GDR—seems to have been neither afraid nor distrustful of their courts. People complained, especially the losers of law suits, but, as Herr Oehmke said: 'This is a business in which people are more likely to criticize than to praise you.' All judges with whom I spoke repeated that in the old days mention of their occupation, whether to acquaintances or strangers, had usually caused curiosity and interest rather than suspicion or alarm. If East German citizens needed legal advice, they were far more likely to turn to the legal information office of their local district court, staffed by judges, than to approach a private attorney. Do you ask those whom you mistrust for help?

'When a citizen walked through the door, we'd drop everything else,' an East Berlin judge once told me. (She did not add: excepting dissidents or *Ausreiser*.) GDR judges were proud of their solicitous concern for the people who had supposedly elected them. They did not notice that the concern contained a good measure of pedagogic condescension. One young judge from East Berlin once described to me how she and her colleagues would immediately interrupt political conversations if citizens appeared on the threshold. Not out of worry that the newcomers could not be trusted but because they did not want their frivolous talk to detract from citizens' respect for their government. '*Pas devant les enfants!*' I thought. West German judges treat their parties more nonchalantly than we used to do, a judge in Potsdam explained to me. The *Wessis*' tone when talking to a plaintiff or defendant is 'rougher' and when citizens complain about some aspect of the process, a West German judge is less likely to humor them than an *Ossi* would have done. But he will also talk the matter over with the parties. 'I always let the participants have their say,' my Potsdam informant told me. But when both sides had unloaded their cares, she would take over and settle the matter. 'This is how it's going to be done.' West German judges will include the parties in their deliberations. 'Maybe we could do it this way. Let's talk about it.' It is a new experience for former GDR citizens. In the past, they were always given directions. 'What are we doing in court if the judge can't make up his mind,' they now think.

The *Spiegel* pictures of the Littenstrasse attic capture nothing of the real relationship between socialist citizens and their courts. The photographs are dramatic and catchy shorthand formulas for a rotten judicial system. But their definition of what was wrong with the East German administration of justice is false. The truth is more complicated, more contradictory, more German. The real disorder is harder to clean up. The fact that even East German citizens seem to accept the photographs' characterization of their own legal past makes it even more difficult fully to know and understand it.

Frau Latzel and I have completed our round. We take a deep breath returning from the chalky dust of the archives to the corridors of the courthouse. Frau Latzel tells me that among its many finds, the attic also held rows and rows of unopened wills deposited during the Second World War. Now West Berlin officials will break the seals and after half a century's delay will try to carry out the wills' provisions. Lord knows who may discover that the house in which he lives and the garden in which he mows his lawn were never intended to be his. Will the world be a better place than if the testaments had never been unearthed? The Germans have a saying for it: *Ordnung muß sein.* There must be order.

18 May 1991

An appointment with Rainer Hannemann; once again in the City Bar. I want to know about his conversation with Herr Ritter's Senate Committee. 'If they'll take anyone, they will take me,' he had optimistically prophesied last autumn. The prediction turned out to have been wrong.

Herr Hannemann's interview took place last March. The questions followed the progress of the candidate's curriculum vitae. Rainer Hannemann had joined the Party while in high school and had gotten into trouble with one of his teachers. The teacher's accusations had in turn led to Party disciplinary proceedings in 1979. The examiners wanted to know more. 'Tell us about the matter. What exactly had given rise to the investigation?' Already at this point, Herr Hannemann had noticed a warning undertone: 'Don't think that we will believe everything you say.' Helplessly, he now shrugs his shoulders. It was not really a political encounter. Just one of those collisions between teacher and pupil. Rainer Hannemann had not meant to challenge socialism, but only one of its representatives.

So when did he first collide with the system itself? His alienation from the Party was a drawn-out process, Rainer Hannemann had said. He could not identify definite turning points. But he remembered one particular event: reading a biography of Stalin. Again, the examiners wanted particulars. Who had given it to him? And when? Rainer Hannemann did not remember. New suspicions among the Senate representatives.

Then came the elections in the Spring of 1989 at which East German citizens had for the first time in their country's history openly complained about election fraud. In May, Rainer Hannemann had joined the first demonstrations. 'But there were no demonstrations yet in May!' one of the Senate people had objected. 'There they sat across from me and told me what had and had not happened in the GDR in May 1989!' says Rainer Hannemann and shakes his head.

And so it went on. The examiners had turned to Rainer Hannemann's letter to Erich Honecker (copy to Party headquarters) in which he had complained about the repression of anti-Party votes. The Senate people wanted details. What exactly had Herr Hannemann said in that letter? Had he kept a copy? He had. But Rainer Hannemann had intentionally not attached that copy to his application. The letter was too tame, he says, and as far as he is concerned 'the protests had come way too late.' In any case, he saw no reason why it should place him ahead of other East Berlin candidates for readmission. 'I did not want to use the letter to justify myself.' And then the next point on the Senate Committee's list: Herr Hannemann's role in the foundation of working-groups at the Contract Court to debate the reform of economic law and to redraft the Party Statute of the SED. New questions by Herr Ritter and his colleagues to undermine the credibility of their witness. Did you let your political opinions be known at the Contract Court? When? To what purpose? And finally the direct attack: 'You don't expect us to believe that you risked your job just to express political disaffectation!'

'Throughout the entire conversation I felt like a suspect', Herr Hannemann says. And then the Senate people finally came out with it: according to information received from the Gauck Agency on State Security files, he had been an informant for the *Stasi*. 'No way could it be true!' Herr Hannemann says. But when five years ago the Stasi officers had

unsuccessfully tried to recruit him, they had also inquired about a friend of
Rainer Hannemann's who at the time was planning a vacation in Yugoslavia. As 'non-socialist economic territory', the destination had caused suspicion. Herr Hannemann had tried to calm the *Stasi*'s fears: his friend was
not the kind of person to run away. But he had also applied for visas for his
children! He is a good Marxist, Herr Hannemann had said. The people from
the firm were not to be convinced. 'If you want, I can give it to you in
writing!' Rainer Hannemann had finally said. And he had given it to them
in writing: an old-fashioned and touching surety for a friend. What a strange
dictatorship this was, I think, that defined its relationship to those it sup-
pressed in such highly personal terms.

But that is my own reaction to the story. Herr Ritter and his colleagues
had not mused over the nature of socialist suppression but had instead
insisted on their 'reports'. Herr Hannemann had contradicted them: besides
that surety, there could be nothing in the files. All right, the Senate representatives eventually had conceded: no real 'reports'. What then? Was his
name included in the *Stasi*'s lists of 'unofficial informants' or not? No, the
Senate people finally admitted. But there was 'something' in the Gauck files
that related to his person. Rainer Hannemann never learned what it was.
'Why don't you call us in a couple of weeks,' he was told at the end of the
interview.

It must have been a strangely asymmetrical encounter. The members of
the Senate Committee, Herr Hannemann says, had remained calm and
polite. But he could barely keep his voice under control. 'I was furious!' Not
least with himself. 'And here I was, playing along for two entire hours!
Buckled under once again, for the sake of a job!' Two days after the
interrogation, Rainer Hannemann went to speak with the management of
an East German construction firm known to him from his days on the
Contract Court. He must have made a good impression. 'You can start with
us,' he was told at the end of the conversation. The written contract followed in the mail. Rainer Hannemann tries to explain his new job to me and
falters in the face of my ignorance of management affairs. But I can see how
pleased he is with his new work. He sent the Senate Administration of
Justice a letter withdrawing his application to the judiciary. It was short; just
something about 'evident mistrust.'

I am pleased to learn that his story has a happy ending, after all. But how
was it possible that Rainer Hannemann's interview with the Senate Committee so decidedly got off on the wrong foot? Herr Hannemann thinks it
was because the West Berliners couldn't make him out. 'I did not fit into
their world of black and white.' I have heard the same explanation from
other East German candidates for the judiciary. 'They couldn't deal with
the ambivalence,' a young woman reported who had recently passed the
vetting process; 'couldn't understand that someone at the same time could

both represent the system and despair over its shortcomings. In my interview, I was constantly pushed back and forth between the roles of victim and villain.' Both are clear-cut categories, allowing for obvious and rational responses. But the in-between conditions, the blending of guilt and innocence, the fact that someone can be both an accomplice and a critic of the system, are hard to handle. Many of the questions posed by Herr Ritter's committee seem to date back to the light-vs.-darkness years of the Cold War. Could she see herself enforcing the law of the class enemy? a (successful) candidate had been asked. 'One knew what to respond.' She had told the examiners that she could no longer understand many of the opinions she had once held. It was even true. But she would have preferred to describe her mental state in its real and confused condition. 'I gave tactical responses,' she said. The members of Herr Ritter's committee 'felt that their views had been confirmed.'

Herr Hannemann tells me that a friend of his who passed the review will in a year's time begin working as associate judge assigned to a *Landgericht*, or regional court, panel. For the time being, he is kept busy as 'Registry judge'; checking additions and deletions from the list of firms and corporations doing business in Berlin. He sits in a little room containing nothing but a desk, two chairs, and a telephone. The work is boring. West judges will do Registry work only if they are too old or too lazy to care for challenges, Herr Hannemann says. He is glad not to have to deal with any of this.

Their suspicion has cost the Senate Administration of Justice a good man.

7 June 1991

I travel for an interview to Potsdam, where I have spent quite a bit of time during the last few weeks. The new East German state of Brandenburg, of which Potsdam is the capital, follows a different road to judicial reform than does the neighboring state of Berlin. Here, former socialist judges are vetted, too. But instead of having been automatically suspended on Reunification Day, each judge continues to hold office until the verdict upon him or her has been spoken. As in Berlin, the vetting process got off to a slow start and is far from completed. But while they are waiting for their turn, Brandenburg judges work side by side with the many guest judges imported from the West German sister-state of North Rhine Westphalia to help with the reform and to acculturate their Eastern colleagues. In the first-instance district court, East German judges sit alone. Even the director of the Potsdam *Kreisgericht*, Bettina Leetz, with whom I am supposed to meet this morning, is a former GDR citizen. At the regional Court of Appeals, where judges sit in panels, the presiding judge is always a West German. But East German associate judges sit right next to her or him. In Potsdam, *Wessis* and *Ossis* thus meet not only in the roles of victors and defeated but also as colleagues. Here, it is not only the past that counts but also the present; not only ideology that governs every debate but also common practical experience. Here in Potsdam, only half an hour by bus from West Berlin's easternmost train station, I find a political laboratory in which each subject's Cold War image of the other is tested daily by the wear and tear of professional co-operation and human proximity. I am curious to see the results of the experiment.

Until now, I have talked with seven lawyers in Potsdam: a West German judge at the Court of Appeals, two West German judges at the Potsdam District Court, three East German judges of that court, and the West German official at the Brandenburg Ministry of Justice who co-ordinates the process of vetting the state's inherited judges and prosecutors. I have learned from these conversations that there are different ways of talking about East–West German affairs: speakers can use the democratic or the hierarchical voice. The hierarchical voice I have encountered often in Berlin: it is used by examiners and examinees alike, and although it makes a difference whether the voice comes from above or from below—sounding condescending or timid, censorious or bitter—speech coming from both directions shares the same proclivity to paint the world in black and white, to generalize, jump to conclusions, and to refer to the other side as 'them' or 'they' who are not to be trusted.

The democratic voice is more specific and more cautious. You sense that the speaker does not ground his observations on general rules but speaks from personal impressions. Often, generalizations are withdrawn or qualified right in the middle of a sentence: it seems the speaker has thought of a person or an incident that does not fit generic descriptions. Your conversation partner will not talk about 'them' but will mention names. Judgments tend to be more lenient: the speaker knows from experience that good and bad are not neatly separated but blurred and shaded. While the hierarchical voice echoes the distance between those at the top and at the bottom, the democratic voice reveals proximity between the speaker and his subjects.

One of the West German judges at the Potsdam *Kreisgericht* is a good example of how human contacts between former ideological opponents can alter a person's voice. We had met last October, at Professor Sendler's talk at the Administrative Court in West Berlin, when the young guest judge from the Rhineland had just arrived in Potsdam to help establish an effective system of judicial review with judges who had never learned to countermand the state. 'To tell the truth, they should all be kicked out,' he had said of his new colleagues at the time. But when I spoke with him last month, he talked differently. Now he was annoyed at a recent spate of newspaper reports predicting the imminent collapse of the administration of justice in Germany's new Eastern states. 'Nothing is collapsing here,' he said. Co-operation between East and West German judges in Brandenburg 'was working just fine.' The work got done. He spoke with blithe matter-of-factness about his ex-socialist colleagues. Why had he changed his views? Because of the daily contacts, the political discussions, the common lunches or suppers, the evenings spent bowling together. 'These guys can hold their liquor,' he said with undisguised respect. Of course, there were some people at the court whom he did not much care for. Why should this place be different from other places? But to him, the Potsdam *Kreisgericht* was no longer staffed with generic people. They were all real and concrete.

'We were lucky to have Frau Leetz as the court's new director,' he also said. When after the *Wende*, Potsdam officials searched for someone willing to manage the district court's transformation into a proper *Rechtsstaat* court, Bettina Leetz, a local 31-year-old family judge, had fearlessly volunteered for the job. In April 1990, she was elected by her fellow judges to the post of District Court Director. Sitting across from me now in her spacious new office—short hair, smart pantsuit, little pearl earrings—she exudes a kind of cheerful chutzpah which I would never have thought could possibly be the product of a socialist upbringing. Even if in the course of our conversation Frau Leetz occasionally claims to be discouraged by Western skepticism and disparagement, I find it difficult to credit her bouts of pessimism. After the collapse of the GDR, she seriously considered emigrating to Australia, Frau Leetz tells me. I am sure she would have done well wherever she went. In the end, she decided to stay home and, with a staff of twenty-five judges and about fifty employees, rebuild the city of Potsdam's District Court.

Even today, more than a year after Frau Leetz took up the job, the differences between East and West German judges at the *Kreisgericht* remain enormous. Sometimes, the Potsdamers are more aware of what separates them from their Western mentors than the Westerners themselves. Is there an unacknowledged pecking order at the court ranking East and West German judges? I asked a guest judge from Cologne. No, he had not noticed anything of the kind. I asked the same question of a local judge from Potsdam. 'I do not feel equal to the Westerners,' was her reply. It seemed to be spoken without bitterness. How equal to the Western colleagues can you be if the dreaded vetting still lies ahead of you? An Eastern judge, awaiting her review, tells me that her husband, already fired from his city job, now trots from firm to firm trying to sell advertisements for the yellow pages, while former West German occupants have raised ownership claims to both her flat and her allotment garden on the outskirts of the city. I stare at her, aghast. Where does she find the strength each morning to face the day?

And then there is the threatening loss of the familiar work routine. Already in the autumn of 1990, Frau Leetz replaced the fixed GDR workday with the flexible hours that Western judges claim as part of their judicial independence. At first, the *Ossis* did not know how to handle their new freedom. They were nowhere to be found. But then they learned to structure their own work schedule. They also had to learn a new professional vocabulary. Do Eastern and Western judges speak a common language? 'Nope,' says an unruffled guest judge from Cologne, who nevertheless praises their co-operation. His Eastern colleagues still have difficulties with West German legal concepts, he says. They misuse unfamiliar terms. It often happens that East and West German judges talk at cross purposes. Then what? You ask, that's all. He has no compunction about asking Western colleagues for their help, an East German judge at the Potsdam District Court tells me. They never say: 'What, don't you know . . . ?' 'We need the *Ossis*, too,' says a Westerner, 'to understand the social context of a case.' So the West Germans must also ask questions. Language differences remain. The East German judges are more straightforward and less apt to speak in legal code, reports a Western judge from the Court of Appeals. They dislike the subjunctive, dislike the idea that an opinion can go either way. They don't say 'on the other hand . . .' nearly so often as the *Wessis*. West German judges are technically more precise, admit the Easterners. They have their own language, inaccessible to laymen. In the old days, GDR judges were always urged to remain comprehensible to ordinary citizens. 'I would be upset if parties left the courtroom bewildered,' an Eastern judge tells me. Her Western colleague explains that many of the linguistic differences between East and West German court proceedings were caused by the respective absence or presence of lawyers. In the Federal Republic, most interactions in the courtroom take place between the judge and the attorneys, and pass way above the heads of plaintiff and defendant. Often, oral arguments are no more than a matter of form and the hearing's intelligibility to laymen 'equals zero.' East German trials were more 'didactic.' 'I hope that judges coming from the GDR will not discard their former social sensibilities,' he adds.

Ossis and *Wessis* also differ in their approach to legal texts. The East Germans tend to be strict constructionists. They feel allegiance to the written word, a Western judge explains, and lack 'interpretive courage.' It cannot be easy for the newcomers to reconcile the seemingly contradictory demands of the West German legal system. On the one hand, they find themselves in unfamiliar 'conditions of stringency' and have to pay more attention than in the past to procedural precision and formality. On the other hand, they are expected to manipulate the law and to rearrange the conceptual components of a case until they fit into a sensible and satisfying pattern. And they can no longer look for helpful instructions from above. But at least there are role models. I talk with a young district judge from Potsdam about his older colleague from the Rhineland. It seems that the West German is an excellent instructor. The young man's admiration and his eagerness to imitate his teacher are very obvious. Yes, there still exist significant differences between Eastern and Western judges in the courts of Potsdam. But these differences are neither presumed nor cast in stone for all eternity.

Some East German qualities are even admired by the *Wessis*. Take the *Ossis'* relaxed attitude towards money. Western judges in Potsdam are paid by their judicial administrations back home and earn three times as much as their colleagues in the East. And yet, both East and West Germans uniformly report that local *Ossis* do not seem to envy their far-flung visitors' greater affluence. Why not? Is unequal access to money not usually the cause of disagreement and strife? Not here, someone points out to me, because disinterest in financial wealth is an important part of an East German judge's self-definition. 'I can't take that gabble over money any more,' says a Potsdam judge. 'Other things are more important.' When recent rumors had it that guest judges were about to lose their compensation for 'special expenses' in East Germany ('bush money' in rude post-unification terminology, and set at higher levels than the regular salary of the locals), many East German judges sided with their protesting Western colleagues. Why this uncalculating generosity? Because GDR judges were nothing special, one of them says. 'Maybe we don't have it in us to be envious,' his colleague adds. Being a judge in the GDR was synonymous with serving. Above all, you served the state, but you also served its citizens. Preserving social peace counted more than money. Frau Leetz, with whom I also talk about the money issue, hopes that she will be able to preserve her former indifference in financial matters. She is not sure whether it can be done. This is one of those things that worries you about the future, she says: 'once you start being envious, they've got you.'

Frau Leetz' own vetting process is complete. She does not take particular credit for having passed. When it was her turn, the Brandenburg Review Commission did not much care whether the candidates had signed arrest warrants in border cases, she says. And they had never heard of the East German practice of dismissing *Ausreiser* labor law suits without oral argument. Instead, the Potsdam examiners were digging for convictions for work-shy behavior under section 249 of the GDR Criminal Code to which the Berlin authorities had never paid attention. Which particular East German judicial practice will be considered most egregious by the Westerners, Frau Leetz suggests, is very much a matter of chance. It would be futile to search the decisions for evidence of social logic. 'They'll never learn it,' she says, when we talk about what it meant to be a judge under Socialism.

I notice her 'they.' I think Frau Leetz would have used a less generic reference had she talked about her Westphalian colleagues at the district court. Our discussion of the vetting process has prompted Bettina Leetz to revert to the hierarchical voice used in relationships between rulers and dependents. Three weeks ago, I had heard the same voice coming from the opposite direction when interviewing Dorothea Schiefer, a Judge of the Superior Administrative Court in the West German city of Münster and now dispatched to the Brandenburg Ministry of Justice to co-ordinate the state's judicial vetting process. When Frau Schiefer explained her tasks, I was struck by her choice of words to describe the East German members of her working group: '*nette Kerlchen*' (nice little fellows), for example, or '*umgängliche Leutchen*' (personable little folks). 'Do you realize how often you use the diminutive?' I finally asked. Frau Schiefer laughed, not the least bit embarrassed by my question: 'but they *are* children!' The East Germans cannot manage without somebody to lean on, she said. They don't identify with their work. At 5 p.m. sharp, ball-point and fountain-pens will drop from *Ossi* hands. To make the simplest decision, they will look for guidance from above. They waste valuable working time commiserating with their fellow citizens. In the end, Frau Schiefer said, she had to put her foot down and shorten her staff's coffee break to its statutory 15 minutes. Now the *Ossis* are hurt: times are hard, they say, and they need to seek solace with each other. 'The GDR was a sheltered workplace!' Frau Schiefer said with good-natured exasperation. And here I complain about her using the diminutive!

But when I checked Frau Schiefer's story with West German judges at the Potsdam District Court and Court of Appeals, I heard a different tale. Were East judges less industrious than their Western colleagues? Hard to tell, said a judge from Cologne, because the East Germans had to spend so many additional hours at retooling classes. As far as he could see, diligence was the kind of quality that, as in the West, varied from person to person. Virtually all of his Eastern colleagues were eager to learn. Did they take a lot of breaks? Not more than judges in West Germany. Did the *Ossis* always need a shoulder to lean on? They struggled professionally and seemed afraid to make mistakes. They often asked questions, and that was as it should be. Were the Easterners less capable of withstanding stress? 'No!' said a guest judge at the Court of Appeals. If he considered how they bore up under the triple weight of work, retooling classes, and the psychological burden of the vetting process, 'he could only take his hat off.' Later, an East Berlin judge who already had passed the review process and was gaining her first experiences as associate judge in West Berlin would explain to me why in Frau Schiefer's working group ball-point pens would have to drop from *Ossi* hands at 5 p.m. 'I am sure those were young women lawyers on Frau Schiefer's team,' she said. Yes. Well, most of them probably had children. You get into trouble if you don't pick up your child punctually from nursury school. West German women judges don't have children or— if they do—they take a leave of absence until their children are older. Did Frau Schiefer have children? No. A simple explanation.

'They don't know enough about us,' says Frau Leetz, using 'they' again. The questionnaires, sent by the Brandenburg Ministry of Justice to be filled out by each employee of Frau Leetz's district court, had asked recipients whether they had worked as unofficial collaborators for the Ministry of State Security. Nobody at the Ministry had known that, like many other public institutions, the district court also employed ten former official *Stasi* members who after the *Wende* had lost their jobs and now worked for the court as secretaries or cleaning ladies. By the way, 'excellent employees,' says Frau Leetz. Their *Stasi* involvement had come to light because the questionnaire had also asked about 'contacts' with the secret police and people had dutifully checked the relevant box. Frau Leetz is as aghast as I am at the *Stasi* horror stories now filling our morning papers. But she will not condemn her new-found cleaning ladies. Again, I notice how human proximity stands in the way of passing moral judgment. 'I have to wait awhile before I confidently can talk about the Stasi,' says Frau Leetz.

Meanwhile, it is impossible to forget the *Stasi* at the Potsdam District Court. The building, designed in the pleasantly romantic fake medieval style of the turn of the century, has always served as a courthouse. But in the years before the *Wende*, it was taken over by the Ministry of State Security. The *Stasi* left its marks. In Frau Leetz's ante-room, her secretary shows me two large wall cabinets filled with cables, now cut off and no longer of use for eavesdropping on anyone. Two red telephones on the secretary's desk— sleeker and heavier than ordinary socialist telephones—are also *Stasi* relics. In one of the courthouse corridors, another wall cabinet reveals, upon my quick and discreet check, more disconnected cables. Over some doors, I spot little light fixtures no longer capable of flashing their signals. And in two rooms I detect mystifying electrical outlets set into a corner of the ceiling. Even the interior decoration of one of the courtrooms matches the *Stasi*'s Philistine and pompous style: heavy, burgundy-colored velvet drapes over white lace curtains. A Halloween house.

Frau Leetz's secretary describes how the Potsdam *Stasi* branched out from its courthouse base: remodelled the building, added on, took over other houses in the vicinity, pulled down a nearby villa under a preservation order and replaced it by a multi-story office building, and like a cancer, grew and grew. I once more raise the *Stasi* topic with Frau Leetz. She seems to think that she and her colleagues had a narrow escape. 'In the end, we would all have been members of the *Stasi*,' she says.

11 June 1991

I have just heard the news: yesterday, the Superior Administrative Court Berlin stopped the closure of the Humboldt University's five 'politically tainted' faculties. Apparently, the court followed the reasoning of the Federal Constitutional Court's recent *Abwicklungs* decision. I remind myself that we are still at the preliminary stages of the battle. At this point, the court only restored the suspensive effect of Humboldt University's lawsuit against its partial closure. For the time being, the Berlin Senate may not proceed with its intended rough-shod policy. In the long run, having both money and power on its side, the city will very likely do with Humboldt University as it pleases. But at least for the moment, Frau Will and her colleagues at the Humboldt Law Faculty have won a short breathing-spell.

IV

Careers

13 June 1991

In Jena, for a cup of tea with Professor Martin Posch, with whom I want to talk about private law scholarship under socialism. Professor Posch, now emerited, is one of East Germany's best known and most productive civil lawyers. Among experts, his name is also known in the United States and Western Europe. Many years ago, we sat just as now on the balcony of his house: sipping tea, enjoying the lovely view over the city and beyond, and talking—gingerly, and careful not to edge too close to any fundamental issue—about the significance of civil law in the GDR. Today, I can come right out with the question that brought me: was it easier to accommodate oneself with those in power in a field seemingly as apolitical as private law?

I know, I know: the term 'apolitical' pretends to an innocence that neither Professor Posch nor I believe in. True, civil law does not deal with state authority but with exchange relationships; not with political power but with property. But to socialists, property equals power. And since it was one of the central goals of socialism fundamentally to change man's attitude towards property, it was to be expected that the new East German state would place a premium on the thorough transformation of its inherited bourgeois civil law system. As it turned out, the task was much more difficult than anticipated. Although the Party had already ordered the drafting of a new East German Civil Code in July 1958, three months after the Babelsberg Conference, it took seventeen years to carry out the task. Until the new ZGB finally entered into force in 1975, the same bourgeois Civil Code of 1900, the *Bürgerliches Gesetzbuch*, or BGB, applied in both German states (although in the GDR, its impact was largely limited to exchange relationships involving private citizens).

But the trials and setbacks during the new Code's lengthy legislative history also testify to its political significance. At every turn of the long road, the Party interfered. Every detail needed its approval. It was the Party that set limits to the new Code's length: not more than 500 sections, draftsmen were ordered, so that ordinary citizens would not get lost in its pages! In the event, the legislative committee managed with only 480 sections, even though it meant omitting important subject-matter under the unspoken assumption that if need be, East German judges could always fall back on the rules of the old BGB. No odious capitalist terminology! the

Party also had commanded. The order was not always easy to follow.
Centuries-old terms, like the word *Pacht* denoting a lease of land, had to be
dropped because they reeked of ground rents and the capitalist commer-
cialization of the soil. But what to put in their place? Endless deliberations.
'Why don't we call it *Picht!*' a committee member is said finally to have
cried out in desperation. In the end, the draftsmen chose the term 'utilization of real estate' (*Nutzung von Bodenflächen*)—not much of an improvement. But, all in all, the ZGB turned out to be a model of simple and
straightforward legal language—way too simple to resolve the weighty and
intricate legal disputes of a complex market economy, but useful in its daily
application to modest socialist consumer relationships.

Professor Posch was one of the intellectual fathers of the ZGB. It was not
his only role in East German civil law development—the field owes much to
his insight and commitment. Today, I want to discuss his most intriguing
contribution to the civil law debate in the GDR: his concept of a 'comprehensive legal relationship' (*allgemeines Rechtsverhältnis*), developed in the
wake of the Babelsberg conference. Walter Ulbricht, in his (and Karl
Polak's) speech in Babelsberg, had complained about the tenacity of bourgeois contract notions in East German legal thought: 'Reading our legal
literature, one is struck by the continued prevalence of the traditional
bourgeois tendency to view the individual as separated from society and to
use contracts as the legal means to reconnect the individual with the collective.' Ulbricht's dislike of contracts—ideologically speaking—could not
come as a surprise. Western contract law presumes the autonomy of the
individual, the equality of partners in the market, and the legitimacy of self-
interest. It is not an autocratic but a democratic instrument. Moreover,
contract law implies social distance between the participants. You don't
need contracts to establish or sustain trust and solicitude between relatives
or friends. Rather, contract law serves people without familial or emotional
connections who enter their agreements in the hope of each advancing his
or her personal interest. How could socialist law overcome the self-centered
rigidity of bourgeois contract law?

By denying, as in the family context, the constitutive power of contracts.
In an article published in December 1959, Professor Posch, for the first
time, advanced the thesis that civil law relationships in the GDR (in particular, the relationships between citizens and the state-owned consumer industry) neither began nor ended with the formation of individual contracts.
Instead, citizen and socialist trade organizations were linked in a permanent
consumption-and-supply relationship that was only substantiated by individual acts of purchase. Even without the establishment of individual contracts—indeed, without any activity from his side—each socialist citizen was
thus legally associated with the state. Professor Posch called this supposedly
permanent civil law connection between individual and society the 'com-

prehensive legal relationship.' His theory, originally confined to consumer relationships, found acceptance in other areas of private law as well. Applying Professor Posch's approach to copyright issues, for example, followers now claimed that, independent of any contract, author and state-owned publishing house were connected by the 'comprehensive legal relationship' and that an author's demands for concrete contractual arrangements thus reflected his 'being captive to capitalist notions of law.'

The jurisprudential implications of Professor Posch's construction are obvious: his theory of the 'comprehensive legal relationship' deprives a citizen of the decision as to whether or not he wants to have anything to do with the state, and instead postulates, even in the area of civil law, a permanent symbiosis between individual and society. 'Did you not find all of this also a bit scary?' I now ask him. Did not the notion of a permanent connection between citizen and state, even in the years after Babelsberg, seem suffocating and debilitating? No, says Herr Posch. He allows that his invention of the the 'comprehensive legal relationship' had been an attempt to translate socialism into law. But he denies the threatening connotations of the concept. At the time, he had been mainly concerned about the state's responsibility to provide for its citizens. To give an example: his 'comprehensive legal relationship' would have included, among other obligations, the state's duty to stock enough spare parts to satisfy consumer requests for repairs.

But this was no legal obligation in the conventional sense, I say. It gave a purchaser no specific claim in court. Indeed, Professor Posch's construct of the 'comprehensive legal relationship' was meant to transcend judicial notions of legal entitlements and, rather than encourage confrontations in court, wanted to unite citizen and state in 'common responsibility' and 'comradely co-operation.' Whether or not the 'comprehensive legal relationship' would have resulted in increased consumer satisfaction thus depended entirely on the generosity of the state. In the event, the concept had no real-life impact anyway. It was dropped as 'impracticable' when the passage of the Soviet Civil Law Fundamentals, much more conservative than the planned ZGB, led to a reorientation of East German civil law doctrine in 1961. Even a late echo of Professor Posch's ideas—the 'obligation' of each state-owned store, established by section 138 of the 1975 Civil Code, to stock 'a comprehensive array of merchandise'—never amounted to more than a wishful dream of the draftsmen. Professor Posch's 'comprehensive legal relationship' remained a figment of scholarly imagination. If nevertheless I am so interested in the idea, it is because it tells me something about the self-definition of its author.

He does not give me the impression of having been particularly devoted to the Party. At the end of the war, Martin Posch was 25 years old and at that time believed in socialism primarily because he shared its hatred of fascism. His faith lasted—unconditionally—until Stalin's death. The ensuing revelations gave rise to doubts. New hopes for a better kind of socialism revived during the Prague Spring and were crushed by the Soviet invasion. When, in the following years, Martin Posch's fifth or sixth attempt to publish politically nonconformist pieces failed, he let things be. 'I was no fighter,' says Herr Posch. And: 'I'm not the type to play the martyr.' Or, as someone else once said of him: 'If Martin Posch makes a political *faux pas*, it is done with the greatest circumspection.' Except for one Party disciplinary proceeding—decided in his favor—he never ran real political risks.

Instead, Professor Posch concentrated on his work. 'I wanted to achieve something in a field in which achievement was possible,' he says. And he did. He became the best-known civil law scholar in the land. When the GDR government needed a legal representative in the United States, it was Martin Posch they turned to. It was Martin Posch who was asked to write the national report for the GDR in the *Encyclopedia of Comparative Law*. He was someone. But someone, it seems to me, without real faith. How would you define justice? I ask him. He avoids an answer: 'That is an extraordinarily difficult question.' What will remain of socialism? 'Nothing.' He corrects himself: 'As a method,' materialism would survive. But the sentence is not spoken with conviction. Nothing in Professor Posch's own work reflects sympathy for materialistic arguments. His 'comprehensive legal relationship,' despite its claim 'to honor socialist reality,' was not the least bit influenced by actual economic conditions in the GDR. Any representative of the Chicago School of Law and Economics is more of a materialist than Martin Posch has ever been.

Explain to me in what ways you and I are different, I ask. 'Personal qualities aside, we aren't,' he says. I think Herr Posch is right. The statement would also explain his scholarly career. We are both in the same business, after all: we know that to build an academic reputation, it is useful—within the limits of what is permissible—to come up with something new. The 'comprehensive legal relationship' was the new idea that established Professor Posch's name among East German legal academics. He argued politically because he defined his work apolitically: not as social service, indentured to a specific political philosophy, but as a personal career, governed by rules to which it would be prudent to adapt. Generically speaking, he and I differ primarily in the amount of intellectual leeway put at our disposal. In American law journals, virtually anything goes. In East German law journals, virtually everything was forbidden. But the 'comprehensive legal relationship'—clever, politically correct, ideologically savvy, practically insignificant—was exactly the right idea for a rising young scholar who in the years after Babelsberg wanted to attract attention.

It seems ironic that in the years under Hitler—whom Professor Posch hated with more passion than he seems ever to have felt for socialism—

German legal academics produced jurisprudential constructs almost identical to his 'comprehensive legal relationship.' Probably for the same political and professional reasons that motivated Martin Posch. Politically, legal scholars in the Third Reich—as Herr Posch under socialism—found themselves operating in a state that feared the cocky individualism of bourgeois contract law and praised instead the altruistic warmth of the community. Professionally, Nazi scholars—as Herr Posch under socialism—sought to gain recognition in an academe surrounded by taboos. The similarities between Professor Posch's ideas and those of his Fascist predecessors are hard to miss. Nazi labor lawyers for instance developed the concept of an 'enterprise community': an all-encompassing labor law relationship between enterprise leader and staff, of which specific employment contracts were only individualized expressions. In Nazi contract law, Professor Larenz wrote in 1936: 'A contract is not a relationship between two isolated individuals, determined solely by the meeting of their minds, but rather a legal relationship embedded in the general charter of the nation, whose quality is primarily determined by the national order.'

I do not want to dramatize Professor Posch's 'comprehensive legal relationship' unduly. It was harmless. Nobody was hurt by Martin Posch's jurisprudential speculations. His many other contributions have greatly enriched East German civil law debate. And even if their theoretical constructs looked similar, there is no denying that Martin Posch and Karl Larenz served fundamentally different political systems. But I am worried by the fact that Professor Posch's and my own professional ambitions in many respects so closely resemble each other and that the ivory tower seems no better a refuge from political contagion than the judge's bench. If anything, it might even be a more precarious site. Judges cannot easily avoid noticing the immediate consequences of their decisions: someone goes to prison, loses his apartment, can see his child only on weekends, or must pay money. In many instances, their obvious impact on other people's lives seems to have operated as a practical corrective to East German judges' indisputable penchant for political conformity. Academics write without immediate and perceptible effect. They only put words on paper. But in the end, even abstract and harmless words can link to form a spider's web of intellectual conformity that may choke an entire political system.

14 June 1991

I have a second appointment today: with Professor Wolfgang Bernet, professor of administrative law at Jena's Friedrich Schiller University. Six years ago, Herr Bernet had invited me to attend a conference on 'Legality in GDR State Administration,' scheduled to take place in Jena from 25 to 27 September 1985. I cannot remember ever having looked forward to an academic meeting with the same excitement and anticipation. But then, only a few days prior to my planned departure, came a letter: the conference, 'for technical reasons,' had been cancelled. Now I can finally find out what really happened.

We have arranged to meet in the University Tower, a tubular high-rise building, like a straight and sterile Tower of Pisa placed brutally in the middle of the ancient Jena town square, where the Law Faculty is housed on the twenty-third floor. Herr Bernet is in shirt-sleeves. When we first met, almost a decade ago, he was also in shirt-sleeves. Despite all reunification worries, Wolfgang Bernet looks quite unacademically fit and energetic.

He started his career in the field of 'state law,' the socialist version of constitutional law, concerned not with the limitation of power but with its exercise. But he found too many political convolutions and too little legal substance in the field. So Wolfgang Bernet switched to administrative law, at the time still called 'law of governance' (*Leitungsrecht*), since, even over a decade after Babelsberg, the term 'administrative law,' reeking of non-committal bureaucratic efficiency, was still politically suspect. But at least the field itself had been rediscovered. Did he believe in socialism in those days? Herr Bernet is not interested in matters of political faith. '*Ach*,' he says 'I'm a pragmatic guy.' He believed 'that the Soviets were not about to relinquish this portion of the globe.' What mattered, therefore, was 'to make life bearable under the existing conditions.' As far as he was concerned, socialism's major weakness was not its opposition to private property but the Party's contempt for ordinary human beings. That contempt found daily expression in East German bureaucratic practice. Like Karl Bönninger in Leipzig—'my hero and role model'—Wolfgang Bernet looked for legal ways to protect a citizen more effectively against administrative interference or apathy than the existing system of informal complaints could do, under which it was left to the administration's own discretion whether or not it wanted to correct self-made injustices.

In 1975, in a paper presented at a conference in Jena dealing with the responsibility of local authorities to protect the rights of citizens, Wolfgang Bernet for the first time came out with the dreaded truth. 'We need the courts to do this,' he said. Outraged objections, and not just at Jena. The conference report in the journal *Staat und Recht* omitted the contentious point and only discreetly mentioned that Professor Bernet had talked about legislative trends in other socialist states. Indeed, all East European sister countries, at least on paper, offered their citizens more extensive legal protection against the executive than did the GDR. It was a fact East German authorities preferred not to mention. When three years later, in his 'B-dissertation' on 'State leadership and the protection of civic rights,' Wolfgang Bernet included a final chapter dealing with issues of judicial review, only one of the four outside examiners—a professor from Hungary—found words of praise.

In 1980 and 1981, Herr Bernet published the results of an empirical study of the effectiveness of citizens' complaints against decisions of local building authorities. I remember well my pleasure and surprise when at my desk in far-away Texas I discovered such real-life insights in the pages of so orthodox and timid a law review as *Staat und Recht*. Today I learn that Wolfgang Bernet managed to pull off the project, 'underground fashion,' with the help of correspondence students and the support of local councils. 'All informal sources,' he says. Nobody noticed anything amiss when the articles appeared in print.

It was the following year, I believe, that Wolfgang Bernet and I met for the first time. We went for a long walk in the hills surrounding Jena and argued about administrative law. It was no accident, Herr Bernet tells me now, that he suggested a hike on that occasion. Safer to stay outside. Administrative law in those days was 'a mine field,' he says. You really had to watch your step. How could he advocate dragging the state into court, people would say. No, not the state, Herr Bernet would reply. Just one of its servants who had violated the state's own rules. But that meant bad-mouthing the existing system of complaints, critics would retort. As if socialist citizens did not have all the legal protections they could wish for! Much of Wolfgang Bernet's energies were taken up quieting ideological fears. He had to watch his vocabulary carefully. Of course, you could not talk about 'separation of powers.' 'Separation of functions' was the most one could get away with.

But there were benevolent observers of his tightrope act and, occasionally, even allies. Of course Professor Bönninger in Leipzig—'we were always on the same wavelength,' Herr Bernet says. Also, Professors Mollnau and Heuer at the Academy of Sciences in Berlin. Professor Wünsche, who in the last days of the GDR would for a short time become Minister of Justice. Closer to home, some colleagues and assistants. Professor Riege, head of Wolfgang Bernet's department, did not openly support his efforts, but neither did he interfere. Instead, he watched with what may have been sympathy. Even local Party officials occasionally showed support or at least lenience. When there was trouble because someone with influence had detected 'separation-of-powers undercurrents' in one of Wolfgang Bernet's public talks, the Jena Party leadership did not ask for a recantation but only advised caution for the future and wrote a 'humble letter' to the event's hosts themselves.

But what about the conference, I remind Herr Bernet. Why that last-minute cancellation? He had better begin at the beginning, Professor Bernet says. Plans for a symposium on socialist 'administrative legality' (meaning: on legal protections against the executive) had first arisen in 1983. But such an undertaking required special legitimization. Wolfgang Bernet received a well-placed 'hint' that it would be useful if he openly disavowed all sympathy for bourgeois theories of judicial review. So he composed an article on 'The development and function of German bourgeois administrative court tradition' which culminated in the statement that 'in the GDR, the law on petitions, formal complaints . . . and many other remedies' had 'done away with the need for court review of administrative decisions.' Never mind that in another article, published the same year, Wolfgang Bernet arrived at the very opposite conclusion: 'I consider it necessary that in a socialist German Democratic Republic, administrative decisions can be subjected to judicial review.' The first piece was 'my entry fee for the conference,' Herr Bernet says. But today, he would rather not have written it all.

In any case, those who decided on these matters accepted the offering. Wolfgang Bernet and his colleagues produced a position paper for the conference, praising conditions in the GDR and interspersing that praise, at judicious intervals, with little bits of the authors' own opinions. By the spring of 1985, practical preparations for the conference had almost been completed. Seventy people had been invited, about fifteen of them scholars from the West. I had mailed a delighted letter of acceptance from Texas. 'Security' had examined and, it seems, approved the list of participants. Rooms had been booked.

In June, a final organizational meeting in Berlin. Once again, the Jena initiators were asked to present their game-plan for the big event. Once again they more or less 'muddled through.' But Herr Bernet and his colleagues already sensed some subcutaneous restlessness among the authorities. 'What the heck are we letting ourselves in for,' the *apparatchiks* seemed to think. The disagreement was played out at the Central Committee, where two departments haggled over the political wisdom of Herr Bernet's plans: the Department for State and Law (as usual, opposed to all intellectual adventures) and the Department for Academic Affairs ('on our side'). It was here, too, that the conditions for approval of the conference were finally hammered out: no Gorbachev quotes; no mention of 'administrative culture' (a term which everyone, correctly, would interpret to mean official corruption and sloth); no press reports. 'I could live with that,' Herr Bernet says.

And so, on 10 August, he left for a well-deserved vacation in Hungary. After Wolfgang Bernet's departure, one further round of worried discussions was held in Berlin. This time, the decision was final: the conference would not take place. Professor Riege, Wolfgang Bernet's head of department, had to sign the letter disinviting the participants; 'I regret that due to technical difficulties. . . .' He could not very well write: 'The Party has put its foot down.' Herr Bernet learned of the disaster only upon his return to Germany. His Hungarian host, not wanting to spoil the guest's vacation, too, had kept the disappointing message to himself.

The months that followed were tough. Not only because all the finessing, the planning, and the labor of two years had come to naught. The Party's decision to cancel the conference also marked Wolfgang Bernet as a political failure: he had fallen from grace. More punishment followed. From the Central Committee and the regional Party leadership came calls for disciplinary proceedings. New Party meetings were arranged to advise Herr Bernet of his errors and to insist on their correction. The Jena district organization did its best to calm the waves. 'We are not against you,' Herr Bernet and his colleagues were told, 'but please, play along and accept the verdict.' The University's Party group sang to a different tune. The conference planners, having expected some prospective guests to decline politely, had invited more participants than their funds would have supported. But since virtually all their invitees had been just as eager to accept as I, the conference, though not allowed to happen, in theory would have been oversubscribed. The miscalculation furnished ammunition for Herr Bernet's critics at the University. 'Violation of financial discipline!' they cried. New Party meetings. 'I went to all of them,' Herr Bernet said. 'Best to stare danger in the face.' Were you afraid? Yes. Above all 'of losing my self-control.' The experience left a sour taste in Wolfgang Bernet's mouth. He thought of leaving the University; at one point went so far as to secure a job in the Attorney's Collegium in nearby Erfurt. In the end, he remained an academic after all.

But it was difficult to get things published. Promotions passed him by: in 1987, Wolfgang Bernet was still a lecturer. The tight-rope walk continued. He wrote an article for *Staat und Recht* voicing approval of the Babelsberg conference and expressing appreciation of Karl Polak. Another 'entry fee'? I notice, though, that Wolfgang Bernet seems to have developed a very personal strategy for dealing with political power. Most of his university colleagues simply delivered the goods which the system expected, accompanied—depending on the ambition and moral self-respect of each author—by generous or stingy doses of sycophancy. A few scholars fell silent or left the university. A little gang of intellectually ambitious and self-confident legal academics developed that 'code-language of the initiated' of which Herr Mollnau spoke, disguising their intended message—again, depending on each writer's courage and ambition—under thinner or thicker layers of dissimulation. 'I turned the undercover transmission of meaning to those whom it was meant to reach into an art-form,' a Jena colleague of Herr Bernet told me—a colleague, by the way, who in faculty debates had not sympathized with Wolfgang Bernet's efforts to propagate judicial controls over the socialist executive, at least not openly. There was something élitist and self-congratulatory about that secret language of East German self-respecting intellectuals. We understand each other, the writers seemed to say. We are better than the rest. We keep among ourselves.

Wolfgang Bernet's method for telling those in power what they wanted to hear was simpler, more brazen: a shirt-sleeve approach, so to speak. He simply said both what he thought, and what he was expected to think. That was his strategy in 1983, when in one and the same year Herr Bernet published one paper supporting, and another one denying the need for judicial review in the GDR. Four years later, the same approach: Herr Bernet, in one article, praised the 'positive intentions' of the Babelsberg conference, and in another, called judicial controls over the executive 'a proper socialist solution' for the GDR. I remember, when talking with one of the 'anti-Babelsbergers' at the time, how furious he had been at Herr Bernet's praise for that ignominious event. 'I won't forgive him those remarks,' my colleague had said. But you know perfectly well that Wolfgang Bernet has fought throughout his entire academic life for better legal controls over the administration, I objected. 'Yes, but how could he say such things!' To Wolfgang Bernet, words did not matter very much. He focused on what you could achieve with them.

Now, looking back, Herr Bernet thinks that those embarrassing passages in praise of Babelsberg might not have been necessary after all. In 1987, 'the Party's grip relaxed.' Those in control began to realize how damaging *Ausreiser* problems were to the GDR's international reputation. The Foreign Ministry complained to the Party: 'People don't talk to us in Vienna anymore.' 'That's when I was dug out,' Herr Bernet says. He was needed to help draft the new 'Statute on the Jurisdiction and Procedure of Courts to Review the Legality of Administrative Decisions' that was passed on 14 December 1988 and entered into force on 1 July 1989. 'Every thing was hush-hush,' Herr Bernet says, and work had to proceed at record speed. During a two-week retreat in Wustrau, a small party of experts slapped together the new decree: much too fast, 'totally unsound,' and without having even half-way faced the crucial problem of how to handle the review of discretionary decisions. At least the new statute 'was planned for growth,' Herr Bernet says. 'We had a foot in the door.'

But at the same time that Herr Bernet and his colleagues in Wustrau managed to move the GDR a little closer to the *Rechtsstaat*, 'a different gang,' in a different location, and with the help of State Security and police officials, cooked up the new East German Travel Decree. It came into force in December 1988. The Decree's intentionally vague rules on the conditions under which GDR citizens were allowed to leave the country had to undermine the effectiveness of the new statute on judicial review, which offered no handle for judicial checks on discretionary decisions. But even Herr Bernet and most of his Wustrau colleagues had not anticipated how thoroughly the Travel Decree would thwart the impact of their own legislative work. Only a few of the Wustrau participants had seen the signs. 'It'll be a flop,' former Supreme Court President Heinrich Toeplitz, for instance, had predicted. And so it was. When a newly-revised statute on judicial review, as a belated and futile afterthought of the Party, was passed in July 1990, Wolfgang Bernet no longer had a hand in it.

And what will happen to him now, I ask. Herr Bernet does not know. He has hopes and plans, writes a lot, and together with colleagues edits a new law review on problems of local administration in the five new eastern states of the Federal Republic. But he is pretty sure that the new West German bosses at Jena University will no longer want him. They don't take academics from the former GDR. I find it hard to believe that East German administrative law should have no use for someone who so readily rolls up his sleeves as Wolfgang Bernet. For him 'the world has not collapsed,' he says. But he is angry at the wholesale Western rejection of things said and done by Eastern jurists. 'As if we never used our heads.'

15 June 1991

Another academic cup of tea; this time with Professor Helmut Gerling, one of the GDR's foremost legal theorists. In pre-*Wende* days, it seemed that he had it all: chair-holder and soul-mate to the anti-Babelsberg intellectual élite; respected by Party officials and academic colleagues alike; *doctor honoris causae* and travel cadre; at home at international conferences and with a long and learned publication list. Even the *Wende* could not touch his luck: Professor Gerling, who has almost reached retirement age, will teach only one more semester and then, like any other Emeritus Professor, will leave, so to speak, with an honorable discharge. No need for him to face the humiliation of the vetting process.

I would have found it difficult, in any case, to picture him before so unimposing and makeshift a tribunal as, for instance, our Humboldt University PSK. Professor Gerling cuts an impressive figure: tall and still dark-haired, with a Byronic profile and the grace and assurance born of many years' success. His study matches the man. I register the innumerable books, the word processor, the old and comfortable furniture, and above all the good taste that was such a rare commodity in the GDR. Helmut Gerling has travelled enough in the West to train aesthetic sensibilities that under the stuffy *petitbourgeois* regime of socialist good taste would have had little room to flourish. How about his beautiful house, I ask; is it, like so many other East German homes these days, the subject of West German restitution claims? No, his ownership rights are unassailable. Here, too, his luck has held. Frau Gerling comes with a plate of exquisite cookies.

How did he find his way to socialism? Helmut Gerling joined the Social Democratic Party in 1945 and had no objections when, one year later, it merged (or, if you listen to a critic of the regime, was forced to merge) with the Communist Party. At the time, he was disturbed by what appeared to him a resurgence of reactionary values and an unseemly tolerance towards former Nazi office-holders in West Germany. The GDR's proclaimed anti-fascism and anti-militarism appealed to him. And what about its Stalinism in those years? Actually, Herr Gerling himself had been eyewitness to an instance of its repressiveness. In the 1950s his best friend, out of the blue, had been arrested and sentenced to life in prison—for espionage. They had been very close. After their simultaneous graduation from law school, the friend had found a job in the Ministry of the Interior while Helmut Gerling had started out in academics. Then came the arrest. Did you believe the accusations? His first reaction had been: 'It can't be true.' His second: 'Can it be true?' Maybe his friend had somehow been 'reckless,' he thought. Maybe there was 'some basis' for the charges against him.

How did the event affect your belief in socialism? Herr Gerling does not answer the question. He wants to move on to other topics. 'Have you read Ingo Müller's *Hitler's Justice*?' he asks in return. He goes on to talk about his loathing for the Third Reich, how he had searched and found an alternative to Adenauer and Globke in the GDR; mentions a piece he once did on Nazi jurisprudence; searches for a reprint. Yes, but your friend, I say. I want to know how one can trust an ideology that has wrecked the life of a close friend. I cite the famous E. M. Forster saying that given the choice between betraying his friend or his country, he hoped to find the guts to betray his country. What does Herr Gerling think? Would he side with his country? Is that what he chose to do when faced with his friend's supposed treason? But had not the friend's incarceration for behavior which probably amounted to no more than criticism of official policies crucially undermined the trust-worthiness of the country?

Herr Gerling will not comment on the Forster quote. His field is legal theory and history. 'Have I read . . . ,' he inquires. No, I have not. But to return to his friend: did Wolfgang Gerling also know the friend's parents? Yes, he knew them well, Herr Gerling says reluctantly. What did one do in those days if someone suddenly disappeared in prison: write a letter to the family? Pay a visit? No, once the arrest had come to light, he had had no further contacts with his friend's parents. 'It would have been risky.' Why, I ask. I know the answer in advance: because they had been such close friends that concern for the family 'might have been open to misinterpret-ation.' Wait a second, I say. Maybe your friend, in some obscure way, had betrayed the cause of socialism—you could not be sure. But you knew that you yourself were not a spy. Yet you feared that the state might mistake you for its enemy and treat you accordingly. You obviously did not trust its legal system. How could you trust its ideology?

This is not the conversation Professor Gerling thought he had agreed to. He steers it back on course: mentions something about 'contradictions' in the political situation at the time, seizes upon the term, and before I know it is talking about 'contradiction as a philosophical category.' It is a topic that has always interested him, he says. He has done quite a bit of work on it. But it was impossible to get articles on the subject published. 'Another instance of repressiveness,' I say, pulling the rudder my way. 'How can you explain that despite its tyranny, socialism maintained such power over people like yourself?' The question suits Professor Gerling better than I had anticipated. Because of its commitment to Germany's humanist heritage, he says. Now he is in his element: mentions Kant and Hegel, their influence on his work, their role in socialist legal theory. But it is a misdescription to say that the Party endorsed German philosophical traditions, I object. It did so erratically and selectively and only if it fitted its political purposes at the time. Maybe, says Herr Gerling. Nevertheless, he had found sufficient sympathy in socialism for the three major themes that dominated his own work: 'universalism, historicism, and humanism.' He reaches for another reprint.

I am puzzled by Herr Gerling's refusal to connect personal experience with political beliefs. His publications have, indeed, maintained remarkable consistency over the years. They speak, unerringly, about the same beautiful subjects: humanism, autonomy, culture, progress, reason. They cite the great spirits of the ages: Plato, Aristotle, Augustine, Kant, Marx. Even their criticism is dignified. Their references to real life are unsullied by concrete proposals. Their equanimity and intellectual poise seem unaffected by the vulgarity of actual events. I make one more attempt to discover the man behind the scholar. 'How could your faith in socialism survive the Soviet invasion of Prague?' I ask. A little pause. 'It survived longer than that,' Herr Gerling says. 'The faith is still alive today.' But the Czech reformers wanted to realize what he, Helmut Gerling, found most attractive about socialism: its humanism. The Soviet army was sent to crush that 'socialism with a human face' with tanks and hand-grenades. Should the event not have caused his political faith to falter? He did not think at the time that the invasion had been 'justified,' Herr Gerling concedes. A rather mild reproof. Had he and his intellectual friends discussed any kind of collective reaction at the time? No. How did they deal psychologically with the invasion? By showing discreet support for people who had been the subject of official criticism. Incidentally, after Hermann Klenner's fall from grace he, Hermut Gerling, had been the first to invite him to participate in a scholarly event. When Klenner was still mayor in that God-forsaken little village?, I ask. No, after he had returned to academia. Was it a risky invitation? 'No, not really,' Herr Gerling says. (He does not lie, I think with renewed respect. He would rather not answer my questions, but if he does, he does it truthfully.) 'Maybe a little,' Hermut Gerling now says upon reflection. 'You did not like to attract the attention of those in control.' Again, he admits that not all was well in socialist academics. How could he—the rationalist, the believer in universal human values—adapt so successfully to its restrictions?

'Where were you on the day the Soviets marched into Prague?' I ask him. Professor Gerling searches a little in his mind. He cannot remember. 'I am sure you can,' I say. 'It was a day everyone remembers, like the day President Kennedy was shot. Think for a bit.' Herr Gerling does, but no, his memory stays mute. I do not conceal my surprise. He cannot remember the day on which every socialist's faith in the essential goodness of his ideology must have received such a devastating blow? Professor Gerling is annoyed. 'You ask questions like a journalist,' he says; 'obsessed with details.' What he means is: unscholarly, unintellectual, concrete. Maybe obsessed with reality, I concede. That includes people's states of mind. 'I want to understand what you really believed in.'

I do not think that I will succeed. Even Professor Gerling's present writings, no longer constrained by the invisible censor, offer no clue—at least none that I can read—to real human convictions, fears, hates or loves, hopes or regrets. The *Wende* has not slowed his productivity. Helmut Gerling's articles are everywhere. As before, they are filled with beautiful ideas, well-turned phrases, and quotations of the great. They may sound a little more elegiac than under socialism, less hopeful (now that hope is no longer officially prescribed), more critical (now that criticism lies in the air). But they are as judicious, measured, and elegant as ever. I get a few more reprints to take home.

Have my questions been unfair? I ask myself. Maybe it is naïve to think that anybody who tosses around ideas for a living will ever, in a personal and existential way, believe in what he or she writes. Maybe all we do is aim for polished, clever, and effective sentences the same way that tennis players aim for well-placed shots. I turn with the question to Herr Gerling. Have I been unfair? 'No,' he replies. I fear that he is too generous. What do I and my colleagues believe in? It is just that the world around us, in most cases, is not so glaringly at odds with the description of it that we put on paper as it was in Helmut Gerling's work.

After lunch, as I stroll through town in search of a cup of coffee, I run into Professor Gerling again. His wife is with him; a grandchild bounces on his shoulders—a family outing. He smiles and waves and we all stop for a little chat. Why does he still talk to me? I asked him questions that were none of my business; drew out a personal story that he wanted to withhold; refused to acknowledge the significance of his great learning; and questioned the sincerity of his beliefs. I did all this from a position of ignorance of his specific field of work and without the legitimacy of someone who herself has gone through the experiences she talks about. I insulted his intellectual honor. Why does he show no anger? Then it occurs to me that intellectual honor is something legal scholars in the GDR may long ago have learned to do without.

17 June 1991

Rededication ceremony and 'open house' at the former *Stadtgericht* in the Littenstrasse. Although the renovations are not yet complete, they have progressed enough to allow the old West Berlin *Landgericht* and a number of new first-instance *Amtsgerichte* (county courts) to move gradually into the building. I walk around and marvel at the changes. Everything smells of paint. The first-floor balconies are ablaze with light. In the ground-floor rotunda, visitors crowd around the many stands where West Berlin judges and paralegals, in honor of the festive occasion, hand out advice and information on everyday legal problems in the new *Rechtsstaat*.

It is a pretty dedication program: a French horn duet, congratulatory remarks by various dignitaries, a speech by the Senator of Justice, Professor Limbach. I am pleased that the day's events also include a talk about Hans Litten, the brave attorney who in the final years of the Weimar Republic defended Communists and workers; who had the courage, in a famous trial in 1931, to subpoena and cross-examine Adolf Hitler on the political goals of fascism; who continued his fight against the Nazis after Hitler came to power; and who, in 1938, in the Dachau concentration camp, took his own life. Long before the *Wende*, the Littenstrasse was named in his honor and in the first-floor gallery of the court-house you will still find his bust: a young, round face, serious as a child's.

I wander into one of the courtrooms. Wasn't I here before? It looks more elegant than I remember: fresh white walls; the wooden panelling polished to a shine; the stucco ornaments on the ceiling carefully outlined in salmon, ink blue, and resplendent gold. As everywhere in the courthouse today, here too representatives of the new judicial system stand ready to answer any legal questions visitors might bring. A man with a reckless tie and a plastic briefcase enquires in broad Saxon dialect about the legality of price-fixing agreements among competitors for public contracts—a fresh-baked capitalist? I check with an official from the justice department about the preparations for the happy day. Did they also invite jurists from East Berlin? Apart from the professional associations, nobody was 'invited,' I learn. Announcements of the event were sent to all courts in West Berlin; the East Berlin members of the city's parliament were told about it; an announcement was placed in the *Tagesspiegel*. I mentally try to compose a tactful invitation addressed at Herr Oehmke and his East Berlin colleagues and give up. If any of the former occupants of this house are here today to inspect its transformation, it is because they, like I, learned of the reopening through the newspaper. But if they have come at all, they will have come incognito.

Frau Limbach enters the room with a little following of officials, gracious as always and visibly pleased with the successful event. Not fewer than forty visitors had made inquiries at the legal information booth dealing with inheritance and probate matters, she says. Family, labor, and social court judges had also been in great demand. And now a small group of distinguished gentlemen appears in the doorway. They make me think of a remark I once heard from a judge in Potsdam: '*Ossis* enter a room; *Wessis* stage an entrance.' The newcomers pause for a second, look around, walk straight to the judges' table and sit down on the three chairs behind it. 'Hm,' the middle one on the seat of the presiding judge says contentedly, 'much nicer than at our Court of Appeals. We might as well stay here.'

Afternoon

A journey to Marzahn to speak with Dieter Feld, one of the first East Berlin judges to face the vetting process and one of the first to fail it. Herr Feld had been a judge for only four and a half years (five, if you count his six-months' stint as assistant judge) and had dealt only with civil law cases. What could have happened in that short and innocuous career to make him permanently unsuitable as a *Rechtsstaat* judge?

Marzahn is a new part of town, to the east of East Berlin, a vast collection of concrete blocks, endlessly filling the window frame as my train approaches, a daunting monument to socialist pre-fab urban architecture. They say that the citizens of Marzahn like it here—young people, mostly, with young children, whose pleasure and gratitude at obtaining their own real little flat with all amenities may have survived the political turnabout. To the outsider, unaware of the web of social relations connecting the neighborhood, Marzahn looks like a gigantic sand-box in which the particularly unimaginative child of a giant has arranged a huge bagful of identical blocks, placing them sometimes flat and somtimes upright. Walking along the wide and windy streets, I notice that each building is equipped with numerous little attachments for displaying flags. It really would look nicer here, I think, if every apartment house were decorated with billowing red banners.

Dieter Feld is a serious young man in his late twenties. Our arrangement was made over the telephone, and he wants to see my ID card before he lets me in. I can offer only my Texas driver's license, but it passes muster. The living-room into which Herr Feld now leads me is tiny, filled to the brim with heavy furniture of bourgeois respectability. Herr Feld is wearing slippers.

His interview with the Senate Administration's Review Committee took place in November 1990. The rejection letter stated no other grounds for the decision than that he had been found 'unsuitable for personal reasons' and therefore 'did not fulfil the prerequisites for employment.' In April 1991, the Parliamentary Judicial Review Commission (which under the Unification Treaty handles the vetting process together with the Senator of Justice, and which tends to be more welcoming towards the East Berliners than the Senate Administration) had endorsed the rejection. Wanting to know more, Herr Feld had gone and asked to see his files at the Ministry of Justice headquarters. He had found no other enlightenment than a memo of February 1991, recording that the interview 'had raised doubts among all members of the Senate Committee as to whether Dieter Feld could be trusted with the office of a judge.' Herr Feld's request for further information had elicited a Senate reply in May 1991, according to which his rejection had been based 'on the reasons stated.'

Maybe a reconstruction of the interview will solve the riddle. What had the examiners asked, I want to know. What, in Dieter Feld's view, had they been after? Primarily, he thinks, they wanted 'to make the candidate feel guilty' about his past. He had known, had he not, that the GDR had signed the Helsinki Agreements which ensured freedom of movement, the Senate examiners had said, for instance. And had he known it? I ask too. Yes, but he had always accepted what he was told, namely, that the agreements required special implementing legislation to be applicable in the GDR. The Senate people also wanted to know why he had specifically noted 'a danger of escape' on some arrest warrants for border violations that he had signed when on occasional weekend duty. 'Because there was a danger of escape!' says Herr Feld, obviously finding the question absurd. 'That was the prerequisite for an arrest!' How many of those warrants did you sign? I ask. The Senate researchers had found two in the archives, says Herr Feld, and although he cannot remember for sure, he does not think that there could have been many more. So what should he feel guilty for seems to be his implication.

Did you ever see anything wrong with what you were doing? I ask him. 'Would I have worked so hard for it if I had?' You never had any doubts about Socialism? 'No time!' says Herr Feld. His workday started early: the alarm clock ringing at a quarter to six, breakfast, then dropping off the kids (now almost 2 and 6 years old) at their respective 'institutions,' and on to work by seven. His wife (who left even earlier for work than he did) would pick up the children by 5:15 p.m., he himself came home around 5:30 p.m. In the evenings, twice a week some collective activity (Herr Feld is organizer of his apartment block's sports association) or a little professional reading. 'The weekends were reserved for the children,' says Herr Feld.

I try to imagine myself in his place. Is a full day enough excuse for not reflecting upon the world around you? Extreme tiredness, I suppose, might be . . . 'But before the *Wende*, you had only one child,' I say. Your life was not so hard as to leave no room for thought. There must have been time for discussions among friends, for reading . . . 'The weekends were for the family,' Herr Feld repeats, firmly. There were the grandparents, the great-grandparents, birthday parties, swimming outings . . . And then comes the real explanation: 'I was happy with family and work.' There might have been time to reflect, but no reason to do so. Here in Marzahn, where everybody had a family, a job, and an apartment and where the evidence of socialist accomplishments was all around you, life in the GDR had looked good to Dieter Feld. 'My work was everything to me,' he says. 'I believed that everybody was well off.' And: 'I believed the Party slogan: our work today determines our life tomorrow.' 'We did not think,' he adds, the first flicker of self-criticism.

Were some of your colleagues more critical of the system than you? I ask. At the time he had not noticed. But now, 'in retrospect,' he realizes that there must have been some who were. Did you watch West German television? 'Rarely.' He regularly watched the East German program denouncing and commenting on Western television; 'to get the arguments.' It seems that, at least occasionally, Herr Feld had found it necessary to arm himself against possible doubts of his own or of others. Did you not miss the possibility of travel? No, not really. 'I was not raised that way.' Confined, he did not notice his confinement. 'We lost the capacity for distant vision,' he says, and it sounds more matter-of-fact than sad.

Why, in your view, did the Senate Review Committee reject you, I ask. Not because of those arrest warrants, thinks Herr Feld. There were just the two, and even if he had signed a few more, that could not have been the reason. And not because of *Stasi* connections: 'there weren't any.' Nor because of pre-*Wende* criticism of his work: 'there had been only one citizen complaint. . . .' And, as Herr Feld launches into a lengthy and still agitated explanation of that complaint's unfoundedness, I agree with him: no, that could not have been it. 'For personal reasons,' the Senate Committee's letter had said. I begin to see what they meant, but Herr Feld cannot and he is entitled to a proper explanation. How could the letter truthfully have read? 'We reject you because you have neither grasped the fundamental flaws of socialist justice nor understood the differences between your and our legal system'?

Do you think that there have been important legal changes since the *Wende*? I ask him. 'That's what they tell us,' says Herr Feld, but he is obviously not convinced. Why not? 'Just look at your and our civil law,' he says, 'they really are not all that different.' If you omit all economic transactions, I say, and Herr Feld concedes the point. Does he perceive important differences between West German and East German constitutional law? Herr Feld thinks for a bit. 'To some extent,' he says hesitantly. Can he explain? 'Well, most of your basic rights we had, too,' he says. On paper, I say. Herr Feld admits that maybe East German rights were not always 'practicable.' What does he mean by that? 'Well, take the right to housing,' he says. Since tenants felt that the state owed them living-space and since, to all intents and purposes, they could not be evicted, they would often fail to pay their rents. If anything, the Constitution was too generous, the answer implies. Hence its lack of impact. It does not occur to Dieter Feld to mention the fact that even on paper, East German constitutional rights were limited, conditioned, or often too vaguely defined to have any meaning and that nobody could sue the state to enforce his rights.

In any case, 'he is through with politics,' Herr Feld says now. He will keep the medals and certificates of appreciation that he accumulated even in his short career—'it really pains me,' he says, 'to see them sold as souvenirs to tourists these days'—but he will not put himself out again for the sake of the collective. He 'has lost heart.' Many of his fellow activists have, too. Will he vote? 'Elections are important,' Herr Feld admits. 'We did not implement our election law,' he adds, again, in his criticism, unwittingly accepting the system's premises and neglecting the fact that even if East German votes had been honestly collected and counted, the one-Party system would have left no room for choice. But politically, says Dieter Feld, he no longer has 'a place he belongs to.' Might I see his correspondence with the Senate Committee, I ask before I leave. Yes, he will make me copies. Could he please send them to my West Berlin address? Again, Dieter Feld's answer echoes the past. 'Not in the mail,' he says, full of suspicion.

21 June 1991

In Leipzig, for an appointment with Doctor Siegfried Seidel, until recently labor law teacher at nearby Halle University. We have arranged to meet at the 'House of the Scientist,' a neo-romanesque villa from the turn of the century that is owned by the University of Leipzig and that comes as close to looking like an English club as you could hope for under socialism. Deep, comfortable armchairs; old oil pictures on the walls; soft light falling from old-fashioned lamps with yellowed silk-fringed shades. In one corner of the room, two middle-aged men, unmistakably professors from the West, converse over a bottle of wine. Behind us, a charming conservatory. I notice for the first time the privilege that accompanied academic life even under socialism.

Herr Seidel does not look like a man whom you would expect to encounter habitually in these rooms. If I did not know him, I would place him in an occupation closer to reality than academics: a farmer, I might guess, or maybe a plumber. He addresses issues in straight, frontal attacks and wastes no time on intellectual deviations. When we first met, about fifteen years ago, and Siegfried Seidel learned of my interest in East German social courts, he simply took me to a session of the Conflict Commission at Halle University which he chaired at the time—to my own and everybody else's amazement. I remember well the startled faces of the Commission's other members when the visitor from Texas was introduced. Siegfried Seidel was also the only one among my conversation partners from pre-*Wende* days who told me that he would inform the Party of our meeting. 'I shall say that I talked with Professor Markovits from the USA about labor law issues,' he explained. Many of Herr Seidel's colleagues, as they were supposed to, must have given the Party more detailed and more accurate descriptions of our respective encounters. But Siegfried Seidel wanted me to know what was going on. He always seemed a little out of place in his surroundings, like a Baptist in a High Church congregation, or like a village mayor in a meeting of slick city managers: someone who thinks what he says, who acts the way he thinks, and who, I am sure, is often accused by friends or colleagues of taking things far too literally. He once explained to me why labor law should be seen as the core subject of legal theory in the GDR. But you are a real socialist! I said, surprised. 'One of the few left in this country,' Siegfried Seidel said.

Now, like everybody else at Halle University, he will be '*abgewickelt*' and will lose his job. But is he not a member of his faculty's Employee Council and therefore immune from dismissal? Ordinarily, it would, indeed, be difficult to fire him. But dismissals in the course of the faculty's political cleansing process do not count as firings. The vetting of Halle University is run by the West German University of Göttingen. It does not provide for hearings. Like his fellow examinees, Herr Seidel has sent all his personal documents to Göttingen and now waits for the results. But he does not expect to pass. With two trips to Angola and no Habilitation thesis he does not have a chance.

No Habilitation thesis. Herr Seidel has been a university teacher since 1956. Why did he never write that second thesis which in both Germanies is a prerequisite for an academic career? Actually, he did write it. But something seems to have gone wrong. What was it? Is it true, as I was once told by a colleague in East Berlin, that Siegfried Seidel's career was one of the few law careers in the GDR to have floundered for political reasons?

No, Herr Seidel would not put it quite that way, although politics were part of the story. He had completed his so-called 'B-dissertation' in 1977: an analysis of 'the legal character of one-man management,'—that is, of the position of socialist enterprise directors. It contained a number of populist assertions: that managers, 'in labor law terms,' were *Werktätige*, that is, ordinary 'toilers' like all other employees; that their legal powers and responsibilities had to be specifically and precisely defined; that 'constant controls' should verify whether a socialist manager lived up to his legal obligations; and that a manager's authority was 'the sole function of his ability and performance.' He had been accused of disregarding the leading role of the Party and, in the process, of putting democratic centralism into question. 'I was not as bold as that,' Herr Seidel says. Still, the customary public defense of the thesis turned into a fierce political debate and, in the end, his dissertation was rejected. But personal animosity between him and one of the examiners definitely played a role in the debacle.

And so Herr Seidel remained stuck in the position of a lecturer. For more than ten years he did not receive a pay rise. Twice he complained to the editor in chief of *Neue Justiz*. Twice, applications for travel to Yugoslavia were rejected. I can imagine how Siegfried Seidel, again, did not quite fit into East German legal academia: too undiplomatic, too direct, perhaps also too naïve. 'I had this notion of taking Marxism at its word,' he says. Is it surprising that the stance led to disappointments?

Where were you when the Soviets invaded Prague? I ask, thinking of my conversation with Professor Gerling. Herr Seidel remembers the event like yesterday. Early in the morning, he had heard the news on the radio. He had immediately gotten into his car to drive to the Konsument department store in Leipzig, where a special stand for Czech consumer products seemed the most natural rallying point for declarations of sympathy with the CSSR that he could think of. But Konsument had been the very picture of normalcy that morning. Everybody else seemed to have opted for 'business as usual.' Maybe it had not been very realistic to hope for spontaneous demonstrations. After hanging around in Leipzig for a while, Herr Seidel, depressed and disappointed, had driven home. He had missed a meeting at the University, but his Dean kindly had covered up for him.

And what does he hope for now, with the additional hindsight of almost a quarter of a century? 'As always, for a more just distribution between north and south and between east and west,' Herr Seidel says. But I no longer hear the old eagerness in his voice. Politically, he would place his bet on neither capitalism nor socialism: 'I have seen so many shortcomings of both during this last year.' Personally, he worries about the future: his wife, who used to head the department for analysis and statistics at the regional court in Leipzig, also lost her job ('that's what the people want,' she had been told) and as to his own prospects, Herr Seidel thinks that he can easily guess how readers in Göttingen will evaluate his file. 'You have done nothing worthwhile in your life and are too old to be of any use in the future,' the *Wessis* will tell him.

I expect Siegfried Seidel to prove their verdict wrong. Even if his hopes for justice remain unfulfilled, he has another resource to fall back upon: his love for modern art. Already at our pre-*Wende* encounters, Herr Seidel,

straying from law talk, would often turn to art: tell me about new East
German artists, recommend galleries, encourage me to branch out and
learn something about painting in the GDR. Now that the barriers of the
Party's official art philosophy have fallen, Siegfried Seidel has big plans. He
is a member of an association for the establishment of an avant-garde
museum in Leipzig. He and his friends hope to enlist the financial help of
the German Federation of Industries. Right now, they are looking for a
suitable building plot. There is this piece of land he has in mind . . . 'Herr
Seidel!' I interrupt, 'you are a sleepwalker!' He is not to be deterred. It
won't be long before the association will be officially established and registered, he continues. Next week the executive officers are scheduled to meet.
'The purpose of life is to enjoy art, literature and science,' he says. 'The rest
we just share with animals.'

24 June 1991

On one of my recent outings to Potsdam I learned that during the 1980s,
several Potsdam judges were made to leave the district court for political
reasons. I even got an address: Peter Peukert, now an attorney here in town,
whose office lies within walking distance of the *Kreisgericht*. We have
arranged to meet this afternoon.

When I arrive, Herr Peukert is in the process of sweeping up the panes of
a broken glass door, at the same time reassuring a client about some drawn-
out dispute with the new administration. Both jobs done, we move to his
unpretentious office. I had expected Peter Peukert to be older. But he had
only been a judge for two and a half years when his troubles began in 1983.
What set them off?

The peace movement. In conversations among family and friends, he and
others had begun to discuss NATO defense policies and to question the
stationing of SS-20 missiles in the GDR. Not that Herr Peukert ever had
attended a peace rally. Nor—specializing in family law and civil law—had
he ever been in the position of having to sentence demonstrators for 'illegitimate assembly' or for 'resisting state authority.' But he began to worry
about what he would do if confronted with those issues: if, while on weekend duty, he were asked to sign an arrest warrant for someone who in the
name of peace had silently stood at some street corner holding a burning
candle in his hand. Herr Peukert first discussed the dreaded dilemma with
colleagues and then, finding no satisfactory answer, with a superior judge at
the courthouse. Could one please 'offer him guidance,' he asked. He 'felt
confused.' And before long: he did not wish to stand as a candidate for the
next judicial elections in May 1984.

'That got things going.' First an angry confrontation with his superiors at
the district court, then four or five citations to attend 'discussions' at the

'Kremlin,' the massive structure on a hill beyond the river Havel that housed the bureau of the Potsdam district Party organization. These talks were 'really quite awful,' Herr Peukert says. He on one side, on the other the gentlemen from the Party, 'doing their best to misconstrue my words.' Accusation heaped upon accusation. And yet, at the end of each conversation, always the same promise: stand as a candidate for re-election and all shall be forgotten.

But by then, Peter Peukert had reached the point where even without the risk of having to sign arrest warrants for peace demonstrators, he no longer wanted to remain a judge. On 16 January 1984, things came to a head at a Party meeting at the Potsdam District Court, called to expel Peter Peukert from the Party. Under the SED Party Statute, two-thirds of those present had to vote in favor of the expulsion. There was a lively but pointless discussion. Herr Peukert and his allies at the courthouse were allowed to speak, but each of their arguments 'was intentionally distorted' by the other side. Finally the vote. Of the twenty-two members of the Party group at the district court, fifteen voted for the expulsion, seven against. Peter Peukert, with only one more vote than needed, was kicked out of the Party. The next day, he handed his current cases over to a colleague, cleaned out his desk, and left.

The story in part confirms my image of justice in the GDR, but in part contradicts it. Peter Peukert's account of the confrontations at the 'Kremlin' reveals the Party I know: authoritarian, intimidating, smug. But I am surprised at his description of the Party meeting at the courthouse. I would not have thought that in the years prior to Gorbachev so sensitive a decision-making process would so religiously have followed the formal voting rules of the Party Statute. Certainly not in a case like this where the outcome was far from certain. And while the debate's conclusion, according to Herr Peukert's report, was predetermined from the start, the process nevertheless allowed the participants to voice conflicting views and to ally themselves in factions. Frau Leetz, for instance, prior to the crucial meeting, had gone around the courthouse trying 'to talk some sense' into Herr Peukert's critics and to persuade them not to cast their vote against him.

The aftermath of Peter Peukert's expulsion from the Party, too, does not conform to the convenient image of law as the lackey of socialist totalitarian rule. Right after his expulsion, Herr Peukert was asked to repay that portion of his salary, already received, that covered the time after 16 January 1984, the day of the Party ballot. He objected: since only the Potsdam district legislature that had elected him could also recall him, he should continue to receive his pay up to the next judicial election date—that is, until 29 February 1984. No, said the cadre official at the court: the expulsion from the Party was the legal equivalent of a dismissal for cause. So Peter Peukert wrote a letter to the Ministry of Justice in Berlin and ten days later received a reply in his favor: the district court was ordered to continue his pay until election day. There was also disagreement concerning the evaluation of Herr Peukert's work. In his opinion, the political reproaches leading to the expulsion from the Party had no place in an assessment of his performance as a judge. When the evaluation was not to his liking, he sued. And although his complaint was dismissed, 'for threadbare reasons,' the evaluation was, nevertheless, re-written two or three times until it no longer contained the objectionable accusations.

What was most painful about the whole experience?, I ask Herr Peukert. Looking for a new job was depressing, he says. Each morning he would leave the house, bracing himself; each evening he would return, hopes dashed. He looked for work as counsel to a state-owned enterprise, but whenever a potential employer requested his files from the district court, he would be told of Peter Peukert's ignominious expulsion. Eventually he found work in the legal department of a large enterprise in Teltow near Berlin. The enterprise director had not cared about the district court's political opinions. Peter Peukert, finally, found himself in human company again. How long had the unemployment lasted? A little over four weeks, Herr Peukert says: from 17 January to 20 February 1984. More than seven years later, he can still recall the dates. Only four weeks!, I think. How sheltered a life in which four weeks of unemployment seem almost unbearable.

But 'the worst had been the feeling of exclusion,' Herr Peukert says. Didn't you feel like a hero? 'Not at all. On the contrary: I felt like an outcast.' Peter Peukert wanted to belong. His mother and grandmother were communists; during the war his uncle had been a partisan in the Soviet Union; he himself had joined the SED while still an apprentice—to Peter Peukert, socialism was home. He could neither understand nor accept the expulsion from the Party and for a long time afterwards fought for his reinstatement. Stormy new confrontations at the Potsdam 'Kremlin.' Ten comrades from the District Party Control Commission 'tore into me.' What was the vocabulary used on those occasions, I want to know: 'Renegade'? 'Traitor'? Perhaps 'criminal'?

No, no, Herr Peukert says. Attacks were not so crude. Mostly, the accusations reflected the disappointment of the Party that despite all its concern for the offender's welfare, things had to take this sorry turn. 'This is a peace-loving state,' he would be told. 'Haven't you learned anything in school?' 'You don't fit in.' 'To think of all the money the state spent on your education.'

I realize: this was no collision between the political system of socialism and a dissident. This was a generation conflict. The parents lament: 'what has become of our child! After all our sacrifices!' The son wants his independence. As often in the case of family disputes, the quarrel arose over some isolated incident. In many other respects, Peter Peukert remained imbued with Party views. I want to know whether he ever signed arrest warrants for 'border violations.' He can't even remember. But whether he did or not, East Germany's criminalization of the right to travel caused him no moral trauma. And although Herr Peukert and his colleagues would occasionally debate specific sentences for 'work-shy behavior' or for leading an 'asocial lifestyle,' the fact that 'crimes' like these were actually listed in the Penal Code did not offend their professional sensibilities. Which particular aspect of the socialist legal system would lead its children to defy the authority of their Party elders seemed almost a matter of chance. The two other insurgents at the district court each challenged the Party for different and very personal reasons. One of them, for example, could no longer swallow the treatment of conscientious objectors in the GDR. What was really at stake in these encounters was the refusal of the Party to grant its children any moral and intellectual room for development. 'I only wanted them to listen!' Herr Peukert says. 'At least occasionally to accept other people's arguments! To admit once in a while that they might be wrong!' But the parents felt too insecure of their authority to make even the tiniest concession. And so, in a single year, three of their sons absconded from the Potsdam City District Court.

But the affair has not destroyed Herr Peukert's relationships with his former colleagues. His friends all stood by him. And because he did not want to attack socialism in its entirety but only the system's self-righteousness and intolerance, Peter Peukert can sympathize even with those colleagues who at that Party meeting in January 1984 voted against him. 'Maybe he was afraid,' he says of someone who at the time had only just joined the district court as an assistant judge—almost in the tone of an elder brother who realizes that it might have been a bit much to expect the younger sibling to take sides against the parents. Would he retain the judge in question under the new order? 'No objections at all.' Herr Peukert seems to consider a former commitment to socialism almost as a professional asset for a judge in the new German states—how else is he or she to understand the past? 'GDR lawyers should not just be treated as political liabilities,' he says. 'There is a lot we have to integrate into the new system, even if it hurts.'

Speaking of himself, he would not wish to become a judge again. Since 1 May 1990, Peter Peukert has worked as an attorney. It has been a period of ups and downs—'downs, mostly,' he says. The months immediately following 3 October 1990 were particularly difficult. During the first two weeks after Reunification Day, not a single client knocked at his door. The fresh-baked citizens of the Federal Republic would only trust attorneys from the West. Meanwhile, they have come to realize that East German lawyers are cheaper and better at empathizing with their stories. Peter Peukert has a lot to learn. He studies the new law on his own, whenever he finds the time. Today, many matters seem routine which only three months ago were unfamiliar. Do you experience the new system as a rule of law? I ask him. Herr Peukert chooses his words with care. 'In comparison to what we had before,' he says.

3 July 1991

A final meeting of the Law Faculty's Personnel Review Commission at Humboldt University. We have to deal with the last complaints against our committee's verdicts. Without exception, all who failed the vetting process have appealed our decision to the University's Central Review Commission. At least in the eyes of those whom we rejected, our PSK has not succeeded in doing justice. Those whom we passed approve of our work— 'because they passed.' 'Actually, it is a shame,' said the candidate who told me of his colleagues' reactions. Both he and I would have wished our commission's efforts to have found more principled acceptance.

By now, the Central University Commission already has rejected most appeals. Today, we are asked to comment on the few remaining cases. We meet in the Dean's office. Behind the windows, the day is glistening with summer heat. But the high-ceilinged room is pleasantly cool. The marble bust of Friedrich Carl von Savigny, which in the days after Babelsberg had been exiled to the university basement, has now been moved into this room and with smooth-faced aristocratic irony seems to observe our uncertain efforts. One of the appeals in particular is troubling us. It comes from a professor who for many years held an important Party office at the university. The job must have entailed tasks and decisions which the office holder, today, would rather not recall. One of my East Berlin colleagues describes what such positions meant for their occupants in the GDR: 'Keep quiet about certain matters, publicly say yes to others, and only occasionally and with great caution distance yourself from Party policies.' Our committee had doubted the applicant's conversion to the *Rechtsstaat* primarily because he had seen no reason to be dissatisfied with his own performance. Not that we wanted demonstrative declarations of guilt. But it seemed to us that a successful new beginning required insight into past mistakes. This candidate had not been willing to find fault with his own behavior. Instead, he had loudly and arrogantly thrown his weight about.

'We must rely on our personal impressions,' a committee member says. 'That's the most credible evidence that we can go by.' Not much consolation. I try to imagine how I, in our candidate's shoes, would have reacted to our committee's questions. 'Maybe he was too proud to concede mistakes in front of people like ourselves,' I venture. Three of my Eastern colleagues interrupt me simultaneously: 'This is no place for pride!'

My heart sinks. How could one ever build a *Rechtsstaat* without pride, I ask myself.

9 July 1991

Back, once again, at the Justice Administration's headquarters near City Hall to speak with Under Secretary Detlef Borrmann about the vetting of the East Berlin judiciary. After Professor Limbach, who as Senator of Justice is responsible for the lustration process, Herr Borrmann is the second in command. I met him last month at a get-together for East and West Berlin judges and prosecutors that the Association of Social Democratic Judges had organized in the hope of getting the alienated brothers to talk. The meeting had been a flop. Instead of the expected hundred participants, twenty-five had come, all but three of them West Berliners, and rather than opening channels of communication we had spent the morning discussing what went wrong. It had been a mistake to choose a venue in West Berlin (thus reinforcing the political hierarchy between *Ossis* and *Wessis* by a hierarchy of place); a mistake to pick a Saturday (when every East Berliner, as one should have known, would spend the day in his allotment garden on the outskirts of the city); a mistake to believe that East Berlin jurists would be eager to listen, once again, to what the *Wessis* had to tell them. Those West Berlin judges and prosecutors who had come— better-intentioned than most of their colleagues—had sat around half-empty tables bemoaning how difficult it was to get reunification matters right. I could hear an undertone of reproach in their lamentations.

But at least the event had provided me with an occasion to meet Herr Borrmann, a gruff and intense man, with whom I had gotten into an argument over the Senate Administration's vetting strategies. It seemed to me that the Western examiners simply were not well enough informed about their candidates' life and work to do them justice, I had said. I cited as evidence the fact that the Senator of Justice herself had, erroneously, told me that the GDR had kept no comprehensive judicial statistics. Would not some insight into the workings of the socialist judiciary help to evaluate its members' adaptability to the rule of law? 'I am not interested in statistics,' Herr Borrmann had angrily replied.

Today I want to find out what he *is* interested in. Our appointment is for 7 p.m. I wonder why Herr Borrmann agreed to the interview: he is a busy man; four times his office had to call to change the date of our meeting; and when, this evening, in the dark and silent corridors of the Justice building, I finally find his name-plate and knock at his door, he looks anything but pleased to see me. Already my first question puts him up in arms. 'So you have come and want to write a book . . .' he says, accusingly, as if the project is something of an imposition. I am interested in the criteria by which we

evaluate the socialist past, I say. I am a lawyer. You and your staff are
lawyers, too. And yet, this evaluation process seems to lack essential elements of fairness. How do you explain that in Berlin, probably no more
than 10 to 15 per cent of the applicants will pass, while in other East
German states the figure will be closer to 50 per cent? That in Berlin, five
arrest warrants for border violations will eliminate you, while in nearby
Brandenburg, reviewers ignore the border cases and instead weed out
candidates who passed harsh sentences for 'asocial behavior'? Are you
not troubled by the haphazardness of the criteria by which you and your
colleagues decide your applicants' fate?

'I'm not the least bit troubled,' says Herr Borrmann, even more annoyed.
But if you care neither about judicial statistics, nor about the uniformity of
your evaluation criteria, what do you care about? Of what do you reproach
your candidates when you declare them to be no longer fit to serve as
judges? Herr Borrmann's irritation rises. 'I don't reproach them of anything!' he barks. Then why . . .? 'Because they are unsuitable!' he shouts.
They knew no separation of powers! They kept their entire country behind
bars! They penalized the exercise of civil rights! 'They don't fit in!' But is
that not a conclusion that needs to be proved in each individual case, I
object. I don't get very far. Herr Borrmann explodes. 'The ignorance!' he
screams. 'The nerve!' 'You have no idea what you are talking about!' Then,
with difficulty, he controls himself. The legal system these judges came from
was totally alien to our own, he says in the strained voice of a teacher
explaining a simple equation to a particularly dense student. They have no
place in the *Rechtsstaat*. East German citizens do not want to encounter the
same old judges as before when they turn to their new courts for help. They
would not trust them. 'The people wouldn't understand!'

Some segments of the American people might not understand the ap-
pointment of black judges either, I say. Objections like these do not count.
Each of your applicants is entitled to a decision on his or her own merits.
Individual rights are not subject to popular vote. 'But they are unsuitable!'
Herr Borrmann screams again. 'They are unpresentable! They don't fit in!'
I am flabbergasted. Why this amazing outburst of temper? In a way, I like
Herr Borrmann's anger better than the glib civility of his colleagues; it
betrays passion about a subject that deserves it. Does it betray something
else? Uncertainty about his own position, perhaps? Or does he have a
point: must judges 'fit in' with the society they serve? Is that why American
judges are elected? But is it not one of the foremost tasks of the Constitution to protect those who do not fit in? 'The Jews did not fit in with the
Third Reich, either,' I say.

Herr Borrmann has had enough. 'Preposterous!' he roars. 'Outrageous!'
He is right. It is outrageous to compare the Jews, unwilling victims of a
corrupt regime, with East German judges, on many occasions only too-

willing accomplices in their regime's corruption. Still, this is the reunification of a divided city, and the almost total exclusion of Eastern jurists from its administration of justice seems to require better reasons than Herr Borrmann will provide. For a while we continue our uneven shouting match: he hollering, I, or so it seems to me, sweet reason herself. I am glad that nobody is any longer around to hear the clamor. Lord knows how I finally get out of Herr Borrmann's office. Did we shake hands? How angry he was! I have never been so yelled at by an official, let alone by an under secretary. Not that I mind, I tell myself, as I wait for the city train. It will make good copy. But I must feel more shaken than I can admit to myself because I pay no attention when I board the train, notice only after many stops that I am travelling in the wrong direction, have to wait an eternity in a cold and deserted station for the return train, and eventually miss my bus connection. It is past 10 p.m. by the time I finally make it home.

10 July 1991

My colleagues at Humboldt University are worried about recent plans of Berlin's Senate Administration to overhaul its Statute on Universities. And rightly so. I have seen a draft of the planned amendments, which are about to be ratified by the Berlin legislature. They significantly limit existing rules on university self-government. Under the new law, only those Humboldt professors who were either appointed under the previous University Statute of 23 October 1990 or who by formal procedure were reappointed to their present posts will be entitled to vote on matters affecting their own school. Since all East Berlin professors obviously obtained their posts prior to 23 October 1990 and since a formal reappointment procedure neither exists nor is likely to be created in the foreseeable future, the new law means in practice that former GDR professors may not participate in university self-administration. To add insult to injury, they may not be elected chair of their department, either. And while at the Free University and the Technical University in West Berlin habilitations and appointments are considered matters of self-government, at Humboldt University they are to be placed in the hands of external state-appointed committees. The new law is thus set to disenfranchise East Berlin professors at the very moment in their history when they should learn to do free scholarship in a free society.

To me, the planned amendments so obviously violate the Constitution's guarantees of academic freedom and equal protection that I ask myself how they could ever have reached the stage of a final draft. After all, these drafts were composed by lawyers. Did it occur to them to consult the Constitution in the process? I have spent almost a year asking East German judges and academics about the influence of socialism on their life and work. Now I realize that I have no idea how important the Basic Law is to the thinking of West German lawyers. Is it just filed as 'Item No. 1' in their *Schönfelder* loose-leaf collection of laws in print? Or has it also taken possession of their hearts and minds? Some years ago, in a Texas newspaper, I found an interview with an illiterate Hispanic farm worker who had enrolled in evening courses in order to learn to read. 'I want to read the Constitution!' he said. Does the Basic Law ever bring a shine to the eyes of those who have been able to read it for many years?

Hence my appointment today with Counsellor Wolf-Dirk Veit, of the Senate Administration's Department of Science and Research, who is in charge of matters affecting Humboldt University. Herr Veit has brought a colleague along. I ask my question: what role did the Constitution play when Senate experts planned the future structure of Humboldt University? Was it perceived as a moral guideline? As a tiresome restriction? Does that famous 'value system of the Basic Law,' so often conjured up in German High Court case-law, exert authority over actual decision-making processes? Or is it an invention of lawyers that gains significance only in litigation?

But I find it difficult to engage Herr Veit in a discussion of constitutional values. I am not sure that he approves of what I am arguing for: to see the Basic Law as a surrogate religion in a secular and pluralist society. All right then, I will phrase my questions more directly: does he have doubts about the constitutionality of the university legislation planned by his department? No. But what about the academic freedom of East Berlin professors? The Basic Law protects only those scholars whose academic credibility has been confirmed by way of a specific selection procedure, says Herr Veit.

That is what the new amendments say. But the Constitution does not intend to shore up actually existing appointment practices but to protect fundamental civil liberties. Its promise of academic freedom must extend to anyone who is seriously committed to the search for scientific knowledge and insight, I say. But Herr Veit does not care for functional interpretations of article five, paragraph three of the Basic Law. Before the *Wende*, East Berlin scholars had no academic freedom either, he says. (He does not add: 'Why now?') But he insists: Humboldt University professors are not scholars in the meaning of the Constitution.

And what does Herr Veit make of their second thesis, the 'Habilitation,' which like its namesake in West Germany served as an author's entry-ticket to an academic career? No proper selection procedure, says Herr Veit. East German universities nominated only one candidate for every open position. Unlike West German universities, they did not draw up lists of three candidates from whom final decision makers would then choose. The system therefore was devoid of competition.

At my law school in Texas, we also vote each candidate for an appointment individually up or down, I say. But the decision lies in the hands of the entire faculty and we would consider it a threat to our independence if, as in West Berlin, a Senator of Science and Research were to choose the winning applicant from a list. What would you say if I attacked the West Berlin appointment process because of its bureaucratic interference with university autonomy? It makes no sense to haggle over different appointment practices, says Herr Veit. They are based on very different political world-views. I agree. In any case, we have lost sight of our original topic: the constitutional weight of academic freedom. The question I started out with—whether deliberations over the fate of Humboldt University were swayed by the decision makers' constitutional faith in the dignity of the unregimented search for truth—has indirectly, I believe, been answered: no. Instead, the planned amendments aim for more regimentation: they are meant to exclude an entire group of university teachers whose backgrounds and intellectual habits seem out of place in West Germany's academic landscape and whose wholesale rejection saves everyone the trouble of acknowledging and facing each individual's specific failures and achievements.

Still, I would like to know how Herr Veit personally views my colleagues in East Berlin. Please outline the intellectual profile of an imaginary Humboldt professor whom you would gladly hire, I ask him, and that of another East Berlin professor who lives up to your worst expectations. Sketch for me the caricatures, as it were, of an East German ideal- and monster-professor. Why not. Herr Veit begins with the monster-professor: someone who owes his position to political connections, a conformist and Stasi informer, spineless, without creativity and without sound scientific knowledge. He can't help smiling as he rattles off the list: it corresponds so perfectly to current Western images of Eastern academics. And now for his portrait of the ideal socialist professor. Preferably a natural scientist, says Herr Veit. No, no, a lawyer, please. Herr Veit hesitates. 'He does not exist,' he says. Still, Wolf-Dirk Veit is willing to give it a try. Someone who has not succumbed to the dictatorship of the Party, he says. Who believes in the rule of law. . . . 'He does not exist,' Herr Veit repeats. Another try: someone who has preserved his intellectual independence, who shares our view of justice, someone like us. . . . 'He cannot exist,' says Herr Veit and gives up.

He is right: we need not look for mirror images of ourselves among East German legal academics, even if what we search for should come closer to reality than Herr Veit's flattering portrait of scholars 'like us.' Let me tell you what my ideal of an East Berlin law professor looks like, I now say. Someone who once truly believed in socialism. Who understands or tries to understand what went wrong, and is resolved to learn from his mistakes.

Who is interested not only in himself but also feels an obligation towards society. Who despite all disappointments rejoices in the rule of law. Who views many aspects of the Federal Republic with skepticism and whose ideas will not reassure our own perception of the world but challenge it! Now I am rolling. 'Someone like Frau Will!' I add for good measure. Herr Veit incredulously shakes his head. But his colleague suddenly speaks up. 'You know, I think you might actually be right,' he says to my amazement.

18 August 1991

My last day in Germany. Tomorrow, my family and I will fly back to the United States. From our holiday cottage in Flensburg, I telephone Frau Will to inquire after the latest news from Berlin. Happily, the Dean reports on the most recent round of law exams at Humboldt University. There had been reason to worry: the candidates belonged to that final group of fourth-year students who had begun their legal education under socialism and who in the middle of their studies had woken up to find themselves in a capitalist legal system. Formally, they were the last generation of students to be tested under GDR examination procedures. But substantively, they had to learn—in two semesters!—as much as possible of those subjects which West German law students take more than seven semesters to cram into their heads! And yet, results had been surprisingly good. The orals—held by examination commissions composed of two East German and two West German professors—had been intentionally rigorous. But of 153 candidates, 140 had passed. One of the students, even with the rare and impressive highest grade available! The Dean makes no mention of her own contribution to the success. But I know: it was largely due to Rosi Will's energy and direction that Humboldt University's law curriculum could so completely and effectively be redesigned and staffed in one short and turbulent year.

What is happening in the fight over Humboldt University's self-governance, I want to know. The Berlin Senate's amended version of the University Decree has now passed. Will Humboldt University challenge it in Constitutional Court? 'Yes!' says Frau Will. 'Good!' I say. That is the way it should be: that the new citizens insist on the full measure of their civil liberties. No, says Frau Will, that's not the way things happened. The vote in Humboldt University's governing body, the Senate, had indeed been seventeen votes in favor of litigation, five against, and one abstention. But only a week earlier, a meeting of the same body had been quite unwilling to risk a constitutional complaint. When Frau Will angrily denounced the discriminatory voting procedures under the new statute, none of her colleagues joined in the attack. 'It's all the same to us,' most other Senate members seem to think. 'It was like banging my head against a wall.' She had been too discouraged to stay until the meeting's end. 'Are you leaving in protest,' the University Rector had asked. 'I could only say yes.'

But a few days after the event, the new conditions of employment for East Berlin university teachers had been published. Unlike in West Berlin, where fastidious pay differentials reflect an elaborate hierarchy of academic rank, the new East Berlin tariffs contemptuously lumped everyone together, as if to say: none of you is worthy of distinction. Every Humboldt teacher with a *Habilitation*, whatever his or her rank, age, or achievement, was scheduled to receive 60 per cent of the pay of a West Berlin junior faculty member. Moreover, everyone, regardless of length of employment, would be legally considered as newly hired—that is, would lose the benefits of seniority. And all who read the new announcements with dismay also knew that in October their rents (still fixed at artificially low socialist levels) would begin to rise. That is what caused the rebellion in Humboldt University's next Senate meeting: financial fears. 'It really didn't have anything to do with people's beliefs in civil liberties,' says Frau Will.

'What a sad story,' I say. 'That's why I am telling it to you.' But I continue to puzzle over the report and much later in the day, after Frau Will and I have long hung up the telephone, I change my mind. What should entitle me to sit in judgment over my colleagues' motives for enforcing their rights? Is it only for love of freedom that the average West German litigant will go to court? Have we not learned from socialism what will happen if we contemptuously rank the pursuit of the public interest over the protection of private rights? No, I was wrong. If the new citizens decide to use the law in defense of their self-defined interests—whatever those may be—then the law will do the job it is supposed to do: protect and strengthen individual autonomy. Not a sad story. Rather an occasion for salute. Welcome, we should say. Welcome to the rule of law!

V

Instead of a Postscript

20 June 1991

In Leipzig, at the 'House of the Scientist,' to meet with Professor Karl
Bönninger for dinner. His name turned up in numerous conversations
during this last year—like a hopeful pennant, popping up here and there
over the heads of marchers in a long and dreary parade. Although clearly a
socialist and clearly, like his colleagues, searching for the true faith, Karl
Bönninger was the only participant at the Babelsberg conference to speak
in his own voice. When in the early 1970s his field, administrative law,
vanished from the official legal canon, he offered instead an optional lecture
on 'Principles of Bourgeois Administrative Law' at the University of Leipzig. Not being able to place articles on the forbidden subject in law reviews,
he wrote administrative law primers for correspondence students. In 1980,
Karl Bönninger was the first to suggest an East German codification of
administrative procedure. 'A straight arrow,' Herr Bernet had called him;
someone who identified a goal and, by the most direct line between A and
B, set out in pursuit of it. Others confirmed the description. East German
political discourse moved in waves, a colleague in East Berlin explained to
me. Some went with the flow. Some took advantage of the crest. Some
followed their own set course independently of the ups and downs: Karl
Bönninger, for example. What did you think of the work of Bönninger? I
asked an administrative law teacher from Humboldt University at one of
the hearings of our Personnel Review Commission. 'I felt ambivalent
about it,' was the answer. Bönninger's goals had not been 'realistic.' Or, to
translate 'realistic,' had not been politically expedient. When we once
met in Leipzig, Professor Bönninger, without ado and over the objections
of the university custodian, invited me into his office—a gesture that
ordinarily required prior permission by a Party committee. Not politically
expedient, either. That was a long time ago. Will I recognize Karl
Bönninger today?

But he looks barely changed: not very tall, now white-haired, lively,
energetic, innocent. His Rhineland accent, a little worn after decades of life
in the other Germany, is still unmistakable. Karl Bönninger studied law in
Bonn where he received his first degree in 1948. Like his father, who had
joined in 1920, he was a member of the Communist Party. What had
attracted him to socialism? Its separation of the individual from the prop-

erty owner. Karl Bönninger believed that law and socialism could be squared. But as a Communist, he was not accepted into the judicial appren- ticeship which in West Germany is the prerequisite for Bar admission. In 1948, his father had been fired from his public service job. Even earlier, the son, then still in university, had like other Communists been expelled from the same Organization of Socialist Students in which he originally, like the future Chancellor Helmut Schmidt, had held a seat on the executive com- mittee. In 1948, thirteen mostly socialist organizations were outlawed in West Germany, Herr Bönninger tells me; two years later, the number of forbidden groups had risen to 132. So he left to become research assistant to Professor Kröger at the East German Academy for Administration in Forst Zinna. 'I went in the conviction that I would join the better Germany,' he says today.

Once, in some academic handbook or other, I came across a photograph of Karl Bönninger that must have been taken in those days. A young man, looking with trusting eyes into an invisible future, whose picture reminded me of old snapshots of my father from the last years of the Weimar Repub- lic, when he and his friends, with their guitars and rucksacks, were travelling the land, singing of the elusive blue flower of German Romanticism. 'But the early 1950s were not just years of hope,' I now remind Karl Bönninger. They were years of extraordinary repression, too, when the possession of leaflets or the participation in political discussions were prosecuted as 'in- citement to boycott' and punished with long prison sentences—had he not noticed? 'Not very clearly.' For Karl Bönninger, it was a time of class struggle. Germany was a battle field in the Cold War. In 1951, five years prior to the decision of the West German Constitutional Court that would outlaw the Communist Party, the Federal Government passed a resolution declaring as 'hostile to the Constitution' all those organizations 'which are officially so characterized by the Federal Government.' In the same year, amendments to the Criminal Code introduced penalties even for those supposedly subversive activities that entailed no concrete threat to any public or private interest. There were years when over a million mailings from East Germany were routinely stopped and investigated by West German custom officials. If GDR citizens travelling in the Federal Republic (it was easier to travel in those days) were reckless enough to ask about matters of political interest, they could be prosecuted under section 92 of the West German Criminal Code for 'gathering information.' In the years from 1951 to 1968, federal prosecutors investigated about 125,000 people for no other reason than their supposed Communist contacts or interests. The figures are considered to be a conservative estimate.

Karl Bönninger once had the opportunity to watch the ideological war- fare from close up. In 1959, a year after Babelsberg, he visited the Federal Republic to observe a trial at the Dortmund Court of Appeals where two

East German local deputies were prosecuted for promoting inter-German talks. He spoke with one of the West German prosecutors about the pitfalls of section 92 of the Criminal Code. Would it be 'gathering of information' if he took a leaflet on the results of recent local elections back to the GDR? It would be 'ill advised,' said the prosecutor. Well, would it be all right for him, Karl Bönninger, to buy a newspaper in West Germany? 'What a question!' was the prosecutor's outraged response. Those two East German deputies, by the way, had each received a nine-month prison sentence for their deeds. No, the rough-and-ready manners of those years matched the notions of class struggle better than the image of West Germany as a *Rechtsstaat*.

And what of the Babelsberg conference, at which Karl Bönninger himself had fallen victim to political warfare? He had been Communist enough in those days to view the event as a struggle over the purity of doctrine. He saw his own conference paper as the contribution to a legitimate discussion; thought of his exchange with Ulbricht as of a 'controversy among equals.' Was he afraid? No. He did 'not feel like a rebel.' Did he conceive of the possibility of maybe being in the wrong? He probably 'wasted too much thought' on questions of doctrine. But he saw himself not as a victim but as a participant in the debate. He explained his subsequent exile to Schkolnitz with the machinations of Karl Polak. 'That was no lawyer!' he now says contemptuously. 'He wouldn't have known how to handle a legal case.' For Karl Bönninger, good theory has to advance social praxis. Anyway, he had not been ready after Babelsberg to renounce a religion only because of the inadequacy of its priests. He had been a true believer in those days. And today? 'Today, too,' says Karl Bönninger and laughs.

As secretary to the local council in Schkolnitz, he had occasion to observe the workings of a socialist bureaucracy from the bottom up. It was not a bad vantage-point for someone who wanted to find out 'what role the law actually played' in everyday administration. When Karl Bönninger was eventually allowed to return to academia, he took the question with him. He wanted to analyze administrative law 'from the viewpoint of the citizen.' But the working conditions at universities increasingly deteriorated. During the early years, at least, discussions 'below' were vigorous and frequent. Ernst Jacobi—'an impressive man' and like Karl Bönninger an administrative lawyer—was Dean of the Leipzig Law Faculty. But with every year, the range of intellectual freedom shrank. Even at one's own faculty there was no room to maneuver. 'You were helpless.' Having work published was no longer fun. 'Whenever I really cared about a passage, I could be sure that it would be cut.' A warning was said to make the rounds in the editorial offices of East German law reviews: 'If you get something from Bönninger, do not only check between the lines, but also check for what he has not written.' Occasionally, he conformed: 'Once in a while, you want to see yourself in print,' he says apologetically. In all these years he produced a lot 'for the drawer': a 250-page manuscript on public law rights, a history of German administrative law—he never even tried to get them published. And what about his colleagues? Well, there was a certain mutual inability to understand the other. Some colleagues took him to be something of a 'malcontent.' For his part, he was puzzled by their caution. A colleague who specialized in criminal law once confided: 'When I teach crimes against the state, I read the entire lecture verbatim from a script.' 'You must be joking,' Herr Bönninger had said, flabbergasted. His wife complained: there was this funny little click on the line whenever she used the telephone. 'I didn't mind,' says Herr Bönninger. But was he not discouraged? '*Ach*, that's not the way I work.' He was annoyed. But he always found lots of support among his students. 'And nobody blew the whistle on me,' Karl Bönninger says with satisfaction.

In a way, the worst disappointment came after the political turnabout. In socialist days, Karl Bönninger had griped about the East German complaint system that provided a citizen's only protection against the state: no publicity, no neutrality, no procedural rigor, no effective participation of attorneys, no teeth to teach administrators respect for ordinary people. Now, finally, the rule of law would vindicate individual rights. Judicial review of administrative decision-making would restore the frazzled autonomy of East German citizens. For a few short months in 1989, it had indeed looked as if the 'socialist *Rechtsstaat*' (until then, no more than an occasional and unconvincing phrase used in East German legal propaganda) might become reality. But hopes soon faltered. It almost seemed as if the new West German rulers wanted to keep the *Rechtsstaat* to themselves. Their present takeover of East German universities, for instance, does not conform to what Karl Bönninger would call the rule of law. He recently asked a West German colleague why of two agricultural research institutes one had been scheduled to survive while the other was ordered closed. Because the second institute had made a very unfavorable 'political impression,' he was told. 'Political impressions' are no legitimate legal criteria upon which to base rule-of-law decisions, Herr Bönninger says heatedly. 'I had to tell that to a *Wessi*?'

But he is also angry at his colleagues. 'How quickly they adapted! How readily they ducked; how meekly they hung down their heads again!' Karl Bönninger agrees that some vetting process had been necessary: 'I would have been selective, too.' It was also necessary to involve West German colleagues in the process: 'There is so much that we do not notice any more.' But not this wholesale rejection! How many of your colleagues would have passed if you had been in charge of the vetting process? 'Three-quarters.' Maybe conjuring up the faces of some people at his university, he corrects himself: 'Two-thirds.' But the old wish to give each his due breaks through, again: 'Perhaps three-quarters, after all.' Now he is an attorney with five dismissed professors among his clients.

But to Karl Bönninger, even the rule of law, once object of so many hopes, no longer holds the certain promise of justice. Nor does he view the old East German complaint procedure as critically as he used to. Its emphasis on collective harmony and warmth might have been artificial and confining. But at least it fostered human contacts between citizen and administration. 'You have to involve people in the solution of their problems,' Karl Bönninger says. 'It is the only way.' Judicial review is an essential weapon to impress upon the state respect for its own laws. But to the weak, the weapon will often be too heavy and unwieldy to be useful. 'What will it cost,' they must now ask before asserting their rights. And with the next breath: 'There is no way we can afford that.' There is more to justice than the possibility of suing the state. 'You've got to face social realities. If you do not, you will commit injustice.'

What kind of *Rechtsstaat* do you still believe in?, I ask. Karl Bönninger shrugs his shoulders, shakes his head over his own obstinacy, and laughs. 'In mine.' I remember the photograph of the young man with that romantic shine of hope on his face. The blue flower justice, I think.